Truth, Love, and Social Change

and other essays on Community Change

Truth, Love, and Social Change

and other essays on Community Change

Roland L. Warren

Brandeis University

RAND McNALLY & COMPANY   Chicago

To ALL THOSE who, eager for a more just American society, will neither destroy what is good in that society nor desist in their struggle to make it better. May their numbers increase!

PREFACE

The writing of this preface has been delayed by still another national crisis that has closed more than a hundred colleges and interrupted normal activities in hundreds of others. As I write this, the National Guard is quelling campus disturbances in one state and putting down a black riot in another. The stands taken by large numbers of Americans have polarized in recent years toward opposite ends of the scale on these and other issues. As usual, communication takes place more readily within like-thinking groups than between antagonists. Two contrary points of view on specific issues have arisen. Two distinct vocabularies have developed to describe any set of events. Along with them, two quite different interpretations of the nature of American society and the root of its problems have emerged as the means by which these strong differences are expressed.

This book examines some of the issues concerned with *how* change may be brought about. All the essays in it take their places under the general rubric supplied by the title essay, "Truth, Love, and Social Change." The truth referred to here is the conviction of each contesting group that it has the truth, that it is right, and that the other side is simply wrong, out of either malice or ignorance. And the love referred to here is the feeling, held more or less strongly by most individuals, that no matter what the substantive disagreement, people should relate to each other as brothers.

How can we reconcile these two imperatives, which most of us recognize even as we are locked in struggle? The answer to that question (through word and action) will determine in large part how much may yet be salvaged from the American dream—whether we may live in peace with each other because there is justice and because there is love.

vii

If these words seem somewhat Victorian for a sociologist, I make no apologies. Apologies are in order, however, for the rather stilted language of some of the essays, a concession to the insistence on scientism and a deceptive objectivity by most sociologists, including me.

During the time when most of this book was being written, I was supported by a research scientist award from the National Institute of Mental Health, for which gratitude is hereby expressed.

It would be impossible to assign due credit to all those to whom I am intellectually indebted; this particular credit card is alarmingly overdrawn. With few exceptions, the materials of this book stem from my period of association with the Florence Heller Graduate School for Advanced Studies in Social Welfare of Brandeis University. To my colleagues there, both faculty and students, an especially large debt is gratefully acknowledged. Mrs. Eleanor Fraser, my secretary, was helpful in the onerous details of manuscript preparation. My wife, Margaret Hodges Warren, deserves much thanks not only for the preparation of the index but also for straight-from-the-shoulder criticism and for help in clarifying muddy passages. Acknowledgment is made in the footnotes to various journals and copyright holders for granting permission to republish these materials in their present form.

ROLAND L. WARREN

Waltham, Massachusetts
May 1970

CONTENTS

SECTION D.   BROADER CONCEPTS, BROADER VALUES

SECTION

A

Strategies of Change

INTRODUCTION

What Karl Marx said about philosophers would seem to apply with even greater relevance to students of social change: "The philosophers have only *interpreted* the world differently; but the point is to change it." Must all knowledge have a specific payoff in bettered human conditions, and if so, must the payoff be immediate? How long are we willing to wait, how much time are we willing to invest in the faith that somehow knowledge is not merely a matter of understanding for its own sake, but that ultimately knowledge is power, as Bacon asserted, that it does—and must—serve the human condition?

A consideration of change strategies lies on both sides of this question. For there is a sense in which one merely seeks understanding, seeks to know, to put things together, to effect closure, to relate some problematical part of experience to that which is known and of which the behavioral regularities are codified. Must such knowledge always pass the mercenary test of immediate practicality? The students of Browning's dead grammarian did not think so:

> Here's the top-peak; the multitude below
>   Live, for they can, there:
> This man decided not to Live but Know—
>   Bury this man there?

The essays in this section range widely over the area between understanding for its own sake and understanding to "change the world."

"Types of Purposive Social Change at the Community Level" leans toward the pole of understanding for its own sake. It was written at a time when the conventional, orthodox method of seeking to bring about social change in the community—the method of collaboration based on consensus—was being chal-

3

lenged both in word and in deed. How relevant to the problems of a desperately divided country are methods of change that assume that through adequate "communication" a meeting of minds can be reached on the basis of which change can be implemented? As one pursues this question, it becomes apparent that change strategies that might be appropriate (in the sense of actually bringing about the change goal) in a situation of general agreement, or consensus, are significantly different from change strategies appropriate for a contest, in which the change goal is attainable only by overcoming or outmaneuvering an active opposition.

Interestingly enough, during the time that this paper was being conceived and written, an empirical study of thirty-five instances of community action was raising questions that my own earlier theoretical conceptualization of community change was unable to answer.[1] The problems raised by the research converged with the theoretical analysis of consensus, difference, and dissensus situations, lending it support while at the same time sharpening the analysis.

In differentiating contest behavior from the types designated as "collaboration" and "campaign," it seemed important to recognize a distinction that several students of the subject were beginning to point out. If one chooses a contest strategy, there is still the question whether the contest is to be carried on within the rules or norms for conducting contests in the community, or whether one or both contestants will violate the rules. Until that time, the question had been considered principally in relation to the rather surprisingly strong behavior of opponents of fluoridation and school bond issues, and of advocates of censoring allegedly communist literature in school and public libraries. In many respects, these contestants violated the usual, conventional norms for conducting debate on hotly contested issues in the community. In "Types of Purposive Social Change at the Community Level" the analysis was extended to include a much broader range of issues.

But how shall one seek to understand the veritable smorgasbord of social protest activities that took the most bizarre forms during the 1960s? Something was apparently happening in American society that generated these types of behavior, and in turn these otherwise diverse types of activity seemed to have something in common—a purposefulness, implicit or explicit. They seemed to be understandable as a strategy for bringing about social change, a strategy different from the usual forms of contest behavior which followed the conventional middle-class norms for conducting disputes over contested issues. In "Social Work and Social Revolution," an attempt is made to analyze this otherwise dis-

---

[1] The results of that study are not included in this collection. They are reported in Roland L. Warren and Herbert H. Hyman, "Purposive Community Change in Consensus and Dissensus Situations," *Community Mental Health Journal,* 2, no. 4 (Winter 1966), reprinted in *Community Structure and Decision-Making: Comparative Analysis,* ed. Terry N. Clark (San Francisco: Chandler, 1968).

parate array of behavior types as constituting methods of influencing social policy which violate the usual middle-class norms for contest behavior.

"Revolution" is a strong word. Why employ it in this context? There is no implication of a violent revolution in the sense of an armed upheaval. What is indicated, though, is more basic than armed upheaval. Perhaps the most important aspect of this situation is the change in values, the lack of loyalty to older ones, the increasing loyalty to newer ones; but also basic is the fact that the usual processes of social control that would contain norm-violating behavior patterns and enforce and reconstitute conventional norms are applied only halfheartedly, and are manifestly inadequate to cope with the growing norm violation. Equally important is the fact that the halfhearted enforcement of the usual norms for contest arises in large part from a gnawing doubt as to their ultimate validity, a loss in morale among those who support the usual norms. These indications are perhaps subtle, not so dramatic as an armed uprising, but more revolutionary as harbingers of change.

Up to this point, the analysis is still in the mode of dispassionate understanding. But here the mask of *Wertfreiheit* is deliberately discarded, and the author bares his ideological teeth, indicating his basic support of much of the norm-violating behavior as being necessary for the survival and regeneration of American society.

It is but a short step from this position to the value-laden and controversial position asserted in "Social Action: Self-Conception and Change Strategies." We need not preempt here the discourse in which the basic position is developed. But one can perhaps capture much of it in the suggestion that the social worker see the protesting client as an ally in the struggle for social justice, rather than as a bad boy who demands much sympathy because he has some just grievances but whose norm-violating misbehavior is to be rejected. The protesting client can be seen as an antagonist, a threat, or he can be seen as a citizen demanding his rights. The professional social worker is trained to see him as a client needing help. This posture appears to be a bridge between seeing him as an adversary and seeing him as an ally, but since the client's behavior is norm-violating, and since the social worker is cast in the role of a supporter of the system, the social worker seldom takes the role of an ally, but most often takes the role of a potential antagonist in support of the existing agency structure. Hence the question: For whom is the change? And with whom? *Cui bono?*

In these tumultuous times, every scholar who is concerned with the improvement of social conditions must sooner or later come to grips with the problem of norm-violating methods of social policy participation. While the second and third chapters in this section represent my own attempt to do this, the next paper is an attempt to deal with another knotty problem that confronts all serious students of social change: the less dramatic but equally perplexing problem of the relation of task to process in planning activities. On the one hand we have the beautiful plans, developed with great technical virtuosity, for, say, a new hospital, or a new freeway through a section of the city, or for a much more efficient (economically speaking) utilization of land than by the substandard dwellings that now occupy it, or for a much more "rational" division of land use into various categories such as industrial, commercial, and residential. On the other hand, there is the pulling and hauling represented in the political process of issue resolution—the exchanges, the bargains, the deals, the special concessions—all necessary in order to muster the essential support for a given proposal. We confront the choice of "rational" plans that haven't the ghost of a chance of implementation, or plans that arise out of a negotiating process whose rationality is difficult to discern.

Is there no alternative between the course of rationality and the course of political reality? And if there is a possibility of some compromise between the two, how shall the mix be conceived?

"Two Models of Social Planning" is an attempt to confront this problem. It was completed and dittoed in 1965, with the admonition at the top right-hand corner: "Confidential preliminary draft—not for circulation or publication." It occasioned a certain catharsis for me, with the usual subsequent euphoria. A problem that had created tension had perhaps not been solved, but it had been resolved in a way that seemed to make sense. Let the paper be circulated to a small group of colleagues for comments, and then age in the files, I thought. On some future occasion it might be redrafted and published.

But gradually the existence of the paper and the nature of the problem it tackled became known, with the result that the paper, though still unpublished, became anything but confidential, turning up in one quotation or another in a variety of contexts. Its central theme is that the concept of rationality need not be confined to the substantive-technical aspects of a plan, but may be, and should be, extended to include the processual aspects of the planning-implementation sequence.

1

TYPES OF PURPOSIVE SOCIAL CHANGE
AT THE COMMUNITY LEVEL

Although social change has been a recognized field of sociological investigation for over a century, there is a vast gap between what is available on the subject and what is being discussed and written today on efforts at social change in American communities. Obviously, part of the explanation for this gap lies in the fact that sociologists put primary emphasis on attempting to build a body of verified theory about social behavior, including social change, rather than themselves trying to induce change. The practitioner, on the other hand, although likewise interested in understanding, is principally concerned with inducing change, rather than merely accounting for it.

But this distinction has never been clear-cut in practice. At present, a growing body of sociologists and other social scientists have joined the ranks of practitioners, while insisting on maintaining their status as scientists—applied scientists, if you will. But even so, they are adding little to systematic knowledge about social change. Practitioners in the field, whether sociologists or not, appear to be guided principally by empirical considerations.

In the practical field of social-change efforts at the community level, there is a ferment of activity associated with the breakdown of the earlier professional tenet that *the* way to go about inducing change is through decisions based upon consensus. Hence the practitioner finds himself with not a single "professional" way to achieve change goals, but a veritable grab bag of change strategies, many

Originally published as Brandeis University Paper in Social Welfare no. 11 (Waltham, Mass.: Florence Heller Graduate School for Advanced Studies in Social Welfare, Brandeis University, 1965) and reprinted in *Readings in Community Organization Practice,* ed. Ralph M. Kramer and Harry Specht (Englewood Cliffs, N.J.: Prentice-Hall, 1969). It was presented in part at the 1965 annual meeting of the Society for the Study of Social Problems. Notes have been renumbered.

of them poorly defined, many of them overlapping. At the same time the values that presumably guide professional choices in this field are being reexamined, and the question of which kinds of strategies are appropriate for which kinds of change context is receiving increasing attention. Although behavioral scientists may be excused if they refrain from presuming to make substantive statements about what values *should* be used as guides to action, one might presume that they would have some meaningful things to say that would be at least indirectly helpful to the practitioner who desires a basis for the choice between one change strategy and another.

At the level of community action, the kinds of change strategy that are now being employed in one context or another include consensus planning, bargaining, protest movements, research-demonstration, social action, nonviolence, organization of client populations, community development, conflict, elite planning, organization of indigenous groups, and civil disobedience. The list could be extended. But a mere mention of these terms indicates their lack of clarity and their considerable overlapping.

THE NEGLECT OF PURPOSIVE SOCIAL CHANGE

Not all of the reluctance of sociologists to examine current purposive change processes is attributable solely to the lack of conceptual clarification in this field. There are at least two other reasons.

One is the relative neglect of social change in general, and of purposive change in particular. Wilbert E. Moore asserts that the field of social change has been largely neglected by sociologists, and adds: "The ordinary intelligent layman, the person innocent of special training in social science, has seemed more acutely aware of changes in life's circumstances than have the 'experts.' "[1] The modest interest that sociologists have shown in social change has been principally on the level of grand theory. Perhaps this in turn was occasioned by the great difficulty involved in setting up operational measures to distinguish social change from other social processes on an adequate theoretical basis.

In contemporary sociology there is the additional reason, asserted by many critics of the structural-functional school, that basically the equilibrium concept has operated to lead sociologists to consider stability as given, social change as problematical.

Within the broad field of social change, the topic of purposive social change has received even shorter shrift. Some decades ago, Sims observed: "In spite of the wide-spread reliance upon and resort to purposive action in modern society, and the important role rationalistic social philosophy has played in history, social science has given relatively scant attention to it."[2] He went on to point out that this is strange when one recalls that Comte, the "founder" of sociology, "projected sociology as a science for prevising and shaping the future." Sims's observation remains pertinent today.

We need not examine here the conflicting views on the possibility or desirability of purposive social change that have been put forward in the century since Comte. Suffice it to acknowledge the wide gulf between Spencer's assertion that social evolution is so fixed in its course that it cannot be speeded up, "yet it is quite possible to perturb, to retard, or to disorder the process,"[3] and Ward's assertion, in direct refutation of Spencer, that "before the science of society can be truly founded, another advance must be made and the actively dynamic stage reached, in which social phenomena shall be contemplated as capable of intelligent control by society in its own interest."[4]

Moore is perhaps representative of the prevailing attitude when he mentions at a number of places in *Social Change* that a characteristic of the present time is the higher proportion of change that is either planned or a secondary consequence of deliberate changes than was the case earlier; but except for his own special interest in the "modernization" process, he treats the subject with only a few words.

In recent times, though, Robert S. Lynd is notable for his insistent plea that social science be put to work for the betterment of society,[5] and Karl Mannheim sees the development of an adequate philosophy and methodology of social planning as a prerequisite for the survival of democracy.[6]

But there is another cause for the comparative neglect of purposive social change within the general study of social change. This is the widely shared conclusion that despite the drama that surrounds it and the apparent sense of autonomy enjoyed by the principal actors in initiating and influencing change, most social change is not the result of purposive direction, but the aggregate of many social forces working themselves out, only one of them—and a minor one—being the deliberate attempt to create social change.

Sumner proclaimed in effect that when attempts at purposive change succeed, the changes would have taken place in any case.[7] A more usual attitude is that of Mannheim, who recognizes the role of social forces in the accomplishment of social change but asserts that planning should be done from "key positions" where comparatively great control can be brought to bear on the institutional structure.[8]

THE LIMITED RANGE OF PURPOSIVE SOCIAL CHANGE

The assertion that most social change is nonpurposive requires further brief elaboration, for, especially in discussions among practitioners at the community level, it is frequently overlooked. Most purposive change at the community level is a response to problems arising from the unplanned aggregate of individual decisions by persons, families, and organizations of one type or another as they pursue their interests and objectives. Such activity, in aggregate, is perceived as population increase or decrease or redistribution, either geographically or by categories of age and sex; or as "suburban growth," "industrial growth," "increasing automation," greater longevity, increased marriage or divorce rates, smaller average size of family, and so forth. Most of what is called planned social change is a relatively modest response to these larger changes that are taken as given, and are not the result of concerted, deliberate, centralized decision-making. Unemployment insurance is instigated to meet the contingency of unemployment, rather than to prevent it; city planning commissions take adaptive measures in view of such changes as population decline in the central city, suburban growth, new industrial location patterns, and the commuting phenomenon; social services are developed to help families whose individual lives dramatize the results of some of the larger changes.[9]

As organizations and activities are thus set up to adapt in part to the largely uncontrolled changes that take place, these organizations themselves become part of the changing scene.[10] In their activities, they may compete with each other in undesirable or wasteful ways, or they may leave gaps in available service, or their aggregate endeavors may not be adequate to accomplish their adaptive objectives. Thus, one particular field of planning has to do with establishing some minimum of purposive order among such adaptive organizations. Much of what is called planned change at the community level is of this adaptive type, rather than of any fundamental type that would change or redirect the major flow of events.

Likewise, of course, most of the basic, uncontrolled changes that take place at the community level do so in relation to forces outside of the local community and not subject to its deliberate control, as in the case of the general price level or changing industrial production techniques.

Similarly, much planned activity on the national level is not subject to conscious control by any single local community, although it may affect what goes on there. An individual community may opt not to collaborate on some federal program, but the pressures to collaborate, both from within and from without, are very great.

Thus most purposive social change at the community level is of a secondary rather than a basic nature, being a response to the uncontrolled aggregate of decisions to do one thing or another by individual actors in the community, or a response to the behavior of various adaptive organizations that have been set up to cope with these basic changes, or a response to changes occurring in the community as part of a national trend and not separable from it.

Having noted this, we are in a position to examine in proper perspective efforts at purposive change at the community level. For any attempt to do so must take notice of their limited context and relatively superficial nature.

The relation between community change and national change is another important topic on which one must report relative scarcity of investigative attention.[11] Otherwise, the work done by sociologists on purposive change at the community level has centered around five principal foci of investigation. Most voluminous in recent years have been the studies concerned with social power in its relation to community issue resolution and action.[12] Another field of investigation has been community action, where analyses have focused on specific action episodes at the community level[13] and on conceptions of the community and characteristics of action episodes that can properly be called community action.[14] A third focus of attention has been conflict in the community.[15] A fourth area has been community development.[16] A final focus of interest is planned cultural diffusion at the community level.[17]

Behavioral scientists have given little direct attention to the investigation of alternative change strategies at the community level, as a part of the overall topic of purposive social change.

PURPOSIVE CHANGE AND THE
VALUE-INTEREST DIMENSION

When one examines instances of change processes corresponding to the empirical types mentioned earlier, two factors become apparent. One is that any given community action may involve a number of such purposive change processes. The other is that these processes vary on a number of identifiable dimensions, such as degree of value consensus, relation of the change system to the existing power configuration, relation of the change system to the target population, and the timing of the proposal, if there is one.

Of these, the consensus dimension appears most promising as an orientation for systematic analysis. Let us examine it. By way of preface, let us simply state the proposition that *different purposive change strategies are based on different configurations with respect to the dimension of issue agreement–disagreement, and that other, intervening variables determine the specific form that the purposive change effort will take.* How far will this proposition take us toward an analytical ordering of types of change effort and a rough association of these types with different situational configurations?

In this analysis we shall employ the terms value, interest, consensus, dissensus, saliency, latency, proposal, and issue. By *values* we mean underlying, implicit bases for judgment and evaluation. Characteristically, they are communicated in the socialization process and are shared by various groups and subgroups, though not necessarily universally within a society or even within a community or segment of one. By *interest* we mean to denote the relation of an actor to specific reality configurations. Presumably, interests are the speci-

fication of values as they are reflected in actual and potential social situations.*
By *consensus,* we wish to denote a situation of agreement on either values or
interests or both. By *dissensus,* we mean a situation of disagreement on values
or interests or both. By *saliency,* we mean the extent to which something (in
this analysis, a value, an interest, or a situation) is a focus of attention and
concern. By *latency* we mean the extent to which something fails to arouse
attention and concern.

Community Response to Issues

Let us now consider a number of situations with respect to these concepts,
each of which has its own implications for social change strategies. Since the
social change we are considering is purposive, let us consider these situations
from the standpoint of the party or actor (one or more persons or groups) who
wants to bring about the change. To simplify terminology, let us refer to this
actor as the *change agent.*†

By *proposal,* we shall mean an explicit change objective that the change
agent wishes to accomplish. By an *issue,* we mean an aspect or possibility of
purposive change which is the subject of active consideration among important
parties in the situation.

From the standpoint of the change agent, the following three situations
can be analytically distinguished. They are conceived as points on a continuum
rather than as discrete states.

1. Issue consensus. In this situation, there is (*a*) basic agreement as to
the way an issue should be resolved, or (*b*) the likelihood of reaching such
basic agreement once the issue is fully considered.

Issue consensus may arise from common interests arising out of common
values. This is the usual implication of the term consensus in the planning
literature, even though such cases may be the exception rather than the rule in
issue consensus.

---

* Thus, values are designated by such general terms as "equality," "freedom," "respect for human personality," etc., interests by "civil rights," "low taxes," "air-pollution
control." In a recent work Sister Marie Augusta Neal has defined "value" similarly, but
has used "interest" to denote "desires for special advantages for the self or for groups
with which one is identified" (*Values and Interests in Social Change* [Englewood Cliffs,
N.J.: Prentice-Hall, 1965], pp. 9–10). In the present chapter, "interest" is more specific
than "value," but not along a dimension of self-orientation–collectivity orientation. Instead
it denotes an area of specific empirical focus for the more general values.

† Two possible misconceptions should be avoided. First, the term "agent" frequently
denotes someone acting on someone else's behalf. That is not the meaning intended here,
though in specific instances this may be the case. Second, the term frequently denotes a
professional person who is inducing change; but in our usage, this specific meaning is
neither intended nor precluded.

Another basis for issue consensus is the convergence of interests even when values differ. An example is the frequent agreement of parties with quite different value orientations to oppose certain urban renewal proposals. Interests in opposing the issue converge, even though the respective values differ. For instance, some may oppose it because it represents a type of welfare state activity that goes against their values of individualism and freedom, while others oppose it because its presumed perpetuation of discriminatory practices goes against their value of equality.* The fact that there can be issue consensus based on different value configurations, though important, is hardly new, as reflected in the dictum that "politics makes strange bedfellows."

2. Issue difference. This is an intermediate term, difficult to denote. What is meant is a situation where there is a live possibility that issue consensus can eventually be reached, but where there is as yet no agreement either (a) that the change agent's proposal constitutes an issue or (b) on the substance of the proposal itself.

The situation is easy enough to describe and to illustrate. In the one case, the change agent is trying to attract attention to a situation and develop it into an issue, but this is not yet accomplished. He may, for instance, be trying to attract attention to building code violations in slum tenements with a view toward remedial legislation or administrative action. His chief obstacle is apathy. He is trying to create an issue.

In the other case, the situation is already an issue; that is, it is a subject of active consideration. There is disagreement among some of the parties to the situation with respect to the change agent's proposal to change the situation. The latter's chief obstacle is opposition, but he believes that he can, through persuasion, convince the opponents that the proposal conforms to their "true" values or interests.

In each case, the change agent believes he can achieve adequate issue consensus for the success of his proposal.

3. Issue dissensus. In this situation, important parties to the situation either (a) refuse to recognize the issue or (b) oppose the change agent's proposal.

From the change agent's point of view, there is little likelihood, merely through explicit statement and substantive discussion, of developing the situation that concerns him into an issue; or, if it is already an issue, there is little likelihood of changing the value or interest orientation of the opposing parties so as to achieve issue consensus.

* Obviously, what one man holds and affirms as the value of equality may differ from another man's value of equality. We are interested in the basic criterion for judgment and evaluation rather than in the label.

The substantive nature of the lack of issue consensus in situations 2 and 3 may be identical. What differentiates them is the possibility of achieving issue consensus. Where the possibility is great, we speak of issue difference; where it is small, we speak of issue dissensus. As we shall see, the distinction holds important implications for change strategies.

Saliency-latency. Before leaving the dimension of value-interest agreement it is important to become explicit about situations 2a and 3a. They involve an independent dimension, that of saliency-latency. All three of the above situations include conditions within which values and interests are salient, a focus of attention. The substantive considerations that surround the issue are being evaluated actively by the change agent and the other parties to the situation. The exceptions are situations 2a and 3a, where there is value and interest saliency on the part of the change agent but value and interest latency on the part of one or more of the other parties, who do not recognize the situation as an issue.

In this connection, there is a mode of orientation toward the situation and toward the change agent's proposal which is not covered by the threefold typology outlined above. This is a condition in which one or more parties to the situation may recognize the situation as an issue but are predisposed to keep the values and interests involved secondary to other values and interests that are not directly involved. Thus, comparatively speaking, the substantive values and interests they see relating to the issue are held latent in favor of more important values and interests. In practical language, they may have a preference in the matter, but they consider the whole matter to be less important than a lot of other things in which they are directly interested. Their posture in the resolution of the issue will depend less on the immediate substantive questions than on other considerations. Such a condition of one of the parties with respect to a specific issue will be called value latency.

Value saliency–latency should be considered as a continuum, for even among those who take a definite position with respect to a proposal, there are various degrees of intensity with which their opinions, favorable or unfavorable, are held.

Issue situations and strategy selection. To summarize roughly, we have described three issue situations. In issue consensus, the change agent is confident of substantial agreement among the principal parties. In issue difference, he doesn't have it, but expects to get it. In issue dissensus, he doesn't have it and doesn't expect to get it. Further, he may occasionally be dealing with parties who do not have a strong position on the issue, even though they may have a definite opinion about it.

The implications for strategy selection are apparent. In the first situation, the change agent will ordinarily employ strategies based on consensus decisions.

In the second case, he will employ strategies based on persuasion. In the third case, he will employ strategies of contest.* With respect to parties for whom the issue is value-latent, he may use either bargaining or exchange strategies.

Further Variations in Change Processes

Let us turn now to a briefer analysis of the other dimensions mentioned earlier.

Relation to the existing community power configuration. Let us side-step, if possible, the heated debate as to whether the power structure is relatively fixed or whether it is merely a series of ad hoc configurations around specific issues. We are interested here in whether the change goal involves a deliberate shifting of the power configuration on the basis of which the issue involved would ordinarily be determined, or whether the change is to be accomplished within the existing power structure.

Relation to the target population. When we speak of the value-interest situation of an issue, we must be quite clear whether we are discussing change techniques for dealing with the change agent's relations to his own group (planning council executive's relation to planning council; community organization worker's relation to the indigenous group to which he is assigned) or the change agent's or the change system's relation to a target population (planning council's relation to service clients or to donors; indigenous group's relation to city hall). The nature of the value-interest situation surrounding the issue may be quite different in the two relationships. For example, the council may work within an issue consensus situation in resolving its own issues, but then, on the same issues, work within an issue difference situation in relation to the target population.

The presence and timing of the proposal. Most issues involve proposals. An important aspect of purposive change analysis is whether the change agent is seeking to put through a proposal that has already been formulated, or whether he is seeking to develop a proposal, and if so, by what methods.

MAJOR TYPES OF CHANGE STRATEGIES

We turn now from issue situations—which we have classified along a value-interest dimension from consensus through difference to dissensus—to a

---

* Not necessarily conflict. We will get to this shortly.

consideration of change strategies. Three major types can be differentiated. *Collaborative strategies* correspond to issue agreement situations, *campaign strategies* correspond to issue difference situations, and *contest strategies* correspond to issue dissensus situations.

Collaborative Strategies

Collaborative strategies are based on the assumption of a common basis of values and interests, through which substantive agreement on proposals is readily obtainable.

The predominant role of the change agent is that of an *enabler,* or *catalyst.* He is not concerned with putting through his own preconceived proposal, but with helping the pertinent group reach consensus on the issue at hand.

Differences are assumed to be based on misinformation or poor communication. Thus, appropriate action calls for "getting the facts," clearing up misunderstandings based on faulty or incomplete information, and reconciling different points of view on the basis of discussion while accommodating the kernel of value in all such differences. The chief obstacle is not opposition, but rather, if anything, apathy and inaction.

Collaborative strategies have strong support in Western culture in a type of philosophical position that was first given systematic portrayal in Plato's reports of Socrates. Socrates enunciated the dictum that goodness, justice, and so on are universal values or "ideas," which are unitary. Disagreement can therefore arise only through the ignorance of one or all of the parties to an issue.

A closely related support for collaborative strategies is a widely held value commitment connected with perceptions of the democratic process which go beyond majority rule and hold unanimous agreement as a higher value.

A third support is undoubtedly the practical situation that agreement of the principal parties to an issue will increase the likelihood of their identifying themselves with the proposal and taking appropriate steps toward its implementation.

These themes, and perhaps others as well, may account for the frequent attempts to apply collaborative strategies in situations where they are not applicable. With respect to the planning process, Jessie Bernard pointed out many years ago:

> We cannot plan until we have solved our conflicts. A plan presupposes
> (as well as creates) a certain degree of consensus. It assumes that we
> are fairly well agreed on what we want. Those who actually profit from
> the *status quo* are not going to support plans to change it contrary to
> their interests.[18]

Most of the problems and decisions confronting American communities involve issues on which there is little value-interest consensus, once the superficialities of the problems are penetrated. As situations are approached in which issue consensus is lacking, collaborative strategies become less relevant. Nevertheless, attempts to apply collaborative strategies in situations where they are not applicable persist. Since collaborative strategies are not appropriate except in issue consensus situations, and since many serious community problems involve issue difference or dissensus, certain adaptations must be made by those who wish to follow collaborative strategies on these issues.

One type of adaptation involves restricting the collaborative process to those parties whose pertinent value-interest configurations are similar. It is possible, for example, to engage in viable collaborative planning on a relatively conservative basis if the parties to the issue are restricted to an elite group, and so long as there are no major threats from other groups to this group's power position.

A second adaptation is to restrict the issues to those on which agreement can be reached. Even at the level of power elites, there remain important differences in value and interest. On value-salient issues, collaboration is possible only if consensus can be reached. Thus issues that cannot be agreed on tend to get shunted off through a tacit understanding that any consideration of them is taboo, or through inability to reach conclusions or take action, or, if action is nevertheless threatened even though consensus has not been achieved, through withdrawal of the opposing parties. Thus there is strong pressure to discuss and act upon only the more innocuous issues.

Hence it is hardly surprising that at the present time community planning councils are coming under severe criticism on precisely these counts:

1. That they do not adequately represent the community on whose behalf they purport to act.
2. That their activities are principally directed at maintaining and patching up the existing system rather than at making changes that would be sufficiently innovative and powerful to have an important impact on the target problems.

In a sociological analysis, Mayer Zald asserts:

The more a C.O. agency has a constituency made up of agencies, everything else being equal, the harder it is to get commitment to an action program which does not have widespread societal consensus and the more likely the agency is to serve as a clearing house for information and coordination.[19]

And Kravitz has challenged a conference of council executives and board members with some pointed questions.

> Can an organization which wishes to act upon broad social welfare issues afford to orient so completely toward a federated fund as its source of support and leadership? Can it afford to have only token governmental leadership? Can if afford only token leadership from racial and ethnic minorities? Can it afford to dodge hard social problems? Can it afford not to be an instrument of change and still stay in the big ball game?[20]

One may raise the question why the welfare councils are only now being criticized for a practice in which they have engaged for a number of decades. The reasons probably include the growing conviction that present health and welfare services are inadequate to the tasks they confront, the increasing attention by social scientists who tend to point out their predominantly system-maintenance role, the growing challenge from community groups other than those that have traditionally been the active parties in welfare issues—notably, the poor—and the not unrelated growth of federal programs as an alternative source of funds to the local governmental or chest-council sources.*

Welfare council planning is not the only context under which collaborative planning by elites occurs. It occurs in various sectors of the community, within various official planning bodies and outside of them, and in both formal and informal organizational contexts. Floyd Hunter gives excellent descriptions of episodes of such planning on a purely informal basis within the power structure of Atlanta,[21] and Carol Estes Thometz reports that in Dallas, the Civic Committee constitutes a formal organization for elite planning,[22] to give but two examples.

Regardless of the other characteristics of the setting, the important consideration in the employment of collaborative strategies is a situation of issue consensus.

---

* Martin Rein has identified and described three strategies for justifying planned community change efforts. He designates the type of planning described here as the "consensus of elites," and contrasts it with the rational-research approach ("the power of knowledge") and with the organization of the poor ("the power of the people") as alternative change strategies. See his "Strategies of Planned Change" (a paper presented at the Orthopsychiatric Association meetings in New York, March 1965). The first two of these are obviously different from the third; in the present analysis both fall largely in the same category, collaborative strategies, corresponding mainly to situations of issue consensus. Where this is lacking, the opposing sides of controverted issues often develop their respective "research findings" to bolster their own arguments rather than reach agreement, such as the research reports surrounding the question of the relation of cigarette smoking to lung cancer, and the research reports by the American Medical Association on hospital, nursing home, and home-care needs of the aged, as contrasted with reports by various parties supporting the expanded social security proposal.

Campaign Strategies

A number of approaches apply to situations of issue difference, that is, where there is at the time lack of agreement among the principal parties that an issue exists or lack of agreement regarding how the issue should be resolved, but where there is a likely prospect of reaching agreement. In these situations, it is not simply a matter of encouraging discussion, on the basis of which a mutually satisfactory proposal can be expected to win agreement. Rather, the change agent has a position that is not shared. He believes that a particular condition is important, it has value-interest saliency, and he has to attempt to get others to assign it more importance on their own saliency-latency scale. Or he needs to persuade differently minded people that his proposal should be adopted. Value-interest differences are not sufficiently great to preclude the possibility of his doing so. Essentially, then, his approach must be either "Let me show you how this matter touches an important interest of yours," or "Our disagreement over the proposal is merely superficial. Let me show you that, contrary to your present impression, my proposal actually does correspond to your *true* or more basic values and interests."

The predominant role of the change agent is therefore that of *persuader.*

According to the nature of the issue and the nature of the parties, this persuasive effort may involve mass-media "educational" campaigns, letters, testimonials, endorsement by prestige figures, organization of ad hoc groups to direct attention to the issue or promote the proposal, activation of existing groups, individual persuasion in conversation, and the like. Strategies directed along these lines can be called campaigns. They are strategies of achieving agreement to a proposal even among differences, by winning over the other parties through persuasion.

But there is another type of effort, which may or may not be closely related to these activities. This has to do not so much with persuading some target parties of the inherent merit of a proposal as with bringing various types of pressure to bear on them to impel them to go along with the proposal, and perhaps to support it actively, even though they are not convinced of the merits of the case. Thus, endorsement by prestige figures merges gradually into getting important prestige or power figures to recommend the proposal with various degrees of specific pressure on the target party. As such techniques pass a certain threshold, they merge into contest strategies based on issue dissensus, which will be discussed later. Short of this threshold, they constitute a widely recognized phenomenon that nevertheless has no generally accepted name. It is perhaps best described as the moderate coercing of consent. It is moderate in the sense that it must stay this side of the threshold beyond which it engenders active antagonism and opposition by the other party.

Another pathway along which extraneous pressures (not having to do with the inherent merit of the proposal) are employed in the persuasive process in a way that rapidly changes the nature of the process itself is the offering of various inducements to the other party to give verbal or functional assent to a proposal he does not affirm from the standpoint of his own value-interest scale. When pressure takes this path, it becomes a bargaining strategy.

Campaign strategies are strategies to accomplish consensus when the chief obstacle is either apathy or opposition. Out of apathy, they attempt to create interest. Out of opposition, they attempt to create agreement. Thus they are quite different from collaborative strategies, which attempt, through discussion or voting or polls or whatever, to create proposals based on consensus.

Commenting on the process of determining policies on the basis of public opinion or pressure groups or other estimates of the current preferences of various publics, Geoffrey Vickers says:

> This account seems to me to miss an essential element. The men and women in England who abolished slavery, created the educational system, or gave women the vote were not acting on hypotheses of what the voters wanted. They were afire with faith in what people ought to want and in the end they persuaded their lethargic compatriots to give them enough support to warrant a change. American presidents, from Lincoln to Kennedy . . . *criticize* contemporary values, urge *revaluation,* and appeal not to what people are thinking now but to what they ought to be thinking and would be thinking if they exposed themselves with sufficient sensitivity to the subject matter of the debate.[23]

Here Vickers captures both the idea of value-interest saliency and the idea of substantive differences.

Apathy, or lack of value-interest saliency, may be related to the social structure of the situation in subtle ways. Thus a person who fails to find himself getting steamed up about someone else's object of concern may simply be responding to a sensed threat to his own interests which has not been made explicit. And the organization that responds apathetically may in turn be reflecting latent functional blockages that may not even have been expressed verbally in the decision-making process.

It is interesting that among practitioners of planned social change, especially in the health and welfare field, a type of change strategy has recently been championed as an explicit alternative to the collaborative model. Quite understandably, its rationale is based largely on the assertion that collaborative methods are simply unable to produce the changes that are necessary to meet today's needs, for reasons closely related to the foregoing analysis.

Probably the foremost proponent of this type of campaign strategy is Robert Morris. He and Martin Rein have characterized the kind of planning strategy carried on by welfare councils as "federated, based on a rational utopianism," concerned with the distribution and redistribution of resources among agencies, clients, personnel functions, and funds, by means of consensus. In contrast, they characterize newer planning structures as

> essentially partisan in character. Their policy-making leadership consists primarily of like-minded persons with a definite image of the change they seek to promote and the objectives toward which they are striving. They seek to modify their environment so that it becomes consistent with their aims and objectives. Cooperation is desired, but primarily around their focal concerns.[24]

I have described a related campaign strategy in contrasting the problem-area specialist with the permissive community organizer. When the problem-area specialist engages in campaign strategy, he is

> task oriented, focusing on the particular task to be accomplished.... He may be democratically oriented with respect to group self-determination, but by the very nature of his role he cannot encourage the community to consider all the possible alternatives for community improvement. He is "selling" a particular program. He thus tends to lean toward the ethical absolutist side, toward the side which knows what is right and wants the right to prevail.[25]

Bernard Coughlin insists upon the necessity for strong leadership in community planning. "Political scientists, educators, labor leaders, social actionists, business executives, industrial leaders—any group in the community that wants to achieve goals in community planning—actively involves the power of the community and directs it toward preconceived objectives."[26] He asks whether this involves an imposition of one's values on the community, stating that of course there are alternative sets of values involved, but asserting, "In itself, the establishment of preconceived social work goals for planning, coupled with strong leadership in effecting these goals, is not an imposition of values upon the community. It is a bargaining for values."[27]

More recently, Robert Morris and Robert H. Binstock have developed a model for this kind of planning, whose outlines are, briefly, the planner's development of a "merit goal" based on both facts and values. The planner then assesses the feasibility of the goal in relation to the likely resistance to it and the influence that he can bring to bear to achieve it. On the basis of this assessment, he adjusts his goal so that it represents a feasible balance between his ideal goal and the real situation, and then follows the appropriate strategies for achieving it.[28]

In contrasting the collaborative strategies and the campaign strategies, it is important to note the systemic relations. If one focuses on an organization that is engaged in policy-making related to social change, the collaborative strategy calls for bringing into the organization's decision-making the various principal parties to the change, especially those who might otherwise be opposed to it. This involves cooptation,[29] along with its disadvantages, as pointed out by James D. Thompson and William J. McEwen.[30] The campaign strategy, on the other hand, is more likely to involve only like-minded persons in policy-making (which may thus well occur through collaborative strategies), but then to confront the other principal parties to the issue with a campaign or contest strategy rather than a collaborative one.

Contest Strategies

When there is issue dissensus, one must pursue one's own goal in opposition to others, if it is to be pursued at all. A number of different kinds of oppositional activity are in operation in American communities today around just such issues. Most notably, the field of racial discrimination and the related field of organization of the poor persistently occasion basic dissensus and controversy. Tenant protests, sit-ins, rent strikes, demonstrations, and so on are examples of contest strategies. Contest strategies are characterized by the abandonment, temporarily at least, of efforts at consensus, and the employment of efforts to further one's own side of an issue despite opposition from important parties to that issue.

The predominant role of the change agent is therefore that of *contestant.*

Coleman states that for controversies or disputes to develop out of specific events at the community level, the event "must touch upon an important aspect of the community members' lives," must "affect the lives of different community members differently," and "must be one on which the community members feel that action can be taken—not one which leaves the community helpless."[31]

The use of the word "conflict" for such situations involves certain ambiguities. Many practitioners apply the term to any process in which one seeks to further his own aims despite opposition. Lewis A. Coser defines it more narrowly as "a struggle over values and claims to scarce status, power and resources in which the aims of the opponents are to neutralize, injure or eliminate their rivals."[32]

Following this usage, and in order to avoid ambiguity, we shall reserve the word "conflict" for processes in which deliberate harmful activity is directed toward an opposing party, and employ the term "contest" to denote not only conflict, but a more inclusive group of processes that may take place under circumstances of issue dissensus. Thus the organization of a group of tenants for the aggressive furthering of their interests in opposition to those of the landlords is a form of contest, but not necessarily of conflict. Similarly, the employment of various nonviolent techniques is more properly considered a contest strategy than a conflict strategy, since, at least in their classical rationale, they do not involve the effort to harm the opponent or eliminate him from the field, even though they do involve the effort to pursue one's own aim in issue dissensus situations.[33]

There is an unfortunate tendency to equate uncritically all issue dissensus situations with conflict strategies. Part of the confusion is caused by the use of the term "conflict" to denote what we have called "issue dissensus," that is, a state in which there are differing positions that appear irreconcilable, at least for the time being. Obviously, this refers to a situation rather than a process. To describe such situations as "conflict situations" and then gradually to denote the behavior within them as "conflict behavior" is to confuse the issue.

But conflict processes and issue dissensus states should not be equated. In the first place, as mentioned earlier, it is possible to agree on issue positions even when there is disagreement on values.

In the second place, not all value-interest disagreements lead to issue contests. We have indicated that situations become issues only when they become a focus of attention and when they acquire value saliency. Not every disagreement does so. As indicated earlier, it is often the object of a campaign to convert a disagreement into an issue, to get people excited about some situation. This is not always easy, as any antivivisectionist or pacifist will tell you.

E. E. Schattschneider points out that "an issue does not become an issue merely because someone says it is. The stakes in making an issue are incalculably great. Millions of attempts are made, but an issue is produced only when the battle is joined."[34]

Finally, there seems to be no discernible correlation between the magnitude of value-interest differences and the degree of conflict. Indeed, some of the most intense conflict takes place among factions whose value-interest positions are relatively close. Witness the crude and harsh in-fighting among slightly different Protestant sects during the past two centuries, and the bitter disputes among various types of socialists which survive to this day.[35]

Hence conflict and issue dissensus, though related, are far from identical.

Interestingly, a revision of earlier scientific and practitioner conceptions of contest in general and conflict in particular as something to be avoided has occurred at roughly the same time as a growth and proliferation of contest strategies for achieving purposive change at the community level. This emphasis on contest strategies in issue dissensus situations is hardly new.

Discussing reform, Jessie Bernard stated many years ago that "it is the attempt of one group to impose its will on an unwilling opponent. It is a naked fight for control."[36] Saul Alinsky, the daddy of much of the current conflict strategy, wrote twenty-five years ago: "A People's Organization is a conflict group. This must be openly and fully recognized."[37] His more recent book *Rules for Revolution* is reported to open with the statement: "Machiavelli wrote 'The Prince' to tell the 'haves' how to keep it; this is a book to tell the 'have nots' how to take it away."[38]

Coleman pointed out some years ago that "the recent increase in community disputes should be not only a cause for concern about democratic processes, but at the same time an indication of a continued and perhaps reawakening interest in the local community."[39] Dan W. Dodson argued persuasively for "The Creative Role of Conflict in Intergroup Relations."[40] And Coser's work on conflict was devoted to the ways in which conflict was functional, rather than dysfunctional, for social systems.[41] Meanwhile, social work community organization practitioners and other professional change agents have gone beyond consensus strategies in the direction of acknowledging the relevance of campaign and contest strategies as well.

The ethical value of conflict has also received supportive attention. Morris Keeton points out that the continual fresh relating of disparate elements in society so as to achieve an increase in realized values "cannot function without conflict," but then adds that "it also cannot function without limits upon the forms which the conflict takes."[42]

One can distinguish four specific types of contest processes in issue dissensus situations.

1. Many contests involve vigorous clashes of opposing positions, but these take place *within accepted social norms* for the confrontation of differing views and the resolution of controverted issues. Examples are legislative debates, legal disputes, and the usual kind of effort through mass media or more personal contact to win over the "public" or some more specific decision-making group to favor one's own position rather than the opponent's.

2. Some contests are occasioned by attempts to *change the distribution of power* in the community. Such attempts naturally arouse opposition on the part of those whose power positions are threatened.

3. Some contests involve a *violation of the usual community norms* for issue resolution in issue dissensus situations. One or more parties break the usual rules of contest. Coleman indicates that community conflict often occasions the rise of new leaders, "who face none of the constraints of maintaining a previous community position, and feel none of the cross-pressures felt by members of community organizations. In addition, these leaders rarely have real identification with the community."[43]

William Kornhauser observes: "People who have fewer attachments to the community are less likely to support the rules according to which community affairs are generally conducted. Such people are less likely to support the right of those with whom they do not agree to express their opinions."[44]

Violation of usual community contest norms has taken two somewhat different forms in recent years. The one to which both Coleman and Kornhauser were addressing themselves has to do with opposition groups that arise around proposals such as fluoridation or school bond issues, and organizations to censor library books or classroom teaching. Another type of norm violation is involved in various "social action" or "social protest" activities. These are norm-violating in three ways. First, the type of action itself is tolerated but not approved by the usual decision-making parties to the issues involved. Thus sit-ins, mass picketing, rent strikes, and related activities are disapproved in and of themselves. Second, they involve a type of participation in issue resolution by parties who are not customarily legitimated for participating in the decision-making process. This is particularly marked in the case of the organization of public assistance clients. Third, when the social change aim is to put an end to segregational practices, the aims themselves sometimes violate the norms of large segments of the issue-resolving parties in the community.

4. An additional type of contest is the deliberate attempt to harm the opponent or remove him from the issue-resolving field, i.e., *conflict in the strict sense of the word*. Specific attempts to depose a particular official, to destroy a career, to bankrupt a firm; harassment of various types; physical violence—all are variations of specific conflict activities.

Combinations of Strategies

In analyzing the strategies of change, we must not lose sight of the fact that a combination of strategies may be associated with the same community change effort. Many types of specific change effort run from a period of a few weeks to a few years, and as the issue develops, different types of situation may characterize it along the dimension of issue consensus–dissensus. At any particular time, as already indicated, the issue situation in one systemic context may differ from that in another, the one reflecting consensus, the other reflecting difference, or dissensus.

But also, as an issue unfolds through time, there may be action episodes within the larger purposive change context which show their own distinct characteristics. Thus, while on a more inclusive level it may be possible to characterize an issue situation as being of one type or another, this does not preclude the possibility that more limited contexts within the total issue situation may have their own distinct characteristics. It is extremely difficult to establish analytical criteria on the basis of which processes and subprocesses such as these can be objectively distinguished, analyzed, and classified. One such effort was made by Willis A. Sutton, Jr., who attempted to operationalize the concepts action course, action subcourse, event, and episode, and to study their interrelationships in nine community action courses in three Kentucky communities.[45]

The present approach, using situations as the basis for analysis, rather than substantive issues or global strategies, permits us to apply a number of strategies to an issue as the situation surrounding it develops and changes.

SOME CURRENT EMPIRICAL CONCEPTS OF
PURPOSIVE SOCIAL CHANGE

In the light of the above analysis, certain brief observations can be made regarding a number of empirical concepts in the field of purposive social change. These do not constitute formal definitions, but rather statements relating the terms and their referents to the foregoing analysis.[46]

Community Development

In customary usage, community development is a campaign strategy out of which a consensus strategy for decision-making is projected for the future. It is ordinarily thought of as activating and bringing into relationship to each other all significant community parties to decision-making. Because it seeks to organize people to express their own needs and to consider action alternatives and then to take action with respect to them, the term has recently been applied to the organization of social action groups of the poor. However, such usage is misleading, since the organization of one segment of the community in a contest relationship to other segments that have not been brought into the process violates the major tenet of inclusiveness in community development principles. This passes no judgment on its desirability or feasibility, but simply indicates that in the commonly accepted sense of the term, it is *not* community development.

Note the systemic relationships. In conventional community development, a campaign type of strategy is employed in order to develop an organization, which then is expected to engage in decision-making using a collaborative strategy, and thereupon to engage in campaign and contest strategies in relationship to groups in the surrounding community. While conventional community development is likely to change the power structure through broadening participation in decision-making, the organization of the poor is specifically designed to do so.

With respect to proposals, there is in each case an initial proposal to organize the community or to organize the poor, and a campaign strategy to gain acceptance and implementation of the proposal. Likewise, in each case subsequent substantive proposals are foreseen as emerging from a collaborative strategy of decision-making within the respective organizations.

Organization of Client Groups

Since the poor and the clients of public assistance agencies, as well as other public agencies such as probation services, tend to overlap, one way of organizing the poor is to organize specific client groups, such as AFDC mothers or other public assistance recipients. The term is also used more broadly to include tenants of public housing projects. As it becomes more inclusive, it merges into the organizing of the poor.

Obviously, though, the organizing of client groups is an empirical or practice term, not an analytical one. For example, a markedly different set of dynamics surrounds the organization of client groups other than the poor, which has also occurred. One of the best examples is the National Association for Retarded Children. Retarded children and their parents are clients, and the service was in an area still somewhat tabooed and still somewhat stigmatized. But the ubiquity of mental retardation throughout the socioeconomic status structure meant that many such clients came from status categories highly legitimated for organizing and presenting their demands, and skillful and experienced in doing so. Hence they were viewed as promoting not only their own interest, but the public interest. The chief obstacle was apathy, not opposition. And they succeeded, with the help of a number of converging pressures, in persuading important decision-makers to move the situation up on their saliency-latency scale. They converted their group concern into a public issue.

Social Action by the Poor

Social action by the poor usually involves a combination of campaign and contest strategies in relation to other groups in the community, analytically distinct from the campaign strategy employed by the change agent in organizing the poor and from the campaign or collaborative strategy (at times contest strategy as well) followed in the decision-making process within the group of organized poor.

George Brager and Harry Specht report three related strategies in connection with Mobilization for Youth in New York City: social brokerage to increase participation, integrative mechanisms to strengthen organizations, and social protest to support social movements.[47] Of these, the last is more specifically social action, as the term is used here.

Lloyd Ohlin outlines four kinds of activities of indigenous movements: (1) mobilizing organizational resources for correcting deficiencies in knowledge and skill in oneself and one's children to eliminate culturally induced handicaps to competition; (2) instituting processes of organizational change to alter the rules and decisions that now control access to existing opportunities; (3) developing liaison with persons and groups external to the local area who indicate a sympathetic willingness to bring pressures to bear on municipal and state-controlled centers of decision relating to the structure of opportunities within the local area; and (4) developing financial resources and recruiting and hiring expert technical assistance for the guidance of indigenous social movements.[48]

In their social-action phase—that is, in relation to other groups in the community—these activities are largely carried out through contest strategies. Murray

Silberman's description of the problem of governmental support of such activities shows why:

> What we have in mind, I believe, are privately operated but publicly financed programs which, though legal, *have little if any prescriptive sanction, and do not (or are not likely to) enjoy widespread public support of a substantial body of public opinion,* and antagonize important economic, professional, and political groups in the community which look upon them as threatening or unduly controversial.[49]

Silberman includes among such programs "the organization of tenant councils, voter-registration campaigns, councils of unemployed. legal actions against administrative agencies over enforcement or non-enforcement of welfare codes, and overt agitational activities."[50]

Martin Oppenheimer and George Lakey have presented a description of direct-action tactics that is broken down as follows: demonstrations (including marches and parades, picketing and holding vigils, fraternization, "haunting," distributing leaflets, renouncing honors), noncooperation (including strikes, hartals, consumers' boycotts or selective buying, renters' boycotts or rent strikes, school boycotts, and tax refusal), and intervention (including sit-ins, fasts, reverse strikes, and nonviolent interjection and obstruction).[51]

Civil disobedience. Civil disobedience is one of the many tactics available in a contest strategy. Conventionally, it is a means of widening a contest by calling to the attention of broader segments of the population the alleged inequity of a particular law, practice, or condition. The deliberate breaking of the law constitutes a dramatic step. In the Gandhian tradition, the persons involved should be fully prepared to take the consequences of their lawbreaking activity, even to the extent of pointing out to authorities that they are breaking the law and should be arrested. The rationale is that the willing submission to the law's "injustice" dramatizes the situation and weakens the morale of those supporting the status quo, while winning sympathetic allies.

Nonviolence. Nonviolence too is a contest strategy designed to weaken the morale of the opponent and to win allies and sympathizers. It takes the form of active demonstration of opposition to existing conditions, and responding to violent or nonviolent negative sanctions nonviolently. Nonviolence thus overlaps civil disobedience, although they are not identical.[52]

Social reform. Social reform is a vaguely defined term used most often to denote relatively long-range efforts to combat specific social conditions, particularly those involving economic exploitation and other target injustices. It is usually a middle-class movement, and usually employs campaign and contest strategies, with emphasis on the latter.

Social movement. A social movement is a long-range effort to accomplish specific goals. C. Wendell King asserts that social movements are "one kind of agency for deliberately altering the social order and for attempting to predetermine events and situations of the future." He defines a social movement as "a group venture extending beyond a local community or a single event and involving a systematic effort to inaugurate changes in thought, behavior, and social relationships."[53] The civil rights movement is an excellent example of a social movement within this conception. Obviously, social movements may employ various strategies at various stages with relation to various groups. By their very nature, though, they emphasize campaign strategies in attempting to create a social issue out of their concern, and contest strategies as the proposals that emerge develop opposition of an ideological nature or of a vested-interest nature, or both.

Bargaining. Bargaining is one of the processes of position formation with respect to a proposal, in which considerations other than those regarding the alleged inherent merits or faults of the proposal prevail. Value-interest positions are relatively latent as to the substantive issue. Support is sought not through consensus-seeking or logical persuasion based on assumed common values and interests, but on the basis of votes, money, favors, or other extraneous considerations.

Consensus planning. The term "consensus planning" is sometimes used to denote what we have called collaborative strategies. But it is often loosely used to mean all manner of joint activity based on agreement of the principal parties, thus virtually eliminating the planning process as a significant dimension independent of consensus. Obviously joint definition of problems, seeking of pertinent data, weighing of alternative solutions, and choice of a mode of action constitute only one type of collaborative process in situations of issue consensus, though admittedly an important one. Its limitations have already been discussed in the section on collaborative strategies. It should be repeated that it is important whether consensus planning takes place among all the principal parties to a community issue, or whether it takes place among only some of them, who thereupon engage in campaign or contest strategies in relation to other parties in order to further the proposal in the community.

CHANGE AND STABILITY

The theoretically curious reader will no doubt long since have noted the possible relationship between the two ends of the value-interest continuum—consensus and dissensus—and the basic theoretical question of social system stability and social system change.

Concerned principally with the problem of how society can exist and persist as a social system, Talcott Parsons takes it as axiomatic that social systems display a characteristic of equilibrium maintenance, behaving in such a way as to restore equilibrium when it has been disturbed, and attempts to show how the various component parts of a social system complement each other in a relation of mutual reinforcement.[54]

Thus, for Parsons, equilibrium is axiomatic, change is problematic. He emphasizes the basis of shared values and norms as an essential element in systems and their maintenance.

It is probably superfluous to point out that a theoretical approach to the social system which emphasizes shared values and norms and a mutuality of social expectations has a certain affinity with the collaborative strategies discussed above. There is an additional point of meaningful relationship. Just as the Parsonian analysis of social systems, emphasizing equilibrium maintenance, is widely held to constitute an essentially conservative orientation, so also the strategies based on consensus, with their tendency to ignore "controversial" issues, serve to perform, however manifestly or latently, a conservative function, having the effect of reconciling system strains through minimal measures, through incrementalism, rather than looking aggressively toward radically new departures.

On the other hand, there are those who see society as constantly in flux, forever pulled and prodded by the interplay of competing and conflicting interests. One of the most important contributions of Karl Marx to social theory was his adaptation of the Hegelian dialectic to the analysis of social structure and change. What in Hegel's case was an implicit Olympian dialogue unfolding itself in history as the development of absolute truth became for Marx the much more mundane struggle of opposing classes, a struggle whose apparent resolution at any point in history merely marked the birth of its successor.

There is a position, based not only on Marx but on a long succession of social and political theorists, which takes not stability but change as the basic characteristic of social systems, and looks upon stability as problematical. Closely associated with this viewpoint is another that acknowledges no such thing as the "public" interest, but rather emphasizes the essential differentiation and incompatibility of important groups of people and the interests they share. For those who hold this position there is no single ideal of truth or justice on which, as Socrates held, all men would agree if they could pursue the matter beyond their own limitations of ignorance. The true situation is rather one of a genuine contest. Dissensus, rather than consensus, is the basic social reality, and social process and social change are the dynamic way in which this dissensus is handled.

Here again one notes the correspondence of this position to the position that emphasizes the values of conflict and which affirms the appropriateness of contest strategies for achieving purposive change at the community level. Let the different interests, with their various value legitimations, compete in the marketplace of the community. Let the differences be clearly stated, rather than played down, and let the changes that "need" to take place actually take place, without such anxious consideration about disturbing equilibrium, offending certain groups, failing to reach agreement, and the like.

From my point of view, the basic theoretical question is almost metaphysical. There is no way in which one validates or invalidates the assertion that society is basically and essentially a stable system, or that society is basically and essentially a dynamic system. One accepts such statements as axiomatic, if at all. They constitute important foci for theoretical analysis, analogous perhaps to the wave theory and photon theory of light.

Actually, the theoretical problem is little different from that posed by certain of Socrates' immediate predecessors. It was Heraclitus who proclaimed that change was the basic law of reality, and that "we step in the same river and yet not in the same one; it is we, and it is not we."* And it was Parmenides the Eleatic who argued the opposite. Persuaded by his own logic, he insisted that basically nothing changes, and concluded: "Hence, becoming is impossible, and passing away is likewise out of the question."

These early philosophers, too, were approaching reality (not specifically the social system) from opposite poles, based on *a priori* conceptions.

In any case, a practical and ethical problem centers around the various kinds of change strategy in use today at the community level. Here again an either-or type of answer is both naïve and inadequate. For there will be situations in which the change agent will value consensus more than his substantive change goal, and act accordingly; and there will be times when he will prefer to pursue his substantive goal at the expense of consensus. Obviously, it would be strange indeed if change agents were in agreement as to which stance to take in all cases.

* Interestingly enough in connection with contest strategies, he also asserted: "Strife is the father of all, the king of all; some he makes gods, others men, some slaves, others free," thus antedating Hobbes's doctrine of the fight of one against all by some two thousand years.

NOTES

[1] Wilbert E. Moore, *Social Change* (Englewood Cliffs, N.J.: Prentice-Hall, 1963), p. v.

[2] Newell Leroy Sims, *The Problem of Social Change* (New York: Crowell, 1939), p. 316.

[3] Herbert Spencer. *The Study of Sociology* (New York: Appleton, 1896), p. 401.

[4] Lester Frank Ward, *Dynamic Sociology* (New York: Appleton, 1893), quoted in Sims, *Problem of Social Change*, p. 324.

[5] Robert S. Lynd, *Knowledge for What? The Place of Social Science in American Culture* (Princeton: Princeton University Press, 1939).

[6] Karl Mannheim, *Man and Society in an Age of Reconstruction: Studies in Modern Social Structure* (New York: Harcourt, Brace, 1940), and *Freedom, Power, and Democratic Planning* (London: Routledge & Kegan Paul, 1951).

[7] William Graham Sumner, *Folkways: A Study of the Sociological Importance of Usages, Manners, Customs, Mores, and Morals* (Boston: Ginn, 1906).

[8] Mannheim, *Man and Society,* p. 153.

[9] Even relatively systematic, long-range, large-scale efforts to modify ecological, economic, and demographic changes may meet with only modest success. See, for example, Donald L. Foley, *Controlling London's Growth: Planning the Great Wen 1940–1960* (Berkeley and Los Angeles: University of California Press, 1963).

[10] See F. E. Emery and E. L. Trist, "The Causal Texture of Organizational Environments," *Human Relations,* 18, no. 1 (February 1965).

[11] Exceptions include Arthur J. Vidich and Joseph Bensman, *Small Town in Mass Society: Class, Power, and Religion in a Rural Community* (Princeton: Princeton University Press, 1958); Floyd Hunter, *Community Power Structure: A Study of Decision Makers* (Chapel Hill: University of North Carolina Press, 1953) and *Top Leadership, U.S.A.* (Chapel Hill: University of North Carolina Press, 1959); and Roland L. Warren, *The Community in America* (Chicago: Rand McNally, 1963).

[12] The literature is too voluminous to cite here. Most of the important reports are cited in a recent article by Charles M. Bonjean and David M. Olson, "Community Leadership: Directions of Research," *Administrative Science Quarterly,* 9, no. 3 (December 1964).

[13] See Solon T. Kimball and Marion B. Pearsall, *The Talladega Story: A Study in Community Process* (University: University of Alabama Press, 1954); Floyd Hunter, Ruth C. Schaffer, and Cecil G. Sheps, *Community Organization: Action and Inaction* (Chapel Hill: University of North Carolina Press, 1956); and Christopher Sower et al., *Community Involvement: The Webs of Formal and Informal Ties that Make for Action* (Glencoe, Ill.: Free Press, 1957).

[14] See Harold F. Kaufman, "Toward an Interactional Conception of Community," *Social Forces,* 38, no. 1 (October 1959); and Willis A. Sutton, Jr., and Jiri Kolaja, "The Concept of Community," *Rural Sociology,* 25, no. 2 (June 1960).

[15] See James S. Coleman, *Community Conflict* (Glencoe, Ill.: Free Press, 1957); and "Trigger for Community Conflict: The Case of Fluoridation," special issue of *Journal of Social Issues,* 17, no. 4 (1961).

[16] See Melvin M. Tumin, "Some Social Requirements for Effective Community Development" (background paper, Conference on Community Development and National Change, sponsored by the Center for International Studies, Endicott House, M.I.T., December 13–15, 1957). *Community Development Review,* no. 11 (December 1958); and Harold F. Kaufman and Lucy W. Cole, "Sociological and Social Psychological Research for Community Development," *International Review of Community Development,* no. 4 (1959).

[17] Such studies are also conducted by anthropologists. Two well-known volumes are Edward H. Spicer, ed., *Human Problems in Technological Change* (New York: Russell Sage Foundation, 1952), and Benjamin D. Paul and Walter B. Miller, *Health, Culture, and Community* (New York: Russell Sage Foundation, 1955).

[18] Jessie Bernard, *American Community Behavior: An Analysis of Problems Confronting American Communities Today* (New York: Dryden Press, 1949), p. 616.

[19] Mayer N. Zald, "Toward a Sociology of Community Organization Practice," mimeographed (revised version of a paper delivered at the National Conference on Social Welfare, Atlantic City, May 24, 1965), p. 27.

[20] Sanford L. Kravitz, *Design out of Discord* (New York: New York State Association of Councils and Chests, 1963), p. 10.

[21] Hunter, *Community Power Structure.*

[22] Carol Estes Thometz, *The Decision-Makers: The Power Structure of Dallas* (Dallas: Southern Methodist University Press, 1965).

[23] Geoffrey Vickers, "Ecology, Planning, and the American Dream," in *The Urban Condition: People and Policy in the Metropolis,* ed. Leonard J. Duhl (New York: Basic Books, 1963), chap. 29, pp. 390–91.

[24] Robert Morris and Martin Rein, "Emerging Patterns in Community Planning," in *Social Work Practice, 1963* (New York: Columbia University Press, 1963), p. 168. See also Rein and Morris, "Goals, Structures, and Strategies for Community Change," *Social Work Practice, 1962* (New York: Columbia University Press, 1962), and Morris, "Social Work Preparation for Effectiveness in Planned Change," *Proceedings of the Eleventh Annual Meeting of the Council on Social Work Education,* January 1963.

[25] Roland L. Warren, "Toward a Reformulation of Community Theory," *Human Organization,* 15, no. 2 (Summer 1956): 10.

[26] Bernard Coughlin, "Community Planning: A Challenge to Social Work," *Social Work,* 6, no. 4 (October 1961): 41.

[27] *Ibid.,* p. 42.

[28] Their model is specifically aimed at "changing the policies of formal organizations for the purpose of improving conditions of social welfare." See Robert Morris and Robert H. Binstock, "Comprehending the Social Planning Process: Towards a Theory of Social Planning," mimeographed (paper presented at the National Conference of Social Welfare, May 1965), and *Feasible Planning for Social Change* (New York: Columbia University Press, 1966).

[29] "Cooptation is the process of absorbing new elements into the leadership or policy-determining structure of an organization as a means of averting threats to its stability or existence" (Philip Selznick, *TVA and the Grass Roots: A Study in the Sociology of Formal Organization* [Berkeley and Los Angeles: University of California Press, 1953], p. 13).

[30] James D. Thompson and William J. McEwen, "Organizational Goals and Environment: Goal-Setting as an Interaction Process," *American Sociological Review,* 23, no. 1 (February 1958).

[31] Coleman, *Community Conflict,* p. 4.

[32] Lewis A. Coser, *The Functions of Social Conflict* (Glencoe, Ill.: Free Press, 1956), p. 8. In a recent article, Raymond W. Mack describes conflict as "opposition or antagonistic struggle, the aim of which is the annihilation, defeat, or subjugation of the other person or group," but he then goes on to equate conflict behavior with the abandonment of "institutionalized norms" ("The Components of Social Conflict," *Social Problems,* 12, no. 4 [Spring 1965]: 391). Conversely, when conflicting parties come to accept rules to govern the limits of the opposition, the "conflict shades into competition" (p. 392). But obviously the two dimensions are independent, for conflict as Mack defines it can take place within institutionalized norms or outside of them, as can competition.

[33] In connection with a bitter strike of Indians in South Africa, Jan Smuts told Gandhi: "If you had hurt an Englishman, I would have shot you, even deported your people. . . . But how long can I go on like this when you do not retaliate?" (M. K. Gandhi, *Non-Violence in Peace and War* [Ahmedabad: Navajivan Publishing House, 1949]), vol. 2, p. 83.

[34] E. E. Schattschneider, *The Semisovereign People: A Realist's View of Democracy in America* (New York: Holt, Rinehart & Winston, 1960), p. 74.

[35] Paraphrasing Simmel, Coser states that "a conflict is more passionate and more radical when it arises out of close relationships. . . . In conflicts within a close group, one side hates the other more intensely the more it is felt to be a threat to the unity and the identity of the group" (*Functions of Social Conflict,* p. 71).

[36] Bernard, *American Community Behavior,* p. 611.

[37] Saul D. Alinsky. *Reveille for Radicals* (Chicago: University of Chicago Press, 1945), p. 153.

[38] *New York Times,* August 2, 1965, p. 33.

[39] Coleman, *Community Conflict,* pp. 3–4.

[40] *Merrill-Palmer Quarterly,* Summer 1958.

[41] Coser, *Functions of Social Conflict.*

[42] Morris Keeton, *Values Men Live By: An Invitation to Religious Inquiry* (New York: Abingdon Press, 1960), p. 203. (The chapter is entitled "... And Come Out Fighting!")

[43] Coleman, *Community Conflict,* p. 12.

[44] William Kornhauser, *Power and Participation in the Local Community,* Health Education Monographs no. 6 (1959), p. 35.

[45] Willis A. Sutton, Jr., "The Socio-Temporal Structure of Community Activities: Event and Episode Comparisons in Three Kentucky Towns" (paper read at the 1964 meetings of the Society for the Study of Social Problems).

[46] On a somewhat different level of analysis, Arthur Dunham has ranged much of this material along a continuum extending from permissive or nondirective types of action to the most directive. See his "Some Types of Community Action Designed to Bring About Community Change," mimeographed (Columbia: School of Social Work and Community Development, University of Missouri, March 1965).

[47] George Brager and Harry Specht, "Mobilizing the Poor for Social Action: Prospects, Problems, and Strategies," mimeographed.

[48] Lloyd E. Ohlin, "Urban Community Development" (paper presented at the UNESCO Conference on Socially Handicapped Families, February 1964).

[49] Murray Silberman, "Securing Change Through Government-Supported Social Action Programs," mimeographed (March 1965), p. 3. (Italics in original.)

[50] *Ibid.*

[51] Martin Oppenheimer and George Lakey, *A Manual for Direct Action: Strategy and Tactics for Civil Rights and All Other Nonviolent Protest Movements* (Chicago: Quadrangle Books, 1964), chap. 7.

[52] For a comprehensive set of readings on nonviolence, see Mulford Q. Sibley, ed., *The Quiet Battle: Writings on the Theory and Practice of Nonviolent Resistance* (Garden City, N.Y.: Doubleday, 1963).

[53] C. Wendell King, *Social Movements in the United States* (New York: Random House, 1956), pp. v, 27.

[54] Talcott Parsons, *The Social System,* 2nd ed. (New York: Free Press, Macmillan, 1964).

2

SOCIAL WORK AND
SOCIAL REVOLUTION

To say that we are living in a period of revolutionary social change is to be so trite as to border on the banal. The assertion must have been made for the first time many centuries ago—I suspect probably by Adam and Eve. One can imagine Eve making that sort of musing statement as she and Adam sat munching an apple. At least, if things hadn't changed much before they munched on the apple, they began to change very soon afterward.

I mention the broad context of social change only in order to go beyond it and point out an order of phenomena that has become increasingly prevalent in the past few years, one that suggests that a social order is beginning to fall apart at the seams, whether or not one sees a new one to take its place. Indeed, the kind of thing I am talking about constitutes a truly revolutionary situation, one that already has begun to have an impact on social work practice and is likely to have an increasing impact for some time to come.

Specifically, I refer to a vast increase in group behavior that represents not the use of conventional methods for bringing about changes in the social order, but rather the use of unconventional methods in order to attack the social order, and through such attack to bring about change.

It appears to me that the impetus for social change today comes more from such revolutionary behavior than from the motivation of incumbents of various

Originally presented as a colloquium paper at the School of Social Service, St. Louis University, April 25, 1968, this paper has also been given in whole or in part at the University of California (Los Angeles), San Diego State University, the University of Alabama, and the University of British Columbia, and as the Dessie E. Kushell Memorial Lecture, American Jewish Committee.

positions, governmental and nongovernmental, in the field of social work or any other field, to bring about changes in their organizations and programs.

We need only look around us to see widely prevalent types of social behavior that are vastly different from the kinds of behavior we were accustomed to fifteen years or so ago.

First we had the beatniks, then the hippies, then the yippies, and God only knows what will take their place tomorrow. We have thousands of suburban housewives descending on Washington to protest the Vietnam war. We have a massive Poor People's March engaging in nonviolent disruption as a tactic for change. We have draft-card burnings, students taking over entire universities in sit-ins, mass picketing of governmental offices, world-renowned medical and spiritual leaders going to jail for allegedly counseling young people to disobey the law, and people refusing to pay taxes as a moral protest. We have people burning down their own neighborhoods, and we have eruptions of simple rapacious looting. We have thousands of young people resigning, as it were, from their own families and revolting against the norms of their parents and resorting to narcotics not primarily as an individual pathology but as a social movement.

One could extend the list. It is already rather long and wide-ranging. My thesis is that the spread of such widely diverse and in some ways bizarre forms of social behavior is not purely adventitious. It represents an important characteristic of current history which merits serious analysis.

NORM-VIOLATING METHODS OF INFLUENCING SOCIAL POLICY

What do all these forms of behavior have in common, besides the fact that most of them were not being practiced so extensively fifteen years ago?

First, they all indicate a discontent with some circumstance of the national social order. Second, whether deliberately or not, they all have an impact on the process of social policy formation in this country.

As an expression of discontent with the national social order, they in turn are part of a larger social phenomenon—a transition from one social order to another. Perhaps the best way to dramatize this transition is to view it from the standpoint of someone who supports the more traditional and conventional norms and values—in short, a cultural conservative.

How dismayed must such a conservative be! His moral and cultural world is disintegrating before his eyes. He sees not only these unintelligible and essentially fearsome behaviors I have catalogued, but he sees other signs of disintegration. Four-letter words permeate contemporary literature. He is exposed to poems with neither rhyme nor meter. He finds metal cylinders suggestive of a factory junk heap offered as sculpture. He sees motion pictures becoming increasingly sadistic and increasingly indecent sexually. He finds church services being held to the accompaniment of a rock combo. He finds people around him with hair hanging below the shoulders, going barefoot, carrying flowers—yes, even the men. He finds youth inclined to laugh at what he always thought of as the eternal verities and the eternal virtues.

One could extend *this* list indefinitely, too. It would indicate the loss of commitment by large segments of the population to the older values, and the taking on of new values that among other things combine a seemingly uninhibited hedonism with diverse new moral injunctions not honored in earlier generations.

Thus the types of social protest activity enumerated earlier are but part of a wider transvaluation—to use Nietzsche's term but not his specific meaning—marking the transition from one set of imperatives to another, whatever that other may turn out to be.

But second, what these activities also have in common is that they influence social policy. This may or may not be what the people who engage in them have in mind. They are thus ways in which people participate in the aggregate process of social policy formulation. The ghetto looter may not have intended it, but his looting and his burning after the assassination of Martin Luther King undoubtedly played a role in the subsequent speedy passage of the Civil Rights Act of 1968, with its remarkably forceful open-housing provisions. The threat of such outbursts constitutes an ever present dynamic in the social policy situation.

Likewise, there seems little doubt that the fact that Lyndon Johnson would have been unable to make personal campaign appearances in 1968 without triggering ugly protest demonstrations and perhaps riots everywhere he went undoubtedly had an impact not only on his decision not to run but also on the assessment of the kind of strategy that would be viable in Vietnam, vis-à-vis both the various Vietnamese and the various Americans here at home.

These are but two illustrations. Actually, all the types of behavior I mentioned earlier can be seen as means of influencing public policy, either on the national or on a more local level. This even includes the hippies, who almost by definition have opted out of the social order—even though they may retain a vestigial psychological (or financial) umbilical cord to Newton or Scarsdale or Grosse Point. For whether or not they consciously planned it so, their opting out has been an influential symbolic act, a pageant both colorful and dramatic. They could not have made a more forceful case against middle-class morality and culture in America than by going off and leaving it, physically, using drugs, sharing in each other's poverty, refusing to fight, sleeping with each other while debasing Eros, proclaiming agape but refusing to acknowledge its biblical origins.

Much the same can be said of those draft-eligible youths who decide to emigrate to Canada in order to escape the draft. They may or may not be primarily preoccupied with their own individual futures, but their act dramatizes a rejection of the total national situation, which includes conscription, and they say no with their feet.

Many of the other types of behavior considered here are much more deliberately aimed at influencing the social process and thus bringing about change. To repeat, what they all have in common is that they represent deviation from the accepted norms of social contest. Whether or not they will it consciously, such deviation is a dynamic for change. As Talcott Parsons has succinctly put it: "Structured deviant behavior tendencies, which are not successfully coped with by the control mechanisms of the social system, constitute one of the principal sources of change in the structure of the social system."[1]

Most Americans are much more familiar with the conventional ways of influencing social policy—the letter to a congressman, the participation in political party activity, the public policy debate, the organized pressure group, the voluntary citizen association. The difference between these ways of influencing policy and the ways of the hippie cult, the draft-card burners, and the Poor People's March is that these latter ways are *not* conventional. Rather, they challenge the conventional ways. They violate the usual norms for contest behavior. They are thus norm-violating methods of social policy participation.

By norm-violating, I do not mean that they violate all norms, but rather that *they violate the conventional norms of American middle-class society for participation in contests over disputed issues.* Nor do I suggest that groups of people engaging in such norm-violating behavior are normless in the sense either of being "amoral" or of being independent of all social sanctions—either of their own group or of others.

Let us examine what is implied by norm-violating methods of social policy participation.

Presumably a democratic, pluralistic society in a period of rapid change must have means through which the diverse values and interests and proposals of various groups receive attention in some type of decision-making process that permits any point of view to affect policy in direct proportion to the number of people who hold it and the depth of feeling with which they hold it.

Political scientists like Edward C. Banfield[2] and Robert A. Dahl[3] and economists like Charles E. Lindblom[4] describe the manner in which pluralistic decision-making allows for adaptive changes whereby social policy is brought into rather close accommodation to the aggregate interests of the diverse parties to policy formulation. Points of view are made known and decisions are reached on controverted issues through a large repertoire of methods of entering the policy-making process—through public debate, through pressure-group activity, through voting, through propaganda campaigns, and through other uses of the resources that each group can muster and bring to bear on the decision-making process.

These are norm-abiding methods of social policy participation, and during most of our history they have generally been considered effective. Why, then, the widespread appearance of norm-violating methods? The simple answer is that many groups find that they are unable to have their views prevail through normal means.

Such an answer helps us little, for this is always the case in a complex heterogeneous society. The crucial point, of course, is that if the system is to be maintained, the losers on any issue, or any combination of issues, have to be willing to suffer defeat but yet support the norms through which the majority will prevails. The system of decision-making is perceived as more important than the particular decision that is reached in any specific case. In a sense, this agreement underlies the social contract.

What makes the difference today, and what makes today's scene truly revolutionary, is that large numbers of people are coming to defect, psychologically, from the established system of decision-making. For their own diverse reasons they are coming to believe that a decision-making system that results in the outcomes they experience as unacceptable is not worth honoring, not worth saving, but rather is in need of radical revision if not utter rejection. They thus feel little commitment to the normal rules of the game for decision-making. Quite the contrary, they may be deliberately hostile to them.

Let me review the discourse to this point. Many types of nonconforming behavior widely prevalent today share two important characteristics. First, they have an effect, whether or not intentional, on public policy. Second, they constitute norm-violating methods of affecting social policy. Their growth indicates a decrease in confidence in the more conventional norms as adequate for bringing about an acceptable social order.

NORM-VIOLATING METHODS AND SOCIAL CONTROL

Perhaps it is well to distinguish, with Robert Merton, between cultural goals and institutionalized norms.[5] There is today a widespread belief that institutionalized norms for achieving the culture's goals are inadequate. This is often the case when an individual or group does not get its way, when the issue is decided against it. In a relatively stable system, however, losers are willing to take their loss and try again tomorrow, still abiding by the conventional norms for contest. Violations of these norms not only would bring about guilt feelings on the part of those responsible for them, but would set in motion various formal and informal social control processes to inhibit the norm-violating behavior and bring the participant back within the more conventional channels.

What is important in today's situation, and what is revolutionary, is the inadequacy of the social control mechanisms that normally assure norm-abiding methods of social contest. The participants have lost the old internalized loyalty to the norms of contest, and the nonparticipants apparently have lost the determination to enforce the norms for conventional contest behavior.

In his *Reflections on Violence,* Sorel quotes Clemenceau approvingly: "There is no better means [than the policy of perpetual concessions] of making the opposite party ask for more and more. Every man or every power whose action consists solely in surrender can only finish by self-annihilation."[6]

Obviously, the prevailing policy can hardly be termed "surrender," as anyone can attest who has seen demonstrating students being swept off their feet with fire hoses or rioters being clubbed into impotence by the police. The point is that despite such countermeasures, norm-violating behavior grows rather than wanes. Why is this so?

One aspect of the situation has to do with powerlessness. Various groups within the population have come to feel relatively powerless to do anything about various conditions that they perceive as undesirable. These various conditions, incidentally, are largely, though not completely, subsumable under two rubrics: the ghettos and the Vietnam war. Tension has mounted with the feeling that something should be done, must be done, and yet little progress is seen, while the problems mount. Since participation through conventional channels seems inadequate to bring about a sufficient response, the alternative to powerlessness is offered by norm-violating patterns.

The second aspect is also fundamental: it is anomie. There is a growing lack of confidence in the basic outlines of American culture and of the American social structure—a sense not merely that somehow the system isn't working properly, but more fundamentally that maybe the system, even when it does work, isn't so good as we thought. What I am trying to indicate here is that the crisis is not only one of institutionalized norms, but also one of cultural goals. And the restiveness about the latter tends to immobilize the control mechanisms that would otherwise be expected to operate to bring those who violate the norms of social policy participation back into line.

DIMENSIONS OF NORM-VIOLATING PARTICIPATION

We come then to one of the important dimensions for analyzing the non-conventional behavior mentioned earlier—the degree of acceptance or rejection of the basic outlines of the American social structure. Obviously, hippies and black militants have in common such a rejection, however much they may differ in their modes of response to it.

Their different modes of response to the rejection, however, illustrate another basic dimension of these various behaviors—the extent to which the norm-violating behavior is purposive in relation to changing the social structure.

By purposive I mean that the behavior is deliberately engaged in as a means of bringing about a change in the social structure. Three examples will indicate the nature of this dimension. The black militant is, generally speaking, purposefully engaged in social policy participation; the hippie is not. Somewhere between them along this dimension is the ghetto rioter engaging in arson or looting.

Another dimension of such behavior is the extent to which the behavior involved actually *is* norm-violating with relation to the major culture. Let us take some examples: Hundreds of college students rang doorbells for Eugene McCarthy in the New Hampshire primary in 1968. In dozens of cities in the United States, weekly anti-Vietnam vigils are held in a perfectly legal manner with the appropriate permits and typically with police protection. Various voter-registration campaigns have been held, particularly among black people who have not yet registered to vote because of fear or apathy.

These instances show that norm-abiding contest behavior merges into norm-violating behavior. The first case was generally perceived, both by the participants and by the voters, as norm-abiding, although it was somewhat unprecedented. In passing, it is important to recall the care with which the participating students were required to abide by middle-class standards regarding haircuts, cleanliness, and attire.

The anti-Vietnam vigils are an interesting case. I do not mean to include all the anti-Vietnam demonstrations, but only a specific set of them which arose from a common source and which involve complete compliance with local ordinances, including police permits and the rest. They are participated in largely by well-dressed, obviously middle-class types—your next-door neighbor. The participants deliberately refrain from incendiary placards, and the vigils are conducted in silence.

What, here, is norm-violating? The vigils certainly are lawful. And they are conducted usually with exemplary demeanor. Yet, in my estimation, they are norm-violating because they involve, and are perceived by both participants and nonparticipants as involving, a symbolic renunciation of the nation's course. They represent, however silent they may be, a huge, reverberating no. They are just the opposite of the little boy's prayer—a classic in simplicity: "Dear God, count me in!" They say, also simply: "Dear Americans, count me out!" As such, they are norm-violating. Many people who agree with the anti-Vietnam position feel that somehow it is basically wrong to stand up in such visible protest. And anyone who has participated can attest to the vicious sneers and verbal denunciations from an occasional "patriot" who quite clearly perceives the threat to the social order.

The third case, voter registration drives in the South, simply illustrates that American society has many subcultures, and what would be norm-violating in one of these, however legal the action, may not be so in another.

These illustrations introduce another important dimension: the extent to which the norm-violating participation is legal or illegal. There is no one-to-one correspondence between behavior that violates the law and behavior that violates the norms of social policy contest. Engaging in illegal behavior is one possible form of norm-violating participation. And where illegal behavior is chosen as a purposeful strategy, it may vary depending on whether the individual is using his own open breaking of the law as a means of pointing out the inequity of the law or of some social condition—in which case he usually does so openly and seeks a legal confrontation—or whether he wishes his illegal act to go unremarked by the law, as in the case of the looter, the hippie drug user, or the political terrorist. But, to repeat, not all norm-violating contest behavior is illegal.

Another dimension along which various types of norm-violating contest behavior are distributed is that of violence–nonviolence. As is well known, both the equal-rights movement and the anti-Vietnam movement are divided on the issue of the acceptability of violent activity as a strategy for change. The point is that both violent activity and nonviolent activity may be norm-violating.

Having defined norm-violating social policy participation and indicated some of the important dimensions on which the diverse forms it takes are distributed, let me make a few additional observations.

First, it would be fallacious to think of all these modes of norm-violating contest behavior as constituting a single social movement. They do not. A social movement is usually thought of as a long-range attempt to bring about a specific change in the social structure or in social behavior. There is no such specific change that unifies the varied types of contest activity under consideration here. What they have in common is not a single goal. A dramatic illustration of this is the grave difficulty that Martin Luther King, Jr., confronted in trying to fuse the anti-Vietnam movement and the equal-rights movement into a single effort.

Second, both norm-violating and norm-abiding methods of social change may be engaged in by the same individuals at different times or in regard to different issues. Thus many of the students who worked for McCarthy saw this effort as their last alternative to working outside the system, to engaging in norm-violating participation. This consideration serves further to reinforce the point that much such protest behavior is associated with powerlessness. It is a plausible hypothesis that *norm-violating behavior may be expected to vary in inverse proportion to the opportunities available for meaningful and effective participation in norm-abiding channels*. And within the norm-violating channels, presumably there is an analogous relationship between the choice of violence and the presumed effectiveness of nonviolence. In both cases, the commitment is for drastic change, change that is perceived as being likely to occur only as a result of norm-violating behavior, with violence resorted to when nonviolence is perceived as ineffective.

Third, some types of norm-violating behavior are employed with the general intent of creating or heightening a revolutionary situation rather than in hopes of effecting any specific outcome. As an example, a student sitting in the path of a Dow Chemical Company recruiter may in fact be attempting through this tactic to keep Dow Chemical recruiters from the campus, but there may be something else involved too. He may at the same time be rebelling against the social order as such, taking this as one tangible way of protesting a much broader spectrum of circumstances. The student who engages in a sit-in because he thinks it will rock the boat and because he thinks the boat ought to be rocked has something in common with the looter who thinks not only of the television set under his arm but that this whole burning and looting will "show them something," and with the young zealot who advocates obscene acts in public, burning dollar bills, and other "shocking" methods of behavior as ways of stirring up the situation, creating a threat to the system, setting things in flux.

Fourth, it is possible to sum up the norm-violating contest behavior as a visceral demonstration of lack of confidence in the will or the ability of the so-called liberals to set the social order right. This is illustrated by the attitude of many black separatists today, that so-called liberals say all the right things but are not able to bring about the necessary changes and, in the last analysis, will side with the system against the inevitable rebellion at continued oppressive conditions. It is akin to Sorel's disdain for the Parliamentary Socialists, who in his view, by seeking to work within the prevailing constitutional system, were actually helping that system to survive without remedying the basic inequities of society, and thus, however inadvertently, having the effect of shoring up a corrupt system and making less likely a basic improvement.[7]

The norm-violator is deliberately dissociating himself from the system. This is the meaning of his norm-violating behavior. In his marrow, he distrusts the system's ability to renew itself. His response, put simply, is either to withdraw from the system psychologically or to try to force the system, as it were, from the outside.

A PERSONAL ASSESSMENT

The discourse so far has been impersonal, but I have no hesitation in giving my own point of view in the matter. I welcome the norm-violating behavior. I welcome it for the simple reason that I believe, with most of the norm-violators, that this society is daily proving its own inability to renew itself within the business-as-usual methods of social policy participation. Nowhere was this more apparent than in the middle of March 1968, when the Kerner Commission report had already been publicized and when in the course of two days the President of the United States declared that despite all the opposition to his policy and the results of the New Hampshire primary, he was going to change his announced course in Vietnam not one whit, and then gave indication that he was considering a cut of eight billion dollars in the federal budget.

I, too, have grave doubts about a system that produces so much inequity at home and so much bloodshed abroad, to the chagrin of the whole world, including former allies. I feel it important to stand up and say no, in just the way we believe the Germans should have done in the 1930s (although I acknowledge that the cases are by no means completely parallel). Like the students who worked for McCarthy in New Hampshire and like Whitney Young in the Urban League, I would prefer to work through norm-abiding methods, and to see others do so. But with Whitney Young I say, "Give us some victories!" There have been precious few in recent years.

I welcome the revolutionary ferment. I, too, believe that the boat must be rocked. But I am for rocking the boat, not drowning its occupants. I certainly do not favor all forms of norm-violating social policy participation, regardless of their consequences. Some I participate in; some I do not participate in, but endorse; and some I do not endorse, like looting and arson, but I think they contribute toward stirring people out of their lethargy; and some I decry.

Misunderstanding is so easy, especially when emotions become aroused. To mention the revolutionary ferment, to say we are living in a social revolution, is not to allude to a one-time event through which large numbers of people will rebel, throw out those in power, and establish a new order. By revolutionary ferment I simply mean a climate in which old values are questioned and established norms for social policy participation are violated. This constant, norm-violating ferment is a much-needed pressure on the conventional processes to change things in order that, among other things, an abrupt violent revolution will not occur. And to repeat, I personally think that our social system needs such impetus, being demonstrably incapable of renewing itself without it.

NORM VIOLATION AND SOCIAL WORK

Norm-violating methods of social policy participation are important for social workers and for social work practice for a number of reasons.

First, I believe that most of the impetus for change in outmoded social institutions of welfare and health care, housing, employment, education, and so on comes not from the occupants of positions within those bureaucracies, but from outside them. Putting this another way, we will see health and welfare institutions changing in response to outside pressures, and through a response by policy-makers, including legislators, to pressures from outside the system in addition to the usual political pressures from within it.

Second, if this is true, then anyone who is interested in trying to bring about changes in the social welfare structure can ill afford to neglect or ignore the dynamic that is coming from the streets. A narrow conception of social planning may ignore it completely.

Third, social workers, caught up as they are between two values that conflict with each other on things that count—the value of social work as a science-oriented profession and social work as a social movement—must make their own individual resolution to the dilemma posed by this conflict. To seek the professional image is to work only within consensus situations, to operate only in the area of the noncontroversial, to accept, deliberately or inadvertently, the present system with its inadequate provision for self-renewal, and, in its worst aspect, to be paid mercenaries of the existing power structure. The other horn of the dilemma is the broad arena of public controversy, which, though it does not necessarily extend to norm-violating contest behavior, extends beyond the bounds of professional norms. But beyond this, social workers can be expected to be no less sensitive than other people—and perhaps rather to be more so—to the utter injustice that usual political processes have proved incapable of overcoming.

I see no ready answer to this dilemma. But in any case, norm-violating contest behavior constitutes an area that the social worker can hardly afford to ignore. I have tried to indicate some of its dimensions, however roughly, in the hope that others may be stimulated to further analysis of this basic characteristic of the contemporary scene and provide us with better tools for understanding it.

NOTES

[1] Talcott Parsons, *The Social System,* 2nd ed. (New York: Free Press, Macmillan, 1964), p. 321.

[2] Edward C. Banfield, *Political Influence* (New York: Free Press, Macmillan, 1961).

[3] Robert A. Dahl, *Who Governs? Democracy and Power in an American City* (New Haven: Yale University Press, 1961).

[4] Charles E. Lindblom, *The Intelligence of Democracy: Decision Making Through Mutual Adjustment* (New York: Free Press, Macmillan, 1965).

[5] Robert K. Merton, *Social Theory and Social Structure,* 2nd ed. (Glencoe, Ill.: Free Press, 1957), pp. 132ff. The present analysis differs from Merton's in that he focuses on the individual's effort to secure culturally defined goals for himself, while the behavior under consideration here involves social change goals for the collectivity and the methods for securing them.

[6] Georges Sorel, *Reflections on Violence,* trans. T. E. Hulme and J. Roth, 2nd ed. (New York: Free Press, Macmillan, 1961), p. 78.

[7] *Ibid., passim.*

3

SOCIAL ACTION:
SELF-CONCEPTION
AND CHANGE STRATEGIES

The somewhat awkward title suggests the central theme of this chapter. In order to talk intelligently of change strategies we must have some conception of what it is we want to change and of who we are who want to change it, and on whose behalf, and with whose help. As we consider these various aspects of the situation, it becomes more meaningful to speak of using this or that particular strategy.

It is difficult to appreciate in any deep sense the truly revolutionary nature of current developments in the society around us. In the field of social work, one often talks of social change, but the social change envisaged is usually of an extremely minor nature. It has to do not with the reorganization of those structural aspects of society that produce hardship and injustice, but rather with the restructuring of service delivery patterns to help those who are their victims.

Let us consider some of the revolutionary ferment that affects social service agencies and the social work profession directly:

A university president recently told a high Washington official that he was simply writing off the university's social work school insofar as a meaningful role in urban problems was concerned, and was looking elsewhere in the university for this kind of relevance.

Hardly a professional social work meeting takes place these days without a black caucus or a social action caucus that registers strong hostility to the

This chapter was prepared as a paper presented at the opening plenary session of the Social Action Workshop, National Conference on Social Welfare, New York City, May 28, 1969.

complacency with which the profession in general and the specific conference in particular are ignoring the implications of today's revolutionary scene.

A few years back, the country's major agency in the much-vaunted attack on poverty adopted the deliberate policy of avoiding the existing social agencies because they were "not in contact with the poor," "not interested in change," and offered little promise.

In a number of social work schools, students are becoming increasingly impatient with curricula that seem outdated and "irrelevant" to the needs of the times.

One could add other such items. There is no need to.

Social service agencies and professional social workers have only recently come to realize that the human problems with which they deal are not merely the products of individual pathologies, but to a large extent are generated by the basic institutional configurations of American society. They do not yet seem to have drawn the relevant implications from this realization. One might expect that if they did so, they would direct their attention increasingly at changing the basic institutions that produce structured unemployment among black youths, serious housing shortages in a land of plenty, migrant workers east, west, and in between working for less than a poverty wage, chronic unemployment in Appalachia, and on through a long list.

One might expect also that from an increased understanding of the structure of American society and of American social institutions would come a realization that social change will not come from the top down. There are two powerful reasons why it will not. One is the fundamental visceral conviction of most professional people and high-status policy-makers that the American social system is fundamentally sound and needs only greater skill in dealing with a few residual problems, which can be met by remedial social agency programs. The other is what Thorstein Veblen would have called their "trained incapacity" —the basic inability we all have acquired, in the course of understanding and adjusting to the existing structure and its supporting norms and values—to recognize alternatives to essentially routine courses of action.

If this is the case, then the needed change will have to come in large part as a result of stimulation from outside the social service agencies as they exist today, and perhaps outside the normal political process of incremental and superficial change, of making minor adaptations—particularly in passive, remedial social services—in order to keep the lid on.

For this reason, social workers who are genuinely concerned with changing those parts of the underlying structure that systematically produce individual pathology—a process as American as baseball—should welcome the growing signs of impatience and the growing strength among their clients and potential clients. The giant masses are stirring, and from their potential threat to the existing institutional structure comes a dynamic for meaningful change, a dynamic that has not yet really been heard but will grow increasingly louder as time goes by. This dynamic may become very cruel and vicious. It has done so already in some instances. Whether or not it continues to do so will depend on the responsiveness not only of social service agencies, but of other parts of the American institutional structure, such as the schools and universities, the police, industry, political parties, and government at various levels.

CONSTRAINTS ON SOCIAL WORKERS

Social workers are hampered in confronting today's needs by three types of constraints.

The first is their claim to professionalism.

The second is their orientation toward system maintenance.

The third is their dependence for legitimation, funding, and support on sources other than their clientele.

The Constraint of Professionalism

Two leading works on planning are indicative of the problem posed by the issue of professionalism. In his book on *The City Planning Process,* Alan Altshuler indicates that city planners, in contrast with social workers, have chosen what I have denoted as one horn of the professionalism dilemma. He states that they attempt in their planning activity to stay within the bounds of their professional expertness. He indicates that this area of expertness is not sufficiently broad even for the relatively narrow spectrum of problems considered under the rubric of comprehensive land-use-planning. He illustrates their ineptness and essential disinclination to engage in a political process in order to get their plans accepted, alluding to this social process aspect (which he implies is wholly outside the field of the professional planner) as opportunism, as distinguished from professionalism.[1] Thus city planners, in restricting the concept of professionalism to the area of their technical expertness, are often confronted with the dilemma of engaging in nonprofessional opportunism or seeing their professional plans go down the drain. (In previous decades they used to "gather dust on the shelf.")

Murray G. Ross, whose *Community Organization* portrays what still remains the underlying rationale of most community workers, took the other horn of the dilemma. He emphasized the process of planning, and subordinated it, together with community integration (which he asserted was more important), to the process of community organization. This he defined as "a process by which a community identifies its needs or objectives, orders (or ranks) them, develops the confidence and will to work at them, finds the resources (internal and/or external) to deal with them, takes action in respect to them, and in so doing extends and develops cooperative and collaborative attitudes and practices in the community."[2]

In so doing, Ross in effect renounces technical-substantive expertness in favor of expertness in utilizing a method of consensus decision-making with "the community." Ross, in other words, frees the social worker from the constraints that Altshuler accepts for the city planner. He sees this not as opportunism, but rather as engaging the community in a process in which action is to be achieved through consensus decision-making on the part of the community.

The price that Ross pays is high, for it is based on the assumption that there is only one "good" for the community, and that, provided the process is adequate, all elements of the community will agree on it. Yet the social worker does not work with the community. He works with people who, because of their official position, or for other reasons that give them high status and considerable power, speak *for* the community, people who define the community's welfare from the vantage point and through the prismatic perspective of high socioeconomic status.

The constraint of consensus planning thus serves as the legitimator that permits the community organizer to engage in social action without being "opportunistic." However, it makes it highly unlikely that he will promote developments that important segments of the elite oppose. He promotes controversial proposals only when a sufficient number of power figures are on his side, so that the decisions that arise within *his* segment of the power structure are based on consensus. And, of course, the issues (such as fluoridation or the need for more mental health services) have a "scientific" basis, and thus are not "really" controversial.

The process of working with all elements of the elite or with sectors of elite support in areas that do not challenge the basic configuration of power is still of great importance and great relevance in many situations. But increasingly these areas of relevance seem to become isolated islands in a sea of larger, more important structural issues for which these methods of professional community organization are ineffective.

To the extent that professionalism is equated with purely "scientific" expertness and is confined to noncontroversial issues based on a consensus of elites, the social worker who casts his lot with professionalism renounces his claim or aspiration to relevance in connection with structural change.

The Constraint of System Maintenance

The second constraint is the orientation of social service agencies and social workers to system maintenance. I allude here to a basic predisposition to identify oneself with the existing American institutional structure and the existing structure of health and welfare services, on the assumption that these structures are capable of meeting today's challenge or, if not, are capable of producing of themselves the changes necessary to meet today's challenge.

Of course, many social workers are active in attempting to induce such changes, either through legislation or through changes in policy within specific agencies. But the principal orientation is nevertheless toward the whole system— to assure that it keeps working, that it meets its challenges, that it preserves basic rights, and so on. Persons who viciously attack the system, regardless of how desperate they may be in response to racism or poverty, are considered disturbances in the system, and remedial action is taken on behalf of the system, to "prevent delinquency," to "prevent riots," and so on, often on the grounds that great economic costs are entailed in a policy of neglect. The system is expected to change of its own accord, through usual policy-formulation processes, provided people are educated to the real state of the situation and are shown that it is in their own eventual self-interest to change.

But as is widely acknowledged, the relevant question today is whether the social worker can work meaningfully and effectively for structural change while operating in the role of a "friend of the court," a gentle gadfly to those in positions of policy-making influence—or whether other types of pressure are not necessary before one can realistically expect meaningful changes. In short, the social worker faces the question of whether he must not, at times, act in the capacity of adversary vis-à-vis his friends in established positions within the system, which may even mean within his own social agency. I say adversary, rather than advocate, and this is deliberate. I want to indicate clearly that I mean something more than advocacy as I understand it—guidance and counsel to disadvantaged groups and representation of their cause in high places. I mean adversary, in the sense of tough and seasoned opposition to existing agency policy—a mode of behavior that may well be interpreted on the part of those in official positions as hostility or betrayal.

I would maintain that we are all in various degrees identified with the existing system and its principal officials, and that this identification debilitates us in our efforts at change, and prevents us from taking an adversary role.

The Constraint of Dependence

The third constraint on social workers is their dependence for legitimation and funding on sources other than their clientele. Many workers have learned to their chagrin that neither city hall nor other powerful organizations and agencies are willing to finance and give moral support to the organizing of disadvantaged groups except under circumstances that ensure that these groups will confine themselves to ineffective strategies, i.e., when they operate in accordance with norms of behavior that usually tip the scales in favor of the people in power.

How often do case supervisors in public assistance line up with protesting welfare mothers to picket the welfare department?

I raise the question not merely for rhetorical purposes—we all know the answer is mighty seldom, if ever—but rather because it illustrates a basic social-psychological aspect of the situation. When the service recipient acts in other than the role of the passive client and takes some type of overt action to exert pressure on the agency, it is expected that the social worker will help the agency to "cool it"; it is not expected that the social worker will ally himself with the client in opposition to the agency. I refer to the expectations not only of agency officials in both governmental and nongovernmental agencies, but of the general public and of most social workers themselves.

I would suggest that most social workers not only are constrained by agency controls; they are constrained by their own attitude toward the client. They identify with him as a person who needs help, which it is to be hoped will be generously given. They do not identify with him as a citizen demanding his legal rights or as a person demanding social justice. They identify rather with the agency, with the system.

Many social workers can testify to the difficulty that social workers encounter when they identify with clients as citizens vis-à-vis their own agencies or vis-à-vis powerful established interests in the community. But many young people who are going into social work are not prepared to let the issue rest there. They have not yet made an adequate "adjustment" to these very real constraints on the social worker. This is the type of thing their older, more experienced colleagues tend to write off as youthful idealism. With a shrug and a couple of friendly clucks, they remind themselves that after a short brush with reality, these youngsters will settle down into comfortable niches in the present structure and work with their elders for gradual change—change that, incidentally, appears to them to be progressing with all the dynamic rapidity of a glacier.

At any rate, these young people are beginning to make "unrealistic" demands that the established institutions support them in their identification with citizen clients rather than with agencies, and that militant effort on behalf of clients must somehow be legitimated.

Is this unrealistic? It seems so. As the saying goes, city hall is not going to support organizations that attack it. But if it is unrealistic, then such unrealism is becoming so widespread and finding such growing numbers of dedicated advocates as to constitute a new dynamic in the social situation and to open up new options.

A business-as-usual attitude regarding change in society and in the established agencies falls far short of realism if it does not recognize these new elements in the situation—the militancy of the disadvantaged and the insurrection within the ranks of young social workers themselves. One might say not only that a proper evaluation of the force of these two dynamisms is essential for the agencies in order that they may perform their tasks in addressing poverty and despair at this late point in the twentieth century, but that it is essential to their very survival.

DIFFICULT ALTERNATIVES

What are the implications of all this for strategies of social change as seen by the social agencies and volunteer and professional workers? One implication seems to be overriding.

Social workers must be clear about the choice that confronts them. On the one hand, they can see themselves as instruments of mercy within a society so structured as to produce misery and despair for millions of its citizens, see themselves trying to develop more effective methods for easing misery and helping individuals to cope with their problems, see themselves trying to plan for more effective delivery systems of social services for those who need them; or they may see themselves as committed to telling their fellow-citizens where the bulk of the problem resides and where the bulk of society's effort must be directed: at the structured poverty, at the unbelievable discrepancies in life chances between a child born in rural Mississippi or in Harlem and a child born in Scarsdale or Winchester, at the unbelievable discrepancies in health care, in treatment by the police and courts, in educational opportunity, in access to the channels of vertical mobility. They can regard the poor not merely with tenderness and sensitivity—though these will never be outdated—but also as citizens justly demanding their rights, as allies in the struggle to bring the changes that are necessary if American society is to redeem itself.

If they choose the former course, if they continue to avoid controversy in the name of professionalism, if they continue to orient themselves to system management and the avoidance of deviancy and disruption, if they continue to identify themselves exclusively with their agencies vis-à-vis the citizen client, they may well avoid some of the hardships they would face if they adopted strategies of contest in regard to their more powerful constituencies. But at the same time, they will find themselves increasingly the target not only of agency clients, who are growing in organization and in strength and in determination to change things, but of other social workers as well—or people who once were social workers or who might have been social workers but who now are not, because they see the social agencies as part of the structure that must be transformed, as part of the problem rather than as part of the solution.

Social action has many facets. It involves working to help ghetto neighborhoods to find greater economic resources; it involves influencing legislators and government officials at local, state, and national levels; it involves utilizing the law and the courts; it involves the public agencies, the church, student power, laymen, voluntary direct service agencies, client organizations, coalitions of various types, and especially black and white coalitions.[3] If it is to be relevant to our condition, it must at times involve taking sides in heated controversies. If this is not the case, then let us not deceive ourselves or others by employing the term "social action."

My plea would be that in any discussion of social action, the truly revolutionary nature of our times be kept in mind—and that we look long and hard at who we are who want to change things, what it is we want to change, on whose behalf, and with whose help.

NOTES

[1] Alan Altshuler, *The City Planning Process: A Political Analysis* (Ithaca: Cornell University Press, 1966), chap. 8.

[2] Murray G. Ross, *Community Organization: Theory and Principles* (New York: Harper, 1955), p. 39. The definition has been slightly shortened in this quotation.

[3] All these facets of social action had been designated for special workshop sessions by the planners of the conference at which this chapter was first presented.

4

TWO MODELS OF
SOCIAL PLANNING

Many converging factors point to the increasing need for inclusive calculation in many types of decisions that formerly were left to the more or less independent discretion of individual agents. Whether the area of decision-making has to do with urban land use or health protection, with the allocation of resources to secure certain national objectives or the distribution of agency services on a community level, or with the myriad other levels and fields where planning has become both relevant and important, the basic consideration is in all cases similar: the allocation of resources and rewards that takes place on the basis of individual decision-making is judged to be inadequate to maximize goal attainment in the aggregate. The simplest example is the traffic light, which permits, through aggregate decision-making, a more rapid and painless flow of traffic than would occur with individual drivers trying to poke and probe their way through the intersection.[1]

What makes the development of interest in inclusive planning especially problematic is that it is fraught with value considerations as well as considerations of the relationship between planning as a process of rational calculation, on the one hand, and the interplay of social forces, on the other.

Two somewhat contrary conceptions of the planning process are in current use in such widely diverse areas as national economic planning, health and welfare planning, city planning, and planning for housing. They imply different courses of action and utilize different methods, calling for different competencies. Let us explore these differences.

The differences are obscured by the generally accepted categorization of

Written in 1965, heretofore circulated in dittoed form.

planning as rational, goal-directed behavior seeking the optimum adaptation of means to ends as guided by a limiting set of social values. There is general agreement that the purpose of planning, in Eckstein's words, "is to 'rationalize' the activities on which planning is imposed; to make subject to calculation what was previously left to chance, to organize what was previously unorganized, to replace spontaneous adjustment with deliberate control."[2]

The difference in the two conceptions centers around the problem of how to relate the social and political context in which planning occurs to the planning process itself.

One conception of the planning process confines itself exclusively to the substantive aspects of the formulation of objectives, the allocation of resources, the disposition of effort, and the appraisal of goal attainment. Values are considered as nonrational elements that are given, not adduced. The exigencies of political party politics or of bureaucratic politics are considered as interfering elements extraneous to the rational planning process. The question of eventual adoption and implementation by the appropriate bodies is likewise extraneous to the planning process as such, and accommodation of such questions in the substantive aspects of a plan is considered a departure from rational planning. Such sociopolitical exigencies are considered irrelevant to the problem of the rational allocation of resources to accomplish predefined ends.

Since, under this conception, planning occurs as a purely rational process abstracted from the realities of the social situation in which it occurs, this approach can be characterized as *abstract* and *rational*.

A substantially different conception of planning has arisen as an alternative approach to the planning process. Rather than starting from the desideratum of perfect rationality in the adaptation of means to ends, it emphasizes gradualism, improvement, the social process of group problem-solving and plan implementation. It formulates its rationale out of the empirical experience derived from specific episodes or "campaigns" to attack this or that problem through concerted action. The problems, whether child labor, housing, income maintenance, or whatever, are situations in which the unimpeded operation of the market does not result in an optimum allocation of resources toward the achievement of maximized need satisfaction. The emphasis is on attacking "social problems" through concerted, purposeful effort.

Since the problems are so apparent and the desired states to be achieved so obviously "better" than the ones being combated, the question of a rigorous methodology for assessing costs and benefits, and more particularly the weighing of quite different kinds of activity in relation to each other in order to obtain optimal allocation of resources and distribution of benefits, are often neglected. The main emphasis therefore is not on choosing between possible courses of action, but rather on mobilizing effort to improve situations that are perceived as social problems.

Thus the emphasis of this conception of planning has been on social process and social action, and the logical rationale of planning has been relatively neglected. There has grown up a considerable literature of "practice theory" in this approach, especially in relation to the field of community welfare organization. Since this conception offers no method for the rational selection of objectives and disposition of efforts, but instead offers a great emphasis on and a considerable body of empirically derived theory regarding the social process of goal-setting and effort distribution, it can be described as *concrete* and *social*.

THE ABSTRACT-RATIONAL MODEL

Max Weber has given the classical depiction of the utility of abstract models of social action:

> For the purposes of a typological scientific analysis it is convenient to treat all irrational, affectually determined elements of behavior as factors of deviation from a conceptually pure type of rational action. . . . The construction of a purely rational course of action in such cases serves the sociologist as a type ("ideal-type") which has the merit of clear understandability and lack of ambiguity. By comparison with this it is possible to understand the ways in which actual action is influenced by irrational factors of all sorts, such as affects and errors, in that they account for the deviation from the line of conduct which would be expected on the hypothesis that the action were purely rational.[3]

This rationale, originally formulated to serve the purposes of scientific investigation, has been adopted quite widely as the basis for the *applied* field of planning. The rational-abstract model places deliberate stress on eliminating all nonrational elements from the planning process as such, confining itself to an adaptation of means to ends in a purely substantive sense. Problems of acceptance and implementation of the plan do not thereby vanish, but are either ignored, delayed, or passed on to another body. Once the rational plan is developed and presented, attention is then turned to its acceptance and implementation.

What this relationship of planning process to implementation process may become in the ebb and flow of issues and politics may best be illuminated by a case illustration. One of the most systematic case studies of the planning process employing the abstract-rational model was made by Meyerson and Banfield.[4] They were painstaking in elucidating the concepts they employed in their analysis, including the concept of planning. They categorized planning as "the rational selection of a course of action," and they described a rational decision explicitly, with reference to Herbert Simon and Talcott Parsons:

> By a *rational* decision, we mean one made in the following manner:
> 1. the decision-maker considers all of the alternatives (courses of action) open to him; i.e., he considers what courses of action are possible within the conditions of the situation and in the light of the ends he seeks to attain; 2. he identifies and evaluates all of the consequences which would follow from the adoption of each alternative; i.e., he predicts how the total situation would be changed by each course of action he might adopt; and 3. he selects that alternative the probable consequences of which would be preferable in terms of his most valued ends.[5]

They employed this conception as the framework for selecting, organizing, and evaluating their data on the planning activities of the Chicago Housing Authority. They acknowledged, though, that no decision can be perfectly rational because of the impossibility of having complete knowledge of all alternatives and all consequences. They differentiated carefully between planning and politics, defining the latter as "the activity (negotiation, argument, discussion, application of force, persuasion, etc.) by which an issue is agitated or settled."[6]

Significantly, the Housing Authority apparently did likewise, first formulating its plan, then deciding on the strategy it would utilize in getting the plan accepted. The plan was decimated in the ensuing struggle for implementation—to such an extent that some of the planning staff thought that no action on housing would have been better than the action that was finally determined in the political process.

The question naturally occurs: Would a different model, one that called for incorporating an accommodation of some of the political realities into the plan, have yielded a more acceptable result? Or would this have been the very negation of the rational planning process?

To clarify the question, let us attempt a systematic description of the abstract-rational model of planning.

1. The planning is *abstract* in the sense that it confines itself to the technical problems to be solved, either ignoring the political process (considered in its broadest terms) or taking certain political conditions and limitations as given, a set of limits within which the technical problem must be solved. It thus abstracts the technical, substantive aspects from the total problem involved in rationalizing decision-making, for it does not seek to rationalize these social factors, but to ignore them or accept them without analysis.

It follows that if the planning body does not engage in rational analysis of the political factors as part of the planning process, these factors become resolved outside of the planning framework and thus are not subject to any process that can properly be called planning; or perhaps rational calculation is given to questions of bargaining, politics, legitimation, and the rest, but as a separate process and perhaps by a different body, *extraneous* to the planning body.

2. Thus, in the abstract-rational model, rational calculation is restricted to the *substantive* aspects of planning. The tangible subject matter—whether it be highway improvement, the provision of health services, or the development of subsidized low-cost housing—thus becomes the principal, if not the exclusive, emphasis in the rational adaptation of means to ends. The social processes that surround this substantive planning function do not receive attention as part of the planning except, as indicated above, where they are considered as limiting the conditions within which planning must confine itself.

3. Although perhaps not logically derivable from the above characteristics, the planning procedure associated with them is usually conceived in relation to specific programs, either self-contained and complete in themselves, or else to be followed by other plans for additional, related programs. Thus such planning often takes the form either of completely separate one-shot ventures or of a series of such discrete plans following each other in time. The latter may take place when a planning body is charged with periodically evolving a plan of operations, usually on an annual basis. In either case, the planning proceeds in *discrete* units, rather than as a continuous process.

4. In this type of planning, along with the substantive considerations, primary attention is given to the objective to be accomplished, in contrast to the alternative of concentrating principally on gradual betterment of the existing situation. The new goal—so many housing units, so many miles of concrete highway, so many new hospital beds—tends to become the focus, with technical calculation being given to the most expeditious technical sequence that will attain it. In this sense, it is primarily oriented not toward improving the present state but toward accomplishing some *final state,* however temporary this "final" state may be acknowledged to be.

5. Because little or no attention is given in the planning process to the social and political aspects of the plan's implementation, the planning body is different from the action system in which decision-making and implementing power reside. Thus the planning system is *separate from the action system,* or else it forms only one small component of the action system.

6. Finally, abstract-rational decision-making tends to be *monistic* in the sense that the planning body, in order to meet its technical requirements, must establish exclusive control over the major components of the planning area. To the extent that other planning agencies and action systems modify the plan in the political arena, the substantive aspects become resolved not by rational calculation but through such processes as bargaining and conflict. But the

planning body does not incorporate these procedures within the planning process, since to do so would vitiate the rationality of the process. The demand that rationality makes for inclusiveness and autonomy thus constitutes a pressure toward unified planning auspices, centralized under hierarchical control.

To summarize, in the abstract-rational model for planning, the substantive aspects are abstracted from the total situation; the political aspects are considered extraneous; rational calculation is confined to the substantive aspects, tends to be organized into discrete units, and is final-state oriented; the action system and planning system do not coincide, and the tendency is toward monistic decision-making.

Certain disadvantages of the abstract-rational model are implicit in the characteristics outlined above. Some of these are clearly documented in the Meyerson and Banfield analysis of the planning of the Chicago Housing Authority.

The Housing Authority developed its plan of site selection and allocation of housing units without any significant interaction with the City Council, the body that would have to approve the housing sites. On completion of the plan, recognizing that there would be resistance by the council, the authority decided to publicize the plan and bring open pressure to bear on the council. The council balked, and a long political controversy ensued.

At first, certain alterations by the City Council were made in the plan as a result of a difficult and somewhat disappointing process of political negotiation. These particular changes, although they were not desired by the Housing Authority, were not judged as unacceptably bad. As a result, the Housing Authority came to accept and support this modified plan, as though it had been dictated not by the exigencies of political compromise but solely by the logic of rational calculation.

But more drastic changes were eventually made, so drastic that to some of the staff the plan finally appeared worse than no project at all. Thus though the adoption of a rational plan had been the goal, the result was just the opposite, with purely political, nontechnical considerations playing an even larger role than might otherwise have been the case.

The above difficulties illustrate the problems of implementing a plan, even when it has been devised in perfect accord with the rational-abstract model. Actually, however, there is another order of difficulties, which are perhaps much more inherent in the process of rational planning itself. Some of these difficulties have been pointed out by Eckstein in his penetrating analysis of planning in the British Health Service.[7] He found the process of rational planning beset with psychological difficulties, logical difficulties, and difficulties stemming from lack of control. The last two are highly illuminating. Regarding logical difficulties, he writes:

In particular, they [the Health Service planners] must always make rationally related, consistent series of decisions where the market de-

manded only single, supposedly self-relating decisions. To cite a simple
example: the Health Service planners have to dole out a limited supply
of capital goods in such a way that the most will be got from the out-
lay: how are they to do this in a rational way? . . . Each individual
decision logically implies a series of further decisions, stretching out
into the most remote recesses of the Service, each one of which should
also be made on rational grounds.[8]

He also points out that certain of the Health Service objectives, such as the
respective goals of rational and democratic administration, were logically inconsistent, as was likewise the choice between minimizing costs and removing
all barriers to treatment.[9]

Of course, it might be asserted that conflicting goals are not exclusive to
the abstract-rational model. This is quite true, but we shall turn later to the
question of whether perhaps other models are better equipped to accommodate
the difficulty of conflicting goals.

Equally important difficulties lie in the area of lack of control. Eckstein
points out that lack of control leads to several types of adaptive behavior by the
planners: (1) the use of routine and stereotyped rules, (2) oversimplification,
(3) rigidity and inertia, (4) political rather than rational decision-making, and
(5) centralization of administration. He points out that these adaptive behaviors
involve either decreasing the area of rational decision-making or resorting to
nonrational modes of behavior.[10] For example, centralization

is clearly designed to facilitate both calculation and control. But insofar
as it increases both the number of factors which must be taken into
account by a single authority and the range of that authority's direct
responsibility for the consequences of decisions, it increases precisely
those tensions which lead to the breakdown of rational action.[11]

And with regard to oversimplification, he writes:

All this illustrates one of the fundamental dilemmas of the planning
process: the need to operate either without standards of calculation or
with overstandardized and oversimplified procedures. . . . They [the
planners] try to maximize the conditions of formally rational at the
expense of substantively rational behavior; in short, they tend to re-
create in the planned system the very faults of the spontaneous
system.[12]

Difficulties of another type confront the rational-abstract model, difficulties
that may be termed *technical*. They are derived in part from the logical difficulties mentioned above. Even if it were theoretically possible to overcome

some of these practical implementational and inherent difficulties, there remains the problem of technical competence at any particular stage of the development of science and technology. The need for multiplying the number of decisions that must be centrally made on the basis of calculation, rather than entrusted to the market, makes extreme demands on planners, who must gather the necessary data, assess the probable results of alternative lines of action, and make the necessary simultaneous adaptations in all the other aspects of the plan.

This technical difficulty posed by the very volume of rational decisions to be made has been a strong handicap to planning in the communist countries, and it is significant that a number of them, notably the USSR, Yugoslavia, Poland, and the German Democratic Republic, have made greater or lesser attempts to decentralize their planning and to turn over certain segments of decision-making to the market. They have found that electronic computers have been of some help, and they are actively exploiting computer possibilities. Yet the trend is definitely toward decentralization of decision-making. It is of course true that decentralized decision-making can also follow the rational-abstract planning model, and most characteristically does follow it; but the difficulty then takes the form of the need for nonrational processes such as political bargaining and conflict in order to reconcile inconsistencies among the various decentralized plans, thus introducing nonrationality at relatively high levels in the planning process.

But perhaps the most decisive critique of rational-abstract planning has been made by Braybrooke and Lindblom in *A Strategy of Decision*.[13] They insist that the rational-abstract model—or the "synoptic ideal," as they call it—is not adapted to man's limited problem-solving capacities; is not adapted to inadequacy of information; is not adapted to the costliness of analysis; is not adapted to failures in constructing a satisfactory evaluative method (whether a rational deductive system, a welfare function, or some other). It is not adapted to the closeness of observed relationships between fact and value in policy-making; it is not adapted to the openness of the systems of variables with which it contends; it is not adapted to the analyst's need for strategic sequences of analytical moves, and it is not adapted to the diverse forms in which policy problems actually arise.[14]

In short, the rational-abstract model, though apparently logical and rational, is beset with grave practical and methodological difficulties. While in their critique Braybrooke and Lindblom were primarily though not exclusively considering welfare economics, the same might be said for abstract-rational models using other logical strategies. Thus, for example, Simon has concluded, with regard to game theory, that "not only does it leave the definition of rational conduct ambiguous in all cases save the zero-sum two-person game, but it requires of economic man even more fantastic reasoning powers than does classical economic theory."[15]

But enough has been said about the difficulties, both theoretical and practical, presented by the abstract-rational model. Perhaps it is well to consider the admonition that Max Weber gave in proposing the use of rational models in scientific investigation:

> Only in this respect and for these reasons of methodological convenience is the method of sociology "rationalistic." . . . It certainly does not involve a belief in the actual predominance of rational elements in human life, for on the question of how far this predominance does or does not exist, nothing whatever has been said. That there is, however, a danger of rationalistic interpretations where they are out of place naturally cannot be denied. All experience unfortunately confirms the existence of this danger.[16]

THE CONCRETE-PROCESSUAL MODEL

Is it either logically possible or methodologically desirable to incorporate the political exigencies surrounding the technical planning process into a planning model?

As a preliminary step toward considering this question, let us review an approach that places emphasis on the total social process of planning rather than on only its technical rational components.

Murray G. Ross has given a widely known formulation of this type of approach. Referring to what we are here calling the abstract-rational model of planning, he writes:

> Surely there is a place for such planning—and one would hope that some of it would find expression in the community planning we are discussing. But, essentially, here we are concerned with "action planning"—planning which leads to action in respect to a problem. For this reason some of the steps to be taken, some of the people to be involved, and some of the considerations allowed to condition the solution differ from those present when action in respect to a problem is hoped for, but the possibility of such action is not permitted to affect the purity of the plan.[17]

On this basis, Ross develops a series of "steps in planning," which include: "1) definition of the problem; 2) study of the nature, meaning, and implications of the problem; 3) decision regarding ultimate solutions; and 4) action on the solution agreed upon."[18] He asserts that the action phase is "not separate from the other aspects of planning," even though it requires distinctive strategy and skills. Political and other social considerations affecting acceptance and implementation are to be intricately connected with the planning process: "In weighing the alternatives and reaching a decision, a large number of factors must be considered by the group. These relate to systems of belief prevalent in the community, power factors present, vested interest that may be threatened, the degree of support likely in the community."[19]

Ross is, of course, not alone in proposing a planning model that incorporates the social and political aspects of acceptance and implementation into the making of the plan itself. The model he proposes is representative of much of the literature in such diverse but related fields as adult group education, community development, community organization for social welfare, and so on.

Yet the proponents of this type of model by and large offer no systematic strategy for rational decision-making within this dynamic planning process. There is no counterpart here for cost-benefit analysis, or for the substantive "engineering" procedures of, say, the city planner. There is, for example, no strategy for the rational modification or realignment of conflicting goals, or for calculating how much of the substantive part of the plan should be exchanged for how much political support. In its purest form, the planning process according to this model becomes not a reasoning process but a social interaction process in which relatively undefined exchanges are made in an operation that approximates bargaining much more closely than rational calculation.

Of course, it is theoretically possible to take a dialectic conception of this interaction process as an actual unfolding of "reason" in the Hegelian sense. Thus the planning group could be conceived as "acting out" a reasoning process in a type of Socratic dialogue whose resultant is the merging of the various partial and fragmentary points of view into a reasoned amalgam. Such a dialectic process in group decision-making has been expounded notably by Mary P. Follett.[20] In this type of "creative experience," the interchange of diverse viewpoints leads to a "higher truth," which was not implicit in the fragmentary viewpoints with which the discussion began. The conception is highly suggestive, but falls far short of a specific rationale for assuring that the solution arrived at is a rational resolution of logical and processual considerations.

Thus the social process model of planning accommodates the processual components but pays the price of giving up rational calculation at the most crucial points—just the reverse of the abstract model.

Is there no prospect, then, for a rational planning model that will incorporate acceptance and implementation components? As a second step toward consideration of this question, let us consider the same dimensions as those that were used to describe the abstract-rational model. In this process, it might be well to keep in mind what is implied in such a model: it would afford a strategy for the simultaneous application of rational calculation to both the substantive-technical and the processual-implementive components of the total planning problem.

1. Such a model would call for a *concrete* type of planning, in that the technical problems to be solved are not abstracted out of their full social situation but are viewed as parts of the total configuration, including both technical and social process components. Technical solutions would not be "superimposed" on an existing social-political situation, since they were not abstracted from the situation to begin with.

2. Rational calculation would be directed at the complete problem, and would have to be able to accommodate both technical and processual factors. Thus it would include *processual* components.

3. Although it is not logically necessary as a corollary, one might expect such a planning process to be a *continuous* interaction process, in which plans would have the status wherever appropriate of tentative working solutions, or integral parts of an emerging action, rather than of a series of discrete, one-shot accomplishments. It is of course obvious that some substantive aspects of planning must be considered in discrete units. Either one builds a bridge or one doesn't—it is hardly feasible to "move toward" building a bridge through building, say, an eighth of it and then testing experience with resultant traffic conditions to decide whether perhaps another eighth, all things considered, would be a reasonable allocation of wealth and effort. Nevertheless, wherever possible, there would be the greatest flexibility to provide for adaptations in plan according to intervening experience; open-ended plans, rather than closed ones.

4. As indicated, such a process, placing emphasis on constant review of experience and evaluation of small steps in the light of the way they alter the existing situation, would be *present-state* oriented, rather than future-state oriented. Thus, though the two are admittedly extreme, the emphasis would be less on how to accomplish some carefully thought-out future state of affairs than on working with the difficulties in the present situation and taking small, tentative, consecutive steps to improve it, each step being subject to review and modification on the basis of experience. A passage from Meyerson and Banfield is suggestive in this regard:

> What was needed was not research, but experiment or, better yet, "pilot" operation of various alternatives. . . . The way to discover and evaluate the advantages and disadvantages of slum rehabilitation as an alternative to slum clearance, for example, was actually to rehabilitate a few blocks and to appraise the results with care. Similarly, a way to find out whether publicly owned but privately managed projects would have fewer status disadvantages in the eyes of white tenants and neighboring property owners was to turn one or two projects over to private management and to study the results.[21]

5. Almost by definition, such planning involves various parties to the problem in the planning process itself. Thus, key figures and groups in the determination of the fate of the plan assume a greater role in the actual planning. The planning process is not left to engineers, social welfare experts, public health experts, or whomever, but involves those people who are crucial for legitimation, implementation, and support of the plan. Thus *the planning body and the action system tend to coincide.* This does not mean that all people who are affected by the plan need participate in the planning process. Although there are various ways for including large numbers of people in goal-setting, as well as in choices among alternative means, representation and delegation can be employed to keep the number of key actors in the interactive planning process to a practical minimum.

Two models for the practical process of planning under this restriction are possible. One calls for the negotiation of various points of view in the action system until a resolution of differences has been reached; then the working out of a technical plan to incorporate the agreed-upon working basis is turned over to a technical staff. The other calls for a closer than usual interaction between technical planning staff and larger action system so that technical aspects enter the calculations as an interaction process, rather than as the second phase of a two-stage model. This second model might be considered more germane to the other characteristics of the concrete-processual model.

Dr. Eugen Pusic, of the University of Zagreb, writes:

> The machinery for planning should correspond to the politico-technical character of the process. In the course of the preparation, already, expertise and political choice go hand in hand. The body responsible for it should, therefore, combine technical competence with political responsibility. The best combination will probably be a small collective body on which political representatives and senior planning technicians have equal standing.[22]

6. Finally, the concrete-processual model tends to be *pluralistic.* It recognizes the multiplicity of planning centers, each with limited power, each having to adapt to the planned behavior of other planning-action systems. It is flexible and emergent rather than rigid and discrete, and it does not depend on the assumption of total rational control of the key substantive aspects of the planning field. It is therefore capable of applying the process of rational calculation to the situation existing at any particular point in time, and it can consider it in conjunction with the more or less uncontrolled (by it) planning and action of other systems. To use the slang expression, it can always "take it from there."

SOME PROBLEMS TO BE SOLVED

This all sounds rather challenging, but is it possible? Particularly, does not such an open system of planning actually reduce the concept to one almost completely devoid of rational calculation in the ordinary sense of the term?

Let us turn for a moment to the question of which actor it is who does the rational calculation, and what his relationship is to the action system. Here again there are two conceptions. The abstract-rational conception posits a purely rational and dispassionate calculator, who plans rationally and who must be assumed to know the answer to each technical problem raised by the planning task or to be able to determine it in the process of rational calculation. One must assume that all relevant problems (all problems appropriate for rational calculation) are of a technical nature, and also that all other problems and viewpoints are irrelevant. But as the plan runs the gauntlet of acceptance or rejection —or concessions in recognition of political or economic pressures, of inevitable modifications—the planner's principal orientation, insofar as he is still one of the principal actors, is to salvage as much of the technical rationality as possible. In this model, not only is rationality limited to the technical aspects of the plan, but the exercise of rational calculation is confined to the planner, as over against all other relevant parties with their values and vested political or economic interests.

In the concrete-social model, the technical expert (the planner of the above model) becomes neither the sole planner nor the sole contributor of rationality. He contributes technical rationality, but either he supplements this with rational calculation designed to embrace and make the "best possible" resolution of all the components—technical, political, bureaucratic, economic, and so on—or he becomes merely one interacting unit in the process that embraces them. Rationality does not consist of his salvaging his plan, no matter how technically perfect, but rather of his contributing an appropriate share of rationality with respect to the technical aspects of the problem, to be evaluated in relation to the rationality contributed by others in bringing different but equally relevant aspects of the total situation under rational calculation—the value aspects, the political aspects, the financial aspects, and so on. Thus the planner is not assumed to have the prescience to know what is the rational "best" and then to further the good by preserving as much as possible of the best. He is assumed only to be competent to participate in the development of a mutually acceptable mix of all the relevant aspects. This is a mix that he does not know beforehand. It is not simply a wearing down of his "better" plan in a grudging concession to reality. It is the development of the optimum configuration on the basis of a reality that includes the major aspects of the total situation.

The question arises: How is the "optimum configuration" to be recognized when it is attained, and what method of rational calculation can be employed in working toward it?

In a paper at a recent national conference on centrally planned change, James Q. Wilson posed the problem as follows: "The problem of centrally planned change is essentially a problem of power. There must be—whatever else exists—some actor who can carry into effect ends that have been arrived at by some method other than the registration of an equilibrium among contending interest groups."[23]

What method? There is the rub. Apparently there is only one example of a method that has been carefully and exhaustively worked out for rational calculation under conditions such as those outlined in the concrete-processual model above. That is the one described in *A Strategy of Decision* by Braybrooke and Lindblom. After subjecting the synoptic ideal (roughly, the rational-abstract model) to a penetrating critique, they describe and explore the implications of an alternative. The strategy is incremental in that it focuses on comparing relatively small increments of change with various alternatives, including the status quo. Further, they insist that such increments can be rationally assessed without being ranged within a preference order of all possible states, such as is demanded, for example, in welfare economics. Alternative policies can be assessed according to their relevance to the actual possible choices that present themselves. Thus their strategy is particularly adapted to the type of open-ended, free-flowing planning that is specified by the concrete-processual model.

The policy analyst concentrates his attention on

> the increments by which value outputs or value consequences differ from one policy to another. He need not ask himself if liberty is precious and, if so, whether it is more precious than security; he need only consider whether an increment of the one value is desirable and whether, when he must choose between the two, an increment of one is worth an increment of the other.[24]

Choices are thus comparative rather than absolute.

The strategy also permits the consideration of only a restricted variety and number of consequences for any given policy, demanding neither omniscience nor a complete exhausting of all possible consequences.

Rather than adjusting means to preestablished ends, the strategy provides for a reciprocal consideration of both, for "clearly what we establish as policy objectives we derive in large part from an inspection of our means."[25] The consideration of the desirable, in other words, is limited to a consideration of the possible, and these, moveover, as matters of degree rather than of kind.

The strategy also provides for a continuous reconstruction of the treatment of the data, being open to reformulations of the problem as well as to a reconsideration of means and ends as their interrelationships are more fully explored. It is characterized by "serial analysis and evaluation," rather than one-shot solutions. Further, the emphasis is on remedying ills rather than achieving abstract goals.

> These characteristics of the strategy again parallel a feature of incremental politics. Policy aims at suppressing vice even though virtue cannot be defined, let alone concretized as a goal; at attending to mental illness even though we are not sure what attitudes and behavior are most healthy; at curbing the expansion of the Soviet Union even though we do not know what positive foreign policy objectives to set against the Kremlin's; at reducing the governmental inefficiencies even though we do not know what maximum level of competence we can reasonably expect; at eliminating inequities in the tax structure even though we do not agree on equity; at destroying slums even though we are uncertain about the kinds of homes and neighborhoods in which their occupants should live.[26]

Finally, it is assumed that analysis and evaluation occur at various loci in society.

Analysis and evaluation are disjointed in the sense that various aspects of public policy and even various aspects of any one problem or problem area are analyzed at various points, with no apparent coordination and without the articulation of parts that ideally characterizes the subdivision of topics in synoptic problem-solving.[27]

A somewhat analogous though less exhaustively elaborated strategy for planning was given much earlier by Herbert A. Simon.[28]

Unfortunately, these strategies appear to fall short of providing an adequate framework and rationale to aid in calculation where the concrete-processual model is used. Braybrooke and Lindblom go far in analyzing the dimensions of analysis and demonstrating their fluid interrelations and the possibility for simultaneous calculation. This in itself is a great service. They have demonstrated that rational calculation can be expanded to include not merely technical considerations but also the whole configuration of values and forces around the planning process. Obviously, we cannot expect to find here such precision of prescription as can be found in welfare economics and game theory; but these, of course, are able to offer such mathematical virtuosity only by assuming powers of rational calculation that virtually do not exist.

In the light of the above analysis, it might be well to consider a definition of rational planning behavior as exemplified in the concrete-processual model: Rational planning behavior is oriented toward a conscious assessment of values, situations, objectives, methods, implementation, and acceptance in their relation to each other and to an aggregate outcome that is the optimum combination of these components, an outcome that emerges in the dynamics of the planning process.

In this connection, it is interesting to note the functions that the director of the Chicago Housing Authority came to ascribe to that agency's planning division. Of the seven listed, three are highly relevant to the present discussion:

> 3. Have a comprehensive knowledge of the plans of effectuating agencies like the Board of Education, transit, etc. Because there is no master plan, it is necessary for the Planning Division to keep in touch with these agencies and to do joint planning with them when feasible.
>
> 4. Collect data on land use; present use and trends, areas of residential and industrial use. Be able to make the best possible case for the best possible site. . . .
>
> 7. Influence the effectuating agencies to serve CHA's ends as well as their own; for example, encourage the Plan Commission to make studies which will be of use to the Authority.[29]

Finally, in the light of the contrast of the two models of rational planning, it is interesting to consider some of the stronger criticisms that have been leveled against social planning, and the directions from which they come. Perhaps the three strongest arguments that have been advanced in recent decades are that social planning is utopian, that it is authoritarian, and that it is inept.

As utopian, social planning comes under serious criticism from two standpoints. The first is that it is so far divorced from reality that it has little practical relevance. The idea is well illustrated in Wayne McMillen's skeptical comment on the Planning Division of the Chicago Housing Authority: "It would be silly to say that Planning applies criteria to sites. There is only one criterion: can we get it approved by the Council?"[30] More frequently, perhaps, planning is criticized for having as its principal output a series of formidable documents, each with massive rationality, each most impressive, each gathering dust on the shelf.

Second, social planning is criticized as being authoritarian and essentially antidemocratic. This attitude stems from at least two sources, which, though not identical, are related. One is a generalized stereotyped image of the planner as someone who seeks total power in order to impose his ends and means, in however rationally conceived a plan, on a grudging citizenry. The other, particularly common among professional process workers in community development, social welfare, adult education, and related fields, is resentment against the outcome of the planner's alleged disregard of the need for democratic value legitimation. It appears to his critics that by coming to dictate rather than negotiate the ends to be achieved and the means of achieving them, the planner inadvertently assures that his plans will be opposed, and that the entire concept of planning will come into disrepute. (Interestingly, though, at other times some of these same professionals speak disparagingly of the "backward" elements in their constituencies, who are not prepared to accept their own particular plans and strategies.)

Third, social planning is criticized as inept. This criticism varies from the course elbow-nudging of the jokesters, with their hilarious stories of oversights and miscalculations in this or that planning program, to the careful analysis of actual oversights and miscalculations, which as a matter of fact do frequently occur in the attempt to apply rationality to highly complex and interrelated planning fields.

Each of these three orders of critique deserves extensive analysis, which space considerations do not permit. I shall make only one observation about them: They all are arguments that apply most directly to the rational-abstract model of planning. The concrete-processual model is more or less deliberately designed to alleviate the difficulties implied in the criticisms.

The concrete-processual model cannot assume that the planning process can free itself of the restraint of actual social reality, of the potentials of actual implementation, as these are mediated, sooner or later, in legitimation, in participation, and in the modifying, accepting, and implementing aspects of the planning process. It assumes a plurality of centers of goal-setting and policy formation, thus not positing, even in its logical prerequisites, a centralized authority with sufficient control to enforce totally integrated planning. Finally, in its more modest scope, in its continuous feedback and modification, in its open subjection to the waxing and waning of specific economic and political forces, it permits a selection of planned activities which corresponds closely to the size and scope that practical wisdom and technological skills can accommodate.

As scientists and professional people become increasingly aware of the configuration of developments that demand increasing application of rational calculation to matters that were earlier left to the market, perhaps more attention will be given to further development of the necessary rational strategy for calculation which is called for by the concrete-processual model. Such attention is necessary if rational calculation is to be extended to the processual aspects of planning. The problems of devising a rationale for calculation are truly formidable, but the potential yield is great.

In any case, it should be helpful to remain aware of the important alternatives that are presented by the two contrasting models of the planning process.

NOTES

[1] More detailed analysis of concerted or inclusive decision-making is given in chap. 9.

[2] Harry Eckstein, "Planning in the Health Service," in *Trends in the National Health*

Service, ed. James Farndale (New York: Macmillan, 1964); originally in Eckstein, *The English Health Service* (Cambridge: Harvard University Press, 1958).

[3] Max Weber, *The Theory of Social and Economic Organization,* trans. A. M. Henderson and Talcott Parsons (New York: Oxford University Press, 1947), p. 92.

[4] Martin Meyerson and Edward C. Banfield, *Politics, Planning, and the Public Interest* (Glencoe, Ill.: Free Press, 1955).

[5] *Ibid.,* p. 314.

[6] *Ibid.,* p. 304.

[7] Eckstein, "Planning in the Health Service."

[8] *Ibid.,* p. 48. It is interesting to note that the same difficulty applies to "single, supposedly self-relating decisions." But in these, the market presumably offers a built-in corrective that does not operate in centrally planned decisions.

[9] *Ibid.,* p. 47.

[10] *Ibid.,* p. 51.

[11] *Ibid.,* pp. 55–56.

[12] *Ibid.,* p. 53.

[13] David Braybrooke and Charles E. Lindblom, *A Strategy of Decision: Policy Evaluation as a Social Process* (New York: Free Press, Macmillan, 1963).

[14] *Ibid.,* pp. 48–54 *passim.*

[15] Herbert A. Simon, "Theories of Decision-Making in Economics and Behavioral Science," *American Economic Review,* 49, no. 3 (June 1959): 266 (quoted in an unpublished paper by Kenneth H. Ives, "Costs-Benefits Analysis: Its Theory and Components, with Applications to the Health and Welfare Fields").

[16] Weber, *Theory of Social and Economic Organization,* pp. 92–93.

[17] Murray G. Ross, *Community Organization: Theory and Principles* (New York: Harper, 1955), p. 134.

[18] *Ibid.,* p. 137.

[19] *Ibid.,* p. 148.

[20] Mary P. Follett, *Creative Experience* (New York: Longmans Green, 1924).

[21] Meyerson and Banfield, *Politics, Planning, and the Public Interest,* p. 282.

[22] Eugen Pusic, "The Needs of Children in Relation to Planning Structures and Processes" (a paper presented at the UNICEF conference at Lake Como, Italy, March 31, 1964).

[23] See Robert Morris, ed., *Centrally Planned Change: Prospects and Concepts* (New York: National Association of Social Workers, 1964), p. 17.

[24] Braybrooke and Lindblom, *A Strategy of Decision,* p. 85.

[25] *Ibid.,* p. 93.

[26] *Ibid.,* pp. 102–3.

[27] *Ibid.,* pp. 105–6.

[28] Herbert A. Simon, *Administrative Behavior* (New York: Macmillan, 1950), pp. 96–97, 99).

[29] Meyerson and Banfield, *Politics, Planning, and the Public Interest,* p. 241.

[30] *Ibid.,* p. 242. McMillen was a member of the Housing Authority at the time.

Community Development
Revisited

INTRODUCTION

There never has been any extensive degree of consensus on a conceptually rigorous definition of community development. The term is elusive, just as are the goals that community development efforts are designed to pursue. Part of the reason, undoubtedly, is the widespread diversity in meaning given the term "community." To the extent that one does not know what it is he is trying to develop, so much more difficult must be the developmental process, and so much less the likelihood for tangible positive outcome.

At times the term has come to be equated with social development, and thus many aspects of social development have been squeezed into a concept and a process based on locality. In national plans, social development, which often gets short shrift compared to physical infrastructure and economic development considerations, is supposed to attend to the "human" aspects of the plan—the question of cultural resistances to change, the anticipated disruption in tribal or peasant life, the development of an institutional structure of social services, the acknowledgment of a democratic imperative toward "participation." These are great tasks, great responsibilities, and the tendency to consider them all as dischargeable through community development programs has overburdened the concept and rendered the task largely impossible.

But the fact that community development was an ambiguous concept, and that the process was burdened with more tasks than it could possibly fulfill, is only part of the reason for the present fairly widespread disillusionment with the notion.

An additional element in the situation has been the enduring dilemma of resolving the task vs. process polarity. Should emphasis be placed on accomplishing certain specific tangible tasks—a new factory or hospital or school or a higher rate of literacy or the elimination of a contagious disease—or should the emphasis be placed on helping people to develop a capacity to help themselves? The banal "both" is no longer an admissible response, at least not to dozens of disillusioned community development workers who have found themselves at the center of conflicting demands that could not be fulfilled simultaneously.[1] So often, the task has virtually *had* to preempt the process, producing the new school or some other tangible accomplishment, but with little or no improvement in the ability of local people to confront their problems. And even when it has been possible to keep the process in the foreground, progress has seemed slow or nonexistent—and likely to recede as soon as the intensive stimulation of the community development worker is removed.

Critics have attacked community development efforts on the basis of a lack of clear definition of objectives and hence the inability to develop adequate evaluational measures. The methodological problems involved in any credible evaluation are tremendous, which is part of the reason that evaluative efforts and guidelines seem so unconvincing.[2] Charles J. Erasmus maintains that the retreat behind vague goals is virtually deliberate, a means by which community development workers can rebut the charge of ineffectiveness by saying in effect: We are trying to develop something both precious and evasive. You can't define it precisely and you can't measure it. (Therefore, you can't demonstrate that we have failed.)[3]

This applies especially to the international field, to community development efforts in so-called underdeveloped contexts, essentially rural contexts. But with only a slight accommodation for the differences, much the same can be said for community development efforts in urban areas, whether in relatively nonindustrialized countries such as India or in industrialized countries such as the United States. And in different ways much the same *has* been said—by Marshall B. Clinard, whose viewpoint is relatively sanguine regarding community development in the urban context;[4] by Marris and Rein, who point to some of the difficult dilemmas and confused and often conflicting goals;[5] and by Daniel Patrick

---

[1] D. C. Dubey and Willis Sutton, "A Rural 'Man in the Middle': The Indian Village Level Worker in Community Development," *Human Organization*, 24, no. 2 (Summer 1965).

[2] Samuel P. Hayes, Jr., *Measuring the Results of Development Projects: A Manual for the Use of Field Workers* (Paris: UNESCO, 1959), and John Donoghue and Iwao Ishino, *Handbook for Community Development Research* (East Lansing: Michigan State University Institute for Community Development, 1962).

[3] Charles J. Erasmus, "Community Development and the Encogido Syndrome," *Human Organization*, 27, no. 1 (Spring 1968).

[4] Marshall B. Clinard, *Slums and Community Development: Experiments in Self-Help* (New York: Free Press, Macmillan, 1966).

[5] Peter Marris and Martin Rein, *Dilemmas of Social Reform: Poverty and Community Action in the United States* (New York: Atherton Press, 1967).

Moynihan, whose treatment is somewhat more oblique but whose verdict is even more pessimistic.[6]

Has community development had its day? Perhaps the term itself is coming to be more diffuse and less meaningful than it was. But the notion that people need help at the local level to organize themselves to confront their problems is not likely to disappear quickly. For despite its patronizing ring, despite the fact that many people who assert this need have vested interests in *giving* that help, there is a strong element of validity in it, particularly if we learn and incorporate into newer strategies some of the lessons of the past two decades—that people can't pick themselves up by their own bootstraps without outside resources, that such developmental efforts stimulate a rise in expectations and inevitable frustration if no tangible advantages are forthcoming from their credence and their efforts, that few people want to organize for the sake of organizing.

The term "community development" has been applied to efforts in the most diverse contexts, even though the conditions and the problems and the relation to the ongoing process of social change may vary enormously. Chapter 5, "The Context of Community Development," which opens this section, comprises an analysis of these differences, relating them to the "great change." It considers many dimensions on which such contexts differ, and points out some of their implications.

Chapter 6, "Theory and Practice in Community Development," had an interesting developmental history itself. The initial request for the preparation of this material came from the Community Resource Development Division of the U.S. Department of Agriculture, which wanted a more or less "definitive" paper that would constitute the focus for a series of regional workshops of Extension Service people across the United States. I was asked to lay out a firm theoretical base for a consideration of community development, and then to draw pertinent implications for practice. Although any reasonably adequate effort to do this would involve a thick volume, I agreed to try to say something helpful in more concise compass, and the paper published here as Chapter 6 was the result. It contains three lines of analysis that may be of some interest and importance. The first is the conception of community development as a problem of making effective decisions and taking effective action when there is no formal organizational unit responsible for the decisions and the action. The second is the related concept of inclusiveness in decision-making, and five types of inclusiveness are considered. The third is a listing and modest analysis of some of the polarities in community development, which in turn form the basis for an

[6] Daniel Patrick Moynihan, *Maximum Feasible Misunderstanding: Community Action in the War on Poverty* (New York: Free Press, Macmillan, 1969).

assessment of how the emphasis is coming to be changed among practitioners in this field.

Chapter 7, "Application of Social Science Knowledge to the Community Organization Field," consists essentially of two inventories. One is an inventory of topics in which a literature is developing in the social sciences (especially, but not exclusively, sociology), a literature that constitutes a modest base of knowledge for the profession of community organization in particular and for community development workers in general. The second is an inventory of the actual utilization of this literature by the writers of articles in the community organization field in two leading professional journals, the *Journal of Social Work* and the *Social Service Review*.

5

THE CONTEXT OF
COMMUNITY DEVELOPMENT

In considering the context of community development, one is faced with the alternatives of relating the analysis to the particular circumstances of one's own country, on the one hand, and of keeping the analysis insofar as possible at a level that is generally applicable, on the other. In this chapter, the latter alternative has been chosen. This choice was made partly because community development is, after all, a widely applied method of bringing about social change, hardly confined to the United States. But it was also made with the deliberate hope that by dealing with the contextual considerations in more general terms, I would be more likely to avoid myopic, situation-bound considerations of limited usefulness, and to emphasize those contextual aspects that are relevant to all community development situations. In bridging the gap between the general considerations and the specific American context at this particular moment, the creativity of the reader is invited.

COMMUNITY DEVELOPMENT AND SOCIAL CHANGE

As a method for bringing about social change, community development is being used at the present time both in situations that are predominantly rural and preindustrial and in situations that are urban and industrialized. It is being used as a means both of promoting industrialization and of coping with its consequences. It is employed in remote villages of traditionally agricultural countries and in the turbulent metropolises of countries that are highly industrialized.

Prepared as chap. 2 of *Community Development as a Process,* ed. Lee J. Cary (Columbia: University of Missouri Press, 1970).

It appears almost as if community development is being asked to bring about a set of conditions—roughly, "modernization"—and then to cope with the conditions it has created. Let us examine this paradoxical situation.

Although community development is a method for bringing about change, change is taking place anyway, both in highly industrialized countries and in the less industrialized ones. The vast changes that are taking place—the population explosion, the "revolution of rising expectations," the establishment of new nation-states, the flight from the land, the growth of cities, the growth of industries, the development of new technologies—all these and others as well are subject to varying amounts of deliberate control at the national or community level.

In many countries, including the new countries with a scarcity of accessible resources and the socialist countries, the deliberate attempt to control or at least to channel or influence these social changes takes place within the framework of a national plan designed to organize various governmental efforts to achieve a set of economic and social objectives. In the United States, on the other hand, such efforts are organized by a multitude of planning organizations, both governmental and nongovernmental, at various levels of geographic inclusiveness, and are seldom brought into direct and deliberate correspondence with each other. There is a wide range of variation among countries as to the degree of centralization or decentralization of planning, both geographically and according to functional fields such as health, education, economic development, and so on.

A widely used classification of these various attempts at deliberate control or influence over change is the threefold one of *economic, physical,* and *social* development or planning. Both terms, development and planning, carry with them the connotation of a deliberate attempt to influence the course of events, with "development" implying the growth of some situation or condition as well as deliberate influence or control. Albert Waterston has combined the terms in his concept of development planning:

A country was considered to be engaged in development planning if its government made a deliberate and continuing attempt to accelerate the rate of economic and social progress and to alter institutional arrangements which were considered to block the attainment of this goal. The attempt had to be a conscious one made by a government and it had to be made often enough to give substance to the government's claim or belief that it was concerting policies and taking action designed to bring about economic and social progress and institutional change.[1]

Such development planning usually has economic, physical, and social aspects, which may be given separate explicit formulation. Community development is sometimes considered to be the local counterpart of such national development planning. It may be incorporated into the national plan as a means of achieving certain specific results. On the other hand, it may be used quite apart from any national development plan, simply as a means of bringing about desired change at the local level, even if the effort is confined to a single locality. Again, in any particular community the effort may be quite minimal, affecting only a small proportion of local people and a narrow range of activities and concern, or it may be much broader.

To summarize, community development is an attempt to influence the course of change at the community level. It may occur as a deliberate part of a national plan or quite apart from one, and it occurs in the most varied settings—rural and urban, highly industrialized and preindustrial. It may be a means used to help bring about industrialization, or it may be a means used to cope with its effects, or both simultaneously.

In order to consider more systematically the context in which community development efforts occur, let us enumerate some of the sweeping changes that are occurring in most parts of the world, and then relate community development efforts to these changes:

1. The increase in population.
2. The movement of people to the cities.
3. The growth of cities and the spread of urban ways to the countryside.
4. The growth of industrial production and the switch to nonagricultural pursuits.
5. The division of labor and consequent multiplication of occupations.
6. The development of large-scale organizations, not only governmental and industrial organizations, but also labor unions, voluntary associations, educational organizations, political parties, and so on.

More or less closely associated with these basic changes are a number of others that are in a certain sense responses or adaptations to the changed conditions brought about by the above:

7. The development of modes of association based on rules and regulations, contract, formal organization, and comparative anonymity rather than on custom, face-to-face relations, common pursuits, homogeneity, and shared values.
8. Changes in the structure of family living and in the roles of husband and wife with respect to each other and their children, and of the members of this nuclear family unit with relation to other kin.
9. The decline of the locality as a central focus of association and the growth of other foci of association, such as employment in the same

company or membership in the same union or religious organization or interest group.

·The reader will notice that all of these changes are interrelated in various ways. It is also significant that although these changes have proceeded in various countries in different sequences and at different rates and are thus apparent in different degrees at any one time, their operation is noticeable in the most diverse countries with respect to geographic location or extent of development.

As an indication of the worldwide prevalence of these trends, a recent group of national delegates from all parts of the world came together to discuss the topic of urban development and its implications for social welfare. It had at its disposal carefully prepared reports from national committees of twenty-seven countries. Although there were vast differences in the conditions they reported, they all reflected the operation of the interrelated combination of trends listed above.[2]

For the purpose of the present discussion, a brief designation for these changes would be useful, and I shall employ a term used elsewhere to denote a somewhat similar list of important social changes: "the great change."[3]

It is helpful to relate community development to this great change. The contexts within which community development occur differ significantly according to the extent to which the particular countries or regions have experienced various aspects of the great change. At one extreme are countries that are generally described as highly developed or highly industrialized.* At the other extreme are countries that are called less developed or underindustrialized. In each case, the meaning usually given to these terms is broad, denoting the wide scope of changes indicated in our list.

As is well known, community development in the decade or two following World War II was thought of primarily in connection with the less developed countries, or the less developed regions of the industrialized countries. Thus it was considered to apply primarily to the smaller and more rural communities. Indeed, much of the thinking that has gone into the very concept of the community as a locality group has been cast in terms, essentially, of the smaller rural communities. Baker Brownell, for example, writes: "A community is a group of people who know one another well. But this is satisfactory only when 'knowing well' means the full pattern of functional and social relationships which people may have with one another."[4] Obviously, this is possible only in a small community. Brownell is consistent in drawing the implication: "The great city rises; the human community declines."[5]

---

* Unless otherwise indicated, the terms "developed," "more developed," "industrialized," and "highly industrialized" are used interchangeably, as are their opposites. They are not employed in an evaluative sense. When a distinction is made, the term "developed" is considered to be more inclusive than the term "industrialized."

Earlier, Arthur E. Morgan had observed: "If the numbers are too large, either community relationships will be restricted and more formal, or the community will break down into aggregates made up of several partial communities, often along economic or other class lines, and the total unity of the community will be partially lost."[6] He does add, however, "Nevertheless, techniques and methods for developing some characteristics of community in larger populations can be developed,"[7] and of course this is precisely the function that community development has been expected to perform in urban settings.[8]

THE LESS DEVELOPED CONTEXT

Let us first consider community development in contexts that have experienced the great change in only a modest degree. These include the so-called less developed countries, but also certain still largely rural, relatively isolated parts of the more developed countries, such as the Appalachian region of the United States. Community development is related to these underdeveloped contexts in two ways: as a means of encouraging the great change and as a response to problems already brought about or anticipated by such changes as are occurring. Typically, both are combined in any particular instance, but for purposes of analysis let us consider them separately.

In a community such as those we are considering, plans for development are typically directed at creating a sound industrial base and integrating the community with the larger society. They also involve the diffusion of new institutions and technical procedures to the people of the locality. Hence the specific programs that are instigated are directed at increasing literacy, developing an industrial base that involves greater specialization of production and consequent greater interdependence with other communities, developing a sense of participation in local institutions and also in the national political arena, utilization of economic and social resources from outside the community, introduction of new health practices, and, withal, the stimulation of organized ways of problem-solving among the local people. Such activities are seen primarily as a necessary prerequisite to the great change, and to such advantages (longer life, higher real income, better nutrition and health) as the great change may be instrumental in bringing about. In this context, community development can be seen as a means of achieving and guiding the great change, and perhaps of guiding it along lines indicated by local values.

Often, though, the context is somewhat different. These underdeveloped communities are already being affected by the great change (especially the growth of industries, the division of labor, the breakdown of older family and other institutional patterns), and the emphasis is on coping with the problems that the great change is bringing with it. As indicated earlier, much of this change may be quite unplanned, and indeed may be apparently inexorable, while some of it may be the deliberate result of governmental policy. In any case, the context is essentially the same. The problem is to find ways through which local action can be taken to avoid some of the more disastrous results of the strains placed on time-worn institutions by modern circumstances.

I have separated these two conditions for purposes of analysis, but they usually appear together in the actual situation. Hence we can summarize this first context of community development by saying that it is a context at the early end of the great change, one in which the problem is to induce the great change as well as to help in the process of coping with its early effects.

It should be noted that not all community development in less developed countries is confined to rural communities. As the great change begins to occur, there is often a mushrooming of city populations caused largely by migration from the rural areas. Vast numbers of people come to the cities, which do not have the economic base to afford them adequate employment and do not have the educational, health, and welfare facilities they need. This circumstance has become a particularly poignant and frustrating context for community development.

It should also be noted that developmental efforts of this type are likewise appropriate for many communities in the more developed countries, which have perhaps had at one time a more viable economic and social base than they have at present. The decline or moving away of particular industries, such as mining or textile manufacturing, may leave communities without an economic base, and hence with widespread apathy and discouragement. The employment of community development as a means of bettering the community's economic base thus becomes appropriate.[9]

THE MORE DEVELOPED CONTEXT

Let us turn now to the other end of the great-change spectrum—the highly urbanized, highly industrialized countries. Here the various processes listed earlier as constituting the great change have run a considerable course. As an example, let us take a large American city along with its metropolitan area. Division of labor is highly intricate, with literally thousands of occupations. Gainful occupations are organized into industrial companies and smaller concerns, governmental and nongovernmental organizations, providing a highly complex network of production and distribution of goods both within the city and in exchange for the produce of other cities. The institutional structure is highly developed, and educational, welfare, and health agencies may be so numerous that there is a problem in coordinating them and utilizing existing resources in these fields for optimum benefit.

A series of structural and personal conditions are seen as problems. On the structural level, there is the question of a viable economic base, with employment opportunities for all, and a fiscal base sufficient to support public services adequately. There is the whole complex of problems regarding the flight to the suburbs and the ghettoizing of the city center, the traffic congestion, the inadequacy of city services, the lack of housing, and so on through a long list.

On the individual level, there are problems of unemployment, marital discord, generation conflict, juvenile delinquency, drug addiction, crime, and on through another long list. Needless to say, all these individual problems have important structural aspects as well.

But these problems, both structural and individual, cannot be solved by accelerating the great change. Quite the contrary, all of these problems are related more or less closely to the impact of the great change. The great change is part of the problem, rather than part of the solution.

In the broadest sense, community development is concerned in this context, as well, with a method through which people can come to confront their problems in a concerted way, using such resources as are available, whether from within the community or from outside—in the United States, most spectacularly in the form of huge grants-in-aid from the federal government for various carefully delineated programs.

But in the larger cities, the face-to-face interaction of any substantial proportion of the population in a process of confronting any substantial proportion of its problems is mathematically impossible. Problems must be confronted by delegation, and this takes place within the contexts of large-scale organizations such as boards of education and schools, chambers of commerce and business and industrial companies, welfare councils and social agencies, the municipal government and its various departments, and so on.

The most broadly developed professional context in which such organizations are brought together has appeared primarily in the field of social welfare agencies, and goes by the name of community organization. But actually, in the larger cities there is no single rubric under which these varied organizations are coordinated. Rather, various segments of organizational activity—education, social services, health services, economic activity—are loosely coordinated in a number of separate organizations. These large-scale coordinating organizations form part of a competitive arena in which they act more or less autonomously with respect to each other, meanwhile achieving varying degrees of coordination within their own special fields of activity.[10]

No way has yet been devised for engaging large numbers of people at any significant level of participation along the whole gamut of community concerns. Hence, in the larger urban setting, community development must take one of two forms. Either it operates at the level of the organization and the superorganization, failing to engage the vast majority of the people in any meaningful way; or it restricts its field of operations to an extremely narrow fragment of the total community picture, such as better schools or better street cleaning—and then only sporadically—or to the various subcommunities that are small enough in scale to afford a basis for broad, meaningful involvement.

Such effort at the subcommunity level has usually taken two forms. One is the usual type of neighborhood association, representing a deliberate attempt to help people to organize in a particular small part of the city to confront the problems and possibilities appropriate to their neighborhood. Hence such associations are usually interested in school facilities, parks and recreational space, the condition of the streets, police protection, and a number of other concerns of immediate relevance to the people living there. Various attempts to interest such associations in the larger problems of the surrounding city or of the larger society have usually met with only minimal success or total failure. But at the level of neighborhood problems, they have proved in many cases to be capable of meaningful and sustained activity.

The other form that such neighborhood activity has taken in the United States has developed more recently. This is the neighborhood organization created not so much to confront the immediate problems of the neighborhood as to confront the larger social structure in which these neighborhood problems are generated. These attempts to "organize the poor" take place on a neighborhood level, but have implications for the structure of the city and of the larger society. One way of looking at them is to say that they are attempts to accomplish three interrelated purposes: to organize the poor for action on their own behalf; to develop a "position" or a series of specific proposals; and to make these positions and proposals known in the larger councils where the affairs of the city are considered.

The rationale is that formerly the poor have not been represented in any effective sense, as indicated by the tendency of social service agencies to place greater emphasis on middle-class clients and the general neglect of the physical, social, and educational aspects of poor neighborhoods. If the poor are to participate meaningfully, they must have a "position." This can be developed only as they discuss their situation and form their points of view in interaction. Then this opinion must be represented. This can be done only if there is sufficient organization so that representatives can be selected who are legitimated to "speak for" the poor. And finally, their position will be given weight in community decision-making only if their spokesmen are backed by some form of power, power that can come only through organization and capacity to take concerted action, whether this be in lobbying, education, protesting, or voting.

To convert poor neighborhoods into effective subcommunities is not an easy task; it is one of the most challenging problems confronting community development in urban areas.

To summarize, in the more developed countries, which have experienced the great change in a large degree, community development is confronted with a different kind of situation than in underdeveloped areas. The problems that communities in developed countries are called upon to face are themselves concomitants of the great change. These problems, too, are economic, physical, and social in nature. But here community development efforts are directed largely at taking effective adaptive action to mitigate the painful consequences of the great change, rather than at bringing about that change. The great change has disrupted older patterns of social relations, and the disruption in turn has brought about adaptive behavior that is experienced as the structural and personal problems of urban industrial life. Action to mitigate these problems can be taken in urban communities by only a small proportion of the people, acting through various relatively fragmented organizations. This affords at least a modicum of deliberate, coordinated problem-solving activity, but it does not resolve the problem of how a substantial proportion of the population can meaningfully and effectively be brought into the process. At the neighborhood level, however, community development efforts can engage a large proportion of individuals over a larger sweep of neighborhood-level issues. Neighborhood-level development has recently come into special prominence because of its utilization as a method for helping the poor to organize themselves so that they can have a voice and exercise power in the community arena.

THE RELEVANCE OF THE COMMUNITY LEVEL

Community development is not only viewed as a means of accomplishing certain specific program objectives, but is also considered intrinsically valuable as a process. It is not merely a question of what things are accomplished, but of how they are accomplished. Community development is often thought of as crucial on the basis of a number of specific affirmations:

(a) That you can't have a healthy society that is not made up of healthy, vigorous communities.
(b) That it is better for community people to plan and work for the things they want in their community than to have these things handed down by a higher governmental authority.
(c) That participation in the development of the community is an important preventive for the alienation of individuals in the mass society, over which they have no control and in which they feel no meaningful sense of participation.
(d) That strong participation in community affairs is a necessary basis for a democratic society.

Nevertheless, it can be seen from our analysis of the contexts of community development that as the great change progresses, and as communities become not more but less self-sufficient, more closely intertwined with the major institutions of the larger society, fewer and fewer of the problems that people face in their communities can be adequately confronted at the community level. The population explosion, the growth of nationhood, the struggle among nations, the broad ideological currents that engulf the world, to say nothing of questions of national prosperity, employment opportunity, the availability of capital for growth and of consumer goods for current standards of living—none of these is subject to the control of any particular community.

There has been no letup in the pace at which large-scale organizations are growing and decision-making is becoming centralized at levels more inclusive than the community. Even in those eastern European countries that are now adopting the economic policy of Libermanism and decentralizing some of their formerly centralized national planning as a deliberate policy change—even here the trend does not seem to be in the direction of dispersing the decision-making function to the community. Rather, the process is one of functional decentralization—by industries and industrial units, which in the most democratic form are under the jurisdiction of workers but not of the whole community, and by regions rather than by communities. Elsewhere, the trend toward centralization increases.

Thus, at the same time that community development is pursued as desirable for a democratic society, much of the basis for it is suffering attrition through the increasing extent to which the community affairs of people are influenced by events and decisions at regional or national or international levels. A number of aspects of this situation can be given brief consideration:

First, it is interesting to observe that what seems to be happening is a gradual switch in emphasis, particularly in the developing countries, to the concept of social development, rather than community development. The two are by no means mutually exclusive, but the growth in importance of the concept of social development is in part, at least, an adaptation to the realization that the consideration for what happens to people, as distinguished from the accomplishment of certain task objectives, is not solely a matter of community development, but involves regional and national action as well; and that many of the institutions that people need if life in their communities is to be at all satisfactory must be initiated at national or regional levels, rather than at the community level.

Second, there appears to be growing recognition that participation at the community level is not the only alternative to alienation in the mass society. As William Kornhauser points out, the need is for participation at intermediate levels between the individual and the large-scale organizations of the mass society.[11] Traditionally, such participation has taken place principally on the basis of locality. But such participation can also occur functionally, in labor unions, political parties, interest groups, religious organizations, and economic activity at various levels—some less inclusive than the community, and some more inclusive. There would seem to be no compelling reason why the local community, as such, should be the indispensable form of social participation.

Finally, even though many functions are not appropriate for community-level participation, many others still are, and presumably will be in the predictable future. Certain locality-relevant functions apparently need to be performed pretty much on the scene where people live, and the people who live in any locality have a common interest in seeing that these functions are performed satisfactorily. Stores have to be available to people where they live, as do primary schools, streets, police and fire protection, and a number of other readily identifiable facilities or services. People who live in a particular locality have a common interest in these locality-relevant functions, even though they do not particularly care about associating with each other in their leisure time and even though they may have diverse individual interests and positions that in many cases orient them much more toward the regional or national scene than toward their neighbors.

There can be no single answer to the question of what is a relevant basis for community organization and interaction around such common interests. In some communities and in some neighborhoods of large cities, the degree of identification with other people in the locality may be at a minimum without catastrophic results. In other cases, the viability of the neighborhood as a wholesome environment in which to live may depend on people coming together on the basis of locality and organizing themselves to confront their problems.

In sum, from the social context alone, there can be no single clear answer to the question of how important it is that people organize themselves strongly on the basis of locality. This must be considered as a variable, to be variously assessed in accordance with the multitude of situations and conditions that surround the lives of people in their communities.

REGIONAL AND NATIONAL RELATIONSHIPS

From the foregoing analysis, the close interrelationship of community problems and the conditions of the region and the nation become apparent. The relationship is reciprocal. Conditions in the region and nation place limits on the setting within which community development occurs. To paraphrase John Donne, no community is an island. Every community needs resources—economic, technical, often political—from the surrounding countryside. Likewise, every community is affected by the economic, technical, and political conditions that exist in the surrounding region and nation. At the same time, what individual communities do affects the well-being of the surrounding region and nation. The practical problem therefore arises of the extent to which attempts will be made to coordinate community development efforts on a regional or national basis in order that regional and national resources can be brought more directly to bear on the local communities, and so that the programs of the local communities are so coordinated that their effect on the region and nation is optimally beneficial.

One of the problems of trying to structure the regional aspects of community development is the fact that the most appropriate regional division for one purpose, say industry, may be rather different from the most appropriate regional delineation for another purpose, say elementary education. And these functional divisions, in turn, may be somewhat different from existing political boundaries of regions, whether we are speaking of an urbanized region—a city and its immediate suburbs—or of a larger political subdivision—a county, a state, a province. For our present purposes, we can use the term "region" most broadly, to include any or all of these as the context demands. What is meant is some geographic district larger than the municipality but smaller than the entire country.

This surfeit of overlapping regions is abundantly apparent in the United States. Among the most problematic instances are the metropolitan regions surrounding large American cities and including suburban communities. Ecologically and economically, these areas are interdependent with the metropolitan center. But in actuality, there is usually no political entity that corresponds to this metropolitan complex. There is the city, and there are surrounding cities, towns, and villages. There are numerous special districts. There are counties. But there is no governmental decision-making apparatus with tax power and with legal authority to administer the affairs of this urban complex, nor is there any likelihood of such an inclusive governmental unit with appropriate powers in the near future.

Many concerns of large cities, such as commuter transit, land-use patterns of the metropolitan area, and highway and bridge authorities, are not only intercommunity problems, but interstate problems as well. On the state level, too, problems in various functional areas do not coincide with state boundaries, and there is no existing governmental organization appropriate to the level at which the problem must be confronted. On the federal level, the many different groupings of states into regions for purposes of banking and finance, census, and the regional administration of various federal agency programs likewise illustrate the problem of lack of correspondence between functional areas and geographic governmental jurisdictions.

This crazy-quilt pattern of functional regions helps account for the lack of organization of the various geographic regions for regional development and planning. It likewise helps explain the great multiplicity of special districts—

ad hoc governmental districts with limited power (often, however, including taxing power) set up for the performance of specific functions, such as water districts, sewage districts, school districts, and so on. It is a commonplace not only that the geographic areas served by district offices of state governmental agencies may not coincide with the areas served by the district offices of other agencies of the same state, but also that district-level offices are seldom brought into any meaningful coordination with each other. Much the same situation exists regarding the regional offices of the federal government.

This rather confused and apparently uncoordinated situation should not be taken *ipso facto* as undesirable. The problems just discussed are virtually insuperable in any fundamental sense, simply because functional areas and geographic areas do not coincide. The most that can be done is to make some sort of optimal resolution of the problems of regional districting and coordination, as the U.S. government sought to do in 1969. The costs in time and effort and other resources of setting up regional systems that would maximize the coordination of the various functional divisions at all appropriate geographic levels would very possibly be much greater than the benefits. This is not to say, however, that the existing mix is optimal.

This situation serves as a good backdrop against which to view a frequent complaint by those interested in community development work at the community level in the United States. As new resources are made available to communities by the federal government, each new federal program sets up its own goals and its own administrative machinery and its own constraints on the local community. Coordination of federal policies in relation to the specific community and its special circumstances would seem to be desirable at the community level. Yet the various federal agencies working in the community are structured so that they are relatively isolated from each other. Each is encapsulated in its own administrative hierarchy, which leads through regional offices to Washington. Each is part of a distinct federal administrative apparatus based on its own federal legislation. Under these circumstances, their functional coordination at the municipal level, though highly desirable, is extremely difficult. This is an area in which attempts at coordination will no doubt be accelerated in the next decade, as clamor from the cities increases. One such attempt is the Model Cities program, instituted in 1966.

A second major consideration in structuring the regional and national aspects of community development is the extent to which goals and programs should be set at the regional or national level and the extent to which they should be set at the community level. Many issues are involved in this large question, not the least of which is that the American record of experience of local community initiative in such matters as health and welfare and educational services is not such as to support the viewpoint that initiative should rest with local people, and that such federal funds as are made available to them should be accompanied by the fewest possible constraints. The great impulse of federal initiative regarding local communities has arisen from a number of sources. Important among these is the inadequate fiscal base for community support of the costly undertakings that are needed (urban renewal, school improvement, housing, etc.). Further, communities are often niggardly and backward in the policies they are prepared to develop with regard to such problems as housing, racial integration, urban renewal, schools, pollution, health care, and so on. Stimulus and constraints are therefore needed from outside the communities if anything more than sporadic progress is desired.

The other side of the coin, however, is the need for communities to be able to modify federal programs in ways that are adapted to their local situations. Often, local programs are based more on the availability of federal funds for a specific purpose than on the conviction of local people that these specific programs are the ones most needed.

A third consideration in regard to the community's relationships with the region and the nation requires only brief mention, although its great importance is apparent. As mentioned in an earlier section, many of the most vital problems that communities face are not resolvable at the community level. This is true of regional and national economic conditions, questions of war and peace which have the most fateful consequences for community living, and even questions of quite a different nature, such as the population explosion, the development of science and technology, the migration of people to the cities, and so on.

In sum, many types of activity are more appropriate for the nation or region than for the community, but difficulties in coordination at national and regional levels are numerous. These difficulties are of various types, some purely administrative, others caused by the apparently unalterable lack of coincidence of functional, geographic, and political areas, others caused by the inappropriateness of the community as a major locus for confronting certain types of problems. These difficulties, in addition to the reticence and conservatism of many communities with respect to confronting their problems in any systematic way, present a complex backdrop against which decisions must be made regarding the way in which regional and national programs are to be structured, and regarding the scope of decision-making and operation to be allocated to national, regional, and community levels, respectively.

OTHER ASPECTS OF THE COMMUNITY DEVELOPMENT CONTEXT

In this chapter, some of the broader aspects of the contexts of community development have been considered, with primary emphasis on the relation of community development to the great change and on the respective roles of the community, the region, and the nation in community development. Yet specific contexts for community development show extreme variations, and these differences must be taken into account in planning or operating or assessing specific community development endeavors. We shall consider a few of these variations in this concluding section.

The most obvious variation has already been mentioned—the degree of modernization, or the extent to which the community involved has experienced the various trends that make up the great change. If one compares the effort at community development within a large modern metropolis with that of a remote agricultural village in one of the less developed countries, a number of important and possibly crucial differences may be apparent: level of literacy and education, experience with democratic institutions, availability of financial and personnel resources, and so on, all of which would have to be considered in adopting appropriate methods and strategies.

Another important variation is in the number of potential sources or sponsors of community development efforts. In some countries, these may be restricted to the specific organization for community development which is included in the national plan, and little else, except for sporadic ventures into community development made by an occasional religious or other nongovernmental organization. In other countries, the sources of sponsorship and of personnel to help stimulate community development may be extremely numerous, including not only a number of different (and often competing) programs of various departments and ministries, but also state or provincial efforts, which likewise may be numerous, as well as university extension, national, state, and local voluntary associations, religious organizations, efforts sponsored by industrial companies, and so on.

A related consideration is the extent to which these various efforts are related in any specific way to the governmental structure. In some settings they are not only largely governmental, but part of the administration of a deliberate, more or less integrated national plan. At the other extreme, they may have little relation to government, being quite independently sponsored, organized, and financed, and may look to various levels and branches of government, if at all, solely for access to financial or personnel resources.

Another type of variation has to do with whether the sponsoring agency is roughly a single-purpose or a multipurpose organization. In countries where numerous agencies are active at the community level, it is frequently the case that many of them are engaging in community development as a means for developing local programs in their own particular areas of interest—health, education, urban renewal, housing, prevention of juvenile delinquency, or whatever. Thus, all according to the sponsorship, such efforts may be perceived as stretching across the entire spectrum of possible community concerns or as being concentrated in only one predetermined field of interest. In the latter case, there is much more likelihood that goals will be primarily determined by a specific organization, whether within or outside of the community, rather than by the people who are the participant targets of the program.

Another obvious variation is in the size and complexity of the community field within which community development occurs. Although other variables may affect the picture, it is perhaps safe to generalize that the larger and more complex the community chosen as a unit for development, the smaller the proportion of the total population that will be involved in it in any direct way, and the greater the number of organizations that will be party to the process. In large cities, where the whole city is considered as the community to be developed, procedures will thus differ drastically from the concept of direct face-to-face interaction by all the citizens, and those who claim that direct interaction is an essential ingredient of the community development method may doubt that community development in the strict sense is possible at all except in smaller units.

Because of the importance of such variations as these, there can be no simple recipe or formula for community development. Community development endeavors can be expected to vary on the basis of the contextual matters that have been discussed in this chapter. They will also vary in the values that people utilize as guides to the selection of their goals and to the determination of their methods.

NOTES

[1] Albert Waterston, *Development Planning: Lessons of Experience* (Baltimore: Johns Hopkins University Press, 1965), p. 21.

[2] See *Urban Development—Its Implications for Social Welfare: Report of Pre-Conference Working Party* (Washington, D.C.: 13th International Conference of Social Work, 1966).

[3] See Roland L. Warren, *The Community in America* (Chicago: Rand McNally, 1963), chap. 3. (The "great change" is also treated briefly in chap. 6.)

[4] Baker Brownell, *The Human Community: Its Philosophy and Practice for a Time of Crisis* (New York: Harper, 1950), p. 198.

[5] *Ibid.*, p. 289.

[6] Arthur E. Morgan, *The Small Community: Foundation of Democratic Life* (New York: Harper, 1942), p. 124.

[7] *Ibid.*

[8] For an extensive treatment of the urban community development context, see Marshall B. Clinard, *Slums and Community Development: Experiments in Self-Help* (New York: Free Press, Macmillan, 1966).

[9] Severyn P. Bruyn makes an extensive analysis of one such effort in the cases he analyzes in his *Communities in Action: Pattern and Process* (New Haven, Conn.: College and University Press, 1963).

[10] This situation is given extensive analysis in chaps. 10 and 11.

[11] William Kornhauser, *The Politics of Mass Society* (New York: Free Press, Macmillan, 1959).

6

THEORY AND PRACTICE IN
COMMUNITY DEVELOPMENT

The emergence of the Community Resource Development Program of the Cooperative Extension Service makes appropriate a review of certain relevant theoretical aspects of community structure and development and of current differences of opinion among professionals as to appropriate change strategies.

THE GREAT CHANGE

Let us begin with the changes which are occurring in American society, changes which presumably make community resource development an important and desirable kind of activity on which to spend the citizen's tax dollar.

Many observers have noted an interrelated cluster of changes which have been associated largely with Western society but which are coming to be recognized as characterizing other societies as well. On the practical level, these changes have been grouped together in such concepts as modernization, urbanization, industrialization, and development. This overriding transition can be designated by the term "the great change." A number of salient dimensions of this great change can be briefly described.

First, as Durkheim noted, there occurs a progressive division of labor. Occupational tasks formerly performed by a single individual become divided

Reprinted by permission from *American Journal of Agricultural Economics,* 50, no. 5 (December 1968). Adapted from a paper prepared for the Regional Community Resource Development Workshops of the Federal Extension Service, U.S. Department of Agriculture, 1968. Notes have been renumbered.

in such a manner that various organizations share in the performance of one or another part of the task, and individuals within these organizations perform even more specialized roles. The obvious historical by-products of this process are well known: the tendency away from self-sufficiency, the intricate network of delicately interrelated parts of the productive system, the dependence on a money economy, the psychological difference between working on aggregate tasks and working on fragments of tasks.

Closely associated with the growing division of labor is another important development, a differentiation of interests and associations. As production tasks become more complex and individuals and organizations accommodate themselves to the various fragmented parts of these tasks, they ally themselves with others of similar occupations to further their own economic interests, and they find themselves associating with each other socially as well. Such social selection takes place not only on the basis of the division of labor, but also on that of a new possibility which the changed situation generates: the possibility of associating with other people for reasons of congeniality of personalities or mutuality of interests, rather than merely on the basis of geographic proximity.

These developments in turn have resulted in the growth of strong relationships of people to systems which extend beyond their community borders. Thus, individual residents of communities have developed strong links to their respective extracommunity occupational and interest groups. The same is true of the various types of organizations which are found in communities, whether governmental or nongovernmental, profit or nonprofit.

A related development, as intricate national systems and organizations arise around differentiated functions and interests, is the growth of bureaucratization and impersonalization. The extremely complex network of organizations and systemic interconnections is literally impossible to maintain without systematizing those interrelationships, clearly defining procedures, developing specific rules of performance, and in the process providing for a regularity and dependability of behavior and relationships. We have the widely heralded situation of the individual presumably "lost" in the web of impersonal relationships of bureaucratized organizations in the "mass society." At the same time, changes operate to weaken many of the older ties based on kinship, custom, and common residence.

Closely related to these processes is a transfer of functions which were formerly performed by family, neighborhood, and local community to voluntary organizations, profit enterprises, and governmental offices. The result is that, increasingly, organized efforts to achieve social objectives occur within the framework of one of these three last-mentioned types of formal organizations. This has direct implications for community development.

To the economic and social developments already enumerated should be added the growth of cities and suburbs. Actually, some of the largest cities are declining in population. But this is only an artifact of the arbitrary political divisions within the metropolitan areas. Indeed, the decline in size of the largest cities is directly related to the increase in size of the metropolitan aggregates of which they are the core. In addition, there is a growth of smaller cities and a growth in the nonfarming components of the rural populations.

As an additional major characteristic of the great change, there are many indications of a change in values. One aspect of this value change is the gradual acceptance of governmental activity as a positive value in an increasing number of fields. Another is the gradual change from a moral interpretation of human behavior to a causal one. That is, increasingly people find themselves placing more stress on the causes of behavior than on moral admonitions to the "sinner" to improve his ways. Associated with this is a changing approach to social problems, from one of sporadic moral reform to one of gradual rational planning. Not so closely related, perhaps, but nevertheless highly relevant, is what seems to be an increasing change of emphasis from work and production to enjoyment and consumption. The much discussed Protestant ethic has tended to become replaced by an ethic perhaps most dynamically captured in the title of a recent book: *Enjoy, Enjoy!*

These are the kinds of development which are referred to here by means of the term "the great change."[1]

Now, community development efforts are related to this great change as both cause and effect.[2] These terms are here used loosely, of course. What is implied is that a good part of the effort to bring about change with conscious intent on the community level is directed at engendering or hastening the great change. Now, of course, what is usually consciously intended in community development efforts is to stimulate only certain aspects of the great change: for example, those of achieving a more viable economic interrelation of the community and the larger society—bringing the community into the national political picture, developing an industrial base, and so on. But of course the whole point is that all these various aspects of the great change are interconnected. It is difficult, if not impossible, to achieve some of them without finding the others tagging along, as more or less unwelcome guests. Right here in the United States, there is intense awareness of the problem of preserving and enhancing the community at the same time that industrial development is encouraged. But, to repeat, much of the effort at community change is in the direction of hastening or encouraging the great change—although the change agent may not be aware of all the implications of this objective.

On the other hand, much of the effort at community change is directed at coping with aspects of the great change which have already become apparent and which are seen as social problems. An effort is made to cope with family breakdown, which is attributed to the great change, to restore a sense of community which many aspects of the great change have destroyed or jeopardized, or to coordinate the numerous social and technical programs which have grown up as by-products of the division of labor, to cope with the very problems which the division of labor itself has helped to generate.

In community change efforts, however, the relationship of social intent to the great change is not the simple "either–or" that I have indicated above. It is not a case of attempting either to induce or to cope with the great change. It is usually a mixture of the two. For though the great change is widely prevalent, different parts of the countryside are ranged differently as to how far they have incorporated it. Some are only beginning. Others are in relatively advanced stages. But there are very few that it has not yet affected; and at the other extreme, there are none where it has fully run its course. Even within a single state, efforts at industrial and educational and social development take place at the same time as efforts to cope with the problems caused by such development.

CHANGE—PURPOSIVE AND NONPURPOSIVE

But how much of the change which takes place is planned in any deliberate way, and how much just grows, like Topsy? In some of the developing countries with a national plan and with the government controlling most or all of the inputs for developmental change, the ratio of control to change may be relatively high. But one need only be reminded of the sweep of industrialization, of the unwanted migration of rural workers to the cities in search of jobs which are not yet there for them, to appreciate the constraints under which national plans must operate.

In our own country, we have nothing which approaches a national development plan, and nothing like a unified program by a single agency charged with community development efforts. The ratio of centralized control to change is relatively low.

The assertion that most social change is nonpurposive, or without aggregate social intent, requires further brief elaboration, for it is frequently overlooked by practitioners at the community level.[3] Most purposive change at the community level is a response to problems arising from the unplanned aggregate of individual decisions by persons, families, and organizations of one type or another as they pursue their interests and objectives. Such activity, in aggregate, is perceived as population increase or decrease or redistribution, either geographically or by age-sex category, or as "suburban growth," or "industrial growth," or "increasing automation," or higher longevity, or increased marriage or divorce rates, or smaller average size of family.

Most of what is called "planned social change" is a relatively modest response to these larger changes which are taken as given and are not the result of concerted, deliberate, centralized decision-making. Unemployment insurance is instigated to meet the contingency of unemployment, rather than to prevent it; city planning commissions take adaptive measures in view of such changes as population decline in the central city, suburban growth, new industrial location patterns, and the commuting phenomenon; social services are developed to help families whose individual lives dramatize the results of some of the larger changes.

As organizations and activities are thus set up to adapt in part to the largely uncontrolled changes which take place, these organizations themselves become part of the changing scene. In their activities, they may compete with each other in undesirable or wasteful ways, or they may leave gaps in available service, or their aggregate endeavors may not be adequate to accomplish their adaptive objectives. Thus, one particular field of planning has to do with establishing some minimum of purposive order among such adaptive organizations. Much of what is called *planned change* is of this adaptive type, rather than of any fundamental type which would change or redirect the major flow of events.

Likewise, of course, most of the basic, uncontrolled changes which take place at the community level do so in relation to forces outside of the local community and not subject to its deliberate control, as in the case of the general price level or changing industrial production techniques, such as automation.

The present situation is characterized by a bewildering number of programs, going into the hundreds, with federal or state or local governmental or voluntary sponsorship, in various combinations, and in various degrees of isolation from each other, constituting resources of money and program stimulation for community development. The complexity is bewildering, and the lack of coordination is notorious; yet the situation is far from chaotic, for there are many kinds of interagency linkages, horizontally at any level, and vertically among federal, state, regional, and local levels.

CONCERTING DECISIONS

Nevertheless, it is difficult for people and organizations to get together on whatever level is appropriate and determine what resources are open to them and utilize these resources optimally in the accomplishment of their goals, whatever these may be. Especially at the regional level, there may be no governmental or nongovernmental unit within which they can operate or even be brought together. But even where there is a governmental unit, only some of the problems and possibilities can be faced in a deliberate way by the established departments of the government. What becomes increasingly evident is the need for getting together about the matters which are not the prerogative of any governmental department or nongovernmental organization, or which are shared by several of them with the result that little concerted action can be taken without interorganizational collaboration.

How can effective decisions be made and effective action be taken when there is no formal organizational unit responsible for the decisions and action? In this question, perhaps, lies the principal rationale for what goes by the name of community development. The term has been used in many ways, and unfortunately it has been given a focus by many community development practitioners which is different from that given above. The focus has been one of seeking to restore the sense of fellowship and participation which people enjoyed in the small agricultural community but which has been largely destroyed by the great change. As a result, much effort has been wasted in trying to restore old-fashioned town-meeting models of social participation under circumstances where they are increasingly irrelevant. At the same time, and for the same reason, community development has come under criticism as being both unrealistic and ineffective.

If the principal problem is one of making effective decisions and taking effective action where there is no formal organizational unit responsible for them, there are, of course, a great number of approaches to that problem, in the form of community development functions or departments or offices of various program-oriented agencies such as the Urban Renewal Administration, the Office of Economic Opportunity, the Social and Rehabilitation Service of HEW with its reimbursement to local welfare departments for community development activity, the programs of the Administration on Aging, the Model Cities Administration, and so on through a long list. Each of these organizations seeks to help citizens to organize to engage in programs which, by their very nature, have broad implications and tend to overlap with each other.

Thus, when the Extension Service develops a bold new program in community resource development it is not a question of whether it will be the agency which helps communities organize themselves to function more effectively. It is entering a field—rather late, incidentally—which is already very much occupied. Two or three years ago I described the burgeoning field of community planning by comparing it to a crowded pool. I think the analogy is still appropriate:

> Perhaps we can picture the individual planner as someone about to jump into a swimming pool. His goals and his methods are clear. He has the special knowledge which he needs. He is an expert swimmer. He will dive into the pool at one end, a beautiful shallow racing dive, and swim directly to the other end, using that enviable form which comes from years of concentration on a particular skill, and the

sacrifice of other interests and skills which such technical perfection demands.

So, he jumps in. But I forgot to mention. The pool is not empty. There are a hundred and fifty other people jumping in or swimming underwater or splashing around in it. As he goes to dive, one of the other swimmers clips him on his way to buy a coke and a hamburger. Our planner no sooner hits the water than someone lands on him from the high dive. This latter is an expert swan-diver, who could do a beautiful job of planning and execution, except for our planner and the other hundred and forty-nine people in the pool. Our planner recovers, makes the necessary changes in course, launches out again, but zowie—someone who has been swimming underwater across the pool tries to surface but comes up on our planner's stomach. Does he ever reach the end of the pool? Let us forgo an answer, but rather leave our planner swimming away in Kafkaesque fashion toward his desired change goals, head down, arms flailing, coming up for air as regularly as possible, and doing the expected amount of kicking.[4]

The implication for the Extension Service would therefore be that in its Community Resource Development Program it is not only concerned with helping other people and organizations to come together at various levels to explore common concerns and set goals and establish procedures for joint decision-making and action; for it, too, is one of these parties, one of these organizations, one of these swimmers in the crowded pool. It cannot coordinate all the other coordinators—and they wouldn't let it, even if it could. So it has to look to its own task of finding ways of working with other organizations, of setting up new coalitions, of developing with other organizations flexible ways of coming together around specific problems without constructing top-heavy organizational structures. It must learn to do these things just as it seeks to help others learn to do them. It is probably more important at this point in interorganizational development to be aware of the whole pool, and the position and direction and speed of the various swimmers in it, than to concentrate exclusively on doing one's own beautiful swan dive.

The whole idea of development in the term "community development" implies a process of what may be termed purposive change. As indicated earlier, most social change is not deliberately brought about in any inclusive way. Nevertheless, the whole implication and rationale of community development are that an attempt will be made through concerted decision-making to influence change in the direction of whatever goals may be involved. This implies a planning process in which the appropriate individuals, organizations, or whatever come together. As has already been indicated, the extent to which social change is controlled by planning of this type is often exaggerated, but in any case the planning function is an important focus. The other important focus, of course, is around the question of what people or groups come together, who makes the decisions, and in what kind of a social process.

INCLUSIVENESS IN PLANNING

Presumably, through deliberate planning, inclusiveness is brought to the decision-making which is taking place at various levels in the normal course of events. This inclusiveness which planning seeks to impose on the flow of events and decision-making can be analyzed into five components: (1) inclusiveness of system level, (2) inclusiveness of scope, (3) inclusiveness of time, (4) inclusiveness of geography, and (5) inclusiveness of participation.

Systemic inclusiveness is involved when parties that have been making their respective individual decisions and actions in a particular field don't like the aggregate result so well as they believe they would like it if they somehow pooled their decisions and made them centrally, in closer relation to one another. Land-use control through zoning is an example; the aggregate benefit is presumed to be greater if decisions as to land use are made on a more inclusive level than that of the individual landowner.

Inclusiveness of scope is involved when the decision in one kind of substantive area—say industrial development—is brought into relationship with decisions being made in a different substantive area—say educational and health facilities.

Inclusiveness of time is involved not only when decision-making is related to solving the problem of the moment, but also when the problem of the moment is approached within the framework of a larger time span. Economists have pointed out the tremendous difference in short-run and long-run analysis. Time inclusiveness relates the short-run decision-making to the long-run situation.

Geographic inclusiveness is well illustrated by the growth of regionalism— the increase in emphasis on the need for some decision-making to take place on the regional level. Thus, a metropolitan planning body is set up to broaden the scope of decision-making to include not only the central city, but also a large part of the surrounding metropolitan area. Or, with a still larger scope, regional planning may involve the efforts of several counties in a fairly large area, or of several states, or indeed of several nations.

Inclusiveness of participation has to do with the matter of who shall participate in the decisions which are made at any particular system level and for any particular geographic area. Shall decision-making be broadly diffused, or shall it be confined to a relatively small number of parties?

As the Cooperative Extension Service proceeds in community resource development (which the ECOP report defines as "a process whereby the people who comprise the community arrive at group decisions and actions to bring about changes which will enhance the social and economic well-being of their community"), it will be engaged in the process of planning or inclusive decision-making, and it will be confronting these five dimensions of inclusiveness: inclusiveness of system level, of scope, of time, of geography, and of participation in decision-making. They constitute one possibly useful outline for approaching community development projects.

TWO VIEWS OF COMMUNITY DEVELOPMENT

But community development is not only a question of planning to enhance social and economic well-being; it is also a question of how the planning takes place. For many years, at least in the published accounts, there was considerable agreement that community development was a facilitating process which helped the people of the community determine their own goals and grow in competence to pursue them.

Murray G. Ross's definition of community organization has been widely quoted:

Community organization is a process by which a community identifies its needs or objectives, orders (or ranks) them, develops the confidence and will to work at them, finds the resources (internal and/or external) to deal with them, takes action in respect to them, and in so doing extends and develops cooperative and collaborative attitudes and practices in the community.[5]

In the past decade or so, newer conceptions have arisen to challenge this conventional community development approach. They offer alternatives in connection with a number of issues which any planning process must confront. These have to do with (1) consensus and dissensus, (2) directiveness or nondirectiveness, (3) process orientation or task orientation, (4) inclusiveness of scope, and (5) inclusiveness of participation. Let us consider them in turn.

1. *Consensus and dissensus.* Is there one course of action appropriate for the community on which all parties can agree? And should development efforts seek and confine themselves to such areas of agreement? Or are there important matters on which consensus cannot be reached but in which planning and action should nevertheless take place?

2. *Directiveness or nondirectiveness.* Should the principal strategy of the change agent be that of helping citizens determine their own set of goals and

their own set of priorities? Or should he propose goals and attempt to persuade appropriate groups to accept them and work toward them? The same questions apply to the manner in which the goals are to be sought. Should he be directive in his approach or nondirective?

3. *Process orientation or task orientation.* Should the principal emphasis in community development be the accomplishment of tangible task goals, such as a new zoning ordinance, or the setting up of an antipoverty program, or the improvement of the local school facilities? Or should the principal emphasis be placed on a process of group growth, trying to help the community develop improved communication and structures, formal or informal, for decision-making and effective action, with the specific immediate task outcome being only secondary?

4. *Inclusiveness of scope.* Should the concerns of the community development program range over a wide spectrum of community problems and opportunities, attempting a more or less "global" process for total community improvement, or rather should efforts be confined to a relatively narrow substantive area, such as education, or industrial growth, or land use, or social services?

5. *Inclusiveness of participation.* Should efforts be made at securing participation by the total community, that is, literally, by as high a proportion of the population as possible? Or should efforts be confined to interested groups and those with decision-making prerogatives?

In these five matters, it is not a question of one or the other, for in each case there are various degrees between the extremes. Generally speaking, the older, more conventional or "puristic" approach to community development was characterized by (1) seeking consensus, even when this delayed or precluded positive action, (2) a nondirective stance on the part of the change agent, (3) emphasis on the process of decision-making and change, rather than on specific task goals, (4) inclusiveness in scope, with the total community and its well-being as the focus of concern, and (5) the broadest possible participation in planning and implementation by the entire population.

Recently, all five of these aspects have been challenged from one source or another. In each case, the challenge does not necessarily imply going clear over to the other extreme, but rather moving away from this more conventional position.

It is pointed out that there is no single set of community goals, but that various individuals and organizations have different goals, which often conflict with each other; and that it is precisely the most important and pressing issues about which people are divided, rather than united. To act only in consensus is to immobilize oneself.

Likewise, the change agent is not alone in his efforts (remember the crowded pool); he is competing with other change efforts with different sets of goals and priorities. He is competing for the time of busy people, often powerful decision-makers; he had better know what he wants and how to express it.

Further, since so much effort nowadays is based on temporary ad hoc coalitions around specific issues, the idea is to get together and get the task accomplished; training for community competence in any other sense than getting the job done often seems beside the point.

Likewise, the various concerns of the community are so comprehensive that an organization which seeks to play a vital role must most likely limit itself to one or a few subject areas rather than spreading itself thinly over a number of areas in which much stronger groups are likely to be involved, with higher stakes in the outcome.

Finally, the idea of trying to approach total citizen participation on all important issues is mathematically impossible in all but the smallest communities. The problem of participation is not so simple as one of "involving the whole community," or "letting the people decide." Hence, choices must be made as to who is to participate and in what capacities.

These points have been presented here in somewhat exaggerated form for purposes of emphasis. The point is that the older model of the nondirective involvement of the whole community in change efforts, with high emphasis on process, is coming to be increasingly challenged as time goes on. It is interesting to note that the manner and direction of this challenge are themselves a result of the great change. American society as it changes is moving away from a situation where the older model of community organization was relevant. Planned change efforts in their aggregate look less and less like an orderly committee meeting with complete participation and unanimous decisions, and more and more like the crowded swimming pool. The point is worth emphasizing, because it poses a set of choices as to community development strategy which the Extension Service will be facing as it considers its own efforts in community resource development.

RELEVANT SOCIAL RESEARCH

The field which community resource development encompasses is extremely broad. There is much social research taking place which should be of relevance. From the many research areas receiving attention today, three would seem to be especially important: the community power structure, community action, and the interorganizational planning, decision-making process. They are all interrelated.

A widely known work is Floyd Hunter's book on *Community Power Structure,* which first appeared in 1953.[6] It pointed out that power to influence community action is unevenly distributed, and that in Atlanta, Georgia, which was the city studied, a relatively small group of top leaders was most important in decision-making. These leaders, who kept in touch with each other, were for the most part not the elected officials of government or of nongovernmental organizations; rather, they were the financial and industrial leaders, who in turn influenced the decisions of the official leaders.

A number of years later, Robert A. Dahl made a somewhat similar study in New Haven.[7] His findings, like those of Hunter, pointed out and documented the unequal distribution of power in New Haven, but differed from Hunter's in emphasizing the plurality of power configurations operating in New Haven and also the more influential role played by officials, both governmental and nongovernmental.

Of course, there have been scores of studies of community power since Floyd Hunter's study in 1953. In his book on *Men at the Top,* Robert Presthus gives a fairly comprehensive and readable summary of the research since Hunter, and also gives the methods and results of his own study of community power in two upstate New York communities.[8]

Likewise, a number of studies have been made of action programs in American communities. A few of them can be mentioned as perhaps being of special interest. A group of sociologists from Michigan State University some years ago made a study of the process through which a rural county went when it undertook a broad health self-survey as a means of gathering facts and stimulating action. The resulting book, *Community Involvement,* has many important implications for community resource development.[9]

In the metropolitan setting, Meyerson and Banfield made a study of the strategy of the Chicago Housing Authority in trying to achieve acceptance of its plan for low-cost housing in that city, and published a most informative book on *Politics, Planning, and the Public Interest.*[10]

A number of books are devoted to the dynamics of planning and politics in urban renewal programs. Rossi and Dentler examined an early Chicago urban renewal venture in *The Politics of Urban Renewal.*[11]

In a book called *Urban Renewal Politics,* Kaplan examined the urban renewal program in Newark, New Jersey, in terms of the social-political dynamics of the action program.[12] Scott Greer has studied urban renewal in a number of American cities.[13] Alan A. Altshuler[14] and J. Clarence Davies[15] have written interesting analyses of the city planning process.

Peter Marris and Martin Rein have studied the dynamics of the Ford gray-areas programs and the programs of the President's Committee on Juvenile Delinquency in a number of American cities, and their conclusions regarding the complex problems of social planning in the cities are particularly important.[16]

There is a burgeoning literature of studies dealing with the nature of the planning–decision-making process itself as a part of purposive social change. The book by Bennis, Benne, and Chin is an excellent collection of research and theory in *The Planning of Change.*[17] My own shorter work on "Types of

Purposive Social Change at the Community Level" is meant to be a contribution to this subject.[18] Robert Morris' book on *Centrally Planned Change* is a collection of papers on the subject by various authors.[19] The book by Morris and Binstock on *Feasible Planning for Social Change* is particularly good in considering attempts to bring about change from the specific standpoint of a change agent, as it were, entering the crowded pool and developing his own strategy in the light of what he would really like, what he thinks he can get, and how he can use what resources he has in order to bring it about.[20]

Naturally, one can but indicate the type of work that is being done in the fields I have mentioned. There are other fields as well, and of course many works have not been mentioned.

To many people who have a concern for the community development field, this paper may appear to be cold and critical. It lacks the warmth often associated with admonitions to work in the good cause of restoring a sense of community to people and localities engulfed by the mass society.

The intent has not been to inspire, but to help clarify. Despite its didactic tone, this paper offers few answers. It raises some questions and points up some issues which must be faced if community development efforts are to be effective.

NOTES

[1] The concept is elaborated and these aspects are developed at greater length in my *The Community in America* (Chicago: Rand McNally, 1963).

[2] The material of the following three paragraphs is given fuller analysis on pages 79–89.

[3] The ensuing four paragraphs appear also in chap. 1, pages 9–10.

[4] Roland L. Warren, "Community Change: Planned or Otherwise" (unpublished paper, 1965).

[5] Murray G. Ross, *Community Organization: Theory and Principles* (New York: Harper, 1955), p. 39.

[6] Floyd Hunter, *Community Power Structure: A Study of Decision Makers* (Chapel Hill: University of North Carolina Press, 1953).

[7] Robert A. Dahl, *Who Governs? Democracy and Power in an American City* (New Haven: Yale University Press, 1961).

[8] Robert Presthus, *Men at the Top: A Study in Community Power* (New York: Oxford University Press, 1964).

[9] Christopher Sower *et al.*, *Community Involvement: The Webs of Formal and Informal Ties That Make for Action* (Glencoe, Ill.: Free Press, 1957).

[10] Martin Meyerson and Edward C. Banfield, *Politics, Planning, and the Public Interest* (Glencoe, Ill.: Free Press, 1955). This book is discussed in chap. 4.

[11] Peter H. Rossi and Robert A. Dentler, *The Politics of Urban Renewal* (New York: Free Press, Macmillan, 1961).

[12] Harold Kaplan, *Urban Renewal Politics: Slum Clearance in Newark* (New York: Columbia University Press, 1963).

[13] Scott Greer, *Urban Renewal and American Cities: The Dilemma of Democratic Intervention* (Indianapolis: Bobbs-Merrill, 1965).

[14] Alan A. Altshuler, *The City Planning Process: A Political Analysis* (Ithaca, N.Y.: Cornell University Press, 1965).

[15] J. Clarence Davies III, *Neighborhood Groups and Urban Renewal* (New York: Columbia University Press, 1966).

[16] Peter Marris and Martin Rein, *Dilemmas of Social Reform: Poverty and Community Action in the United States* (New York: Atherton Press, 1967).

[17] Warren G. Bennis, Kenneth D. Benne, and Robert Chin, *The Planning of Change: Readings in the Applied Behavioral Sciences* (New York: Holt, Rinehart & Winston, 1961).

[18] Chap. 1 of this volume.

[19] Robert Morris, ed., *Centrally Planned Change* (New York: National Association of Social Workers, 1964).

[20] Robert Morris and Robert H. Binstock, *Feasible Planning for Social Change* (New York: Columbia University Press, 1966).

7

APPLICATION OF SOCIAL SCIENCE KNOWLEDGE TO THE COMMUNITY ORGANIZATION FIELD

A review of contributions by the social sciences—principally sociology—to community organization indicates that they tend to fall into two principal categories: (1) knowledge about the social context in which community organization is practiced, especially the nature of the community setting; (2) the broad area of social change, and within this, the narrower, more immediately relevant area of purposive social change. Each of these topics has been approached in two ways. The first was to review the literature and develop what seemed to be appropriate categories within which to group the most meaningful or relevant social science contributions. The second was to review all papers in the community organization field in the *Journal of Social Work* and in the *Social Service Review* for a five-year period, 1961–1965, and to note and classify the social science sources that were cited.

MAJOR AREAS OF SOCIAL SCIENCE CONTRIBUTIONS

Let us look first at a brief review of the topics on which significant work has been done by social scientists and which appear to be directly relevant to the field of community organization. These topics do not constitute a logical outline, but simply a convenient grouping that avoids some, but not all, overlapping.

Reprinted by permission from *Journal of Education for Social Work,* 3, no. 3 (Spring 1967). Originally presented at the annual program meeting of the Council on Social Work Education, Salt Lake City, January 1967. Notes have been renumbered.

Values and Value Orientations

Value orientations within the larger society form part of the constraints within which community organization must operate, but they also raise questions as to whether community organization workers have a mandate to try to change those values.[1] On a somewhat different level, differing value configurations provide part of the context within which any specific community organization activity is conducted, and numerous studies point out the way in which these value configurations vary from one community to another, as well as through time.[2] There is a considerable literature on the value structure of American society as well as on variations within this broad configuration in different localities, communities, ethnic groups, and social strata.[3] An important aspect of the value situation is that of value conflicts among groups in the community, a factual, researchable, and, to some extent, researched area[4] that would seem to be an important knowledge base for the practice decisions that must be made regarding values and the goals derived from them.

Ethnic Group Studies

This is a general rubric for the numerous studies that have been made regarding ethnic and racial group subcultures and the ways in which ethnicity is related to position in society, modes of participation, and the availability or non-availability of particular types of resources or opportunities. There is a vast literature of research findings and theoretical conceptualizations in this field.[5] Such concepts seem to have two points of special relevance to community organization. The first is perhaps most obvious: the community organization worker will neglect or ignore ethnic group culture and behavior patterns at his peril, if he is engaged in working with ethnic groups. The second is the growing attention to the social-structural aspects of the life situation of various ethnic groups. We shall turn to the matter of the structural aspects of social problems later.

Voluntary Associations

Community organizers confront voluntary associations in a number of contexts: the voluntary agency, the numerous voluntary associations related directly to the field of health and welfare, and the numerous voluntary associations that afford avenues of participation for individuals and that constitute important actors in the community field. A principal contribution of the social scientists has been the large number of studies indicating the direct correlation between socioeconomic status and organizational participation.[6] In this field, small-group theory, as well, has made an important contribution on a different level.[7] It is my impression that, although numerous social science studies have been made on various aspects of voluntary organizational behavior,[8] they have nowhere been pulled together in the kind of clear and rigorous conceptual framework that would make them directly useful to the community organization worker.

Organizational Theory

The broad field of organizational theory, on the other hand, is a burgeoning one, with great potential usefulness for community organization—a usefulness that is already being exploited.[9] The principal contributions from this field to date seem to lie in the study of bureaucratic organization,[10] as well as some of its pathologies;[11] the extent to which bureaucratic organization is supplemented by informal social processes;[12] the phenomenon of goal displacement,[13] through which organizations can thrive for long periods while devoting a large portion of their activities to goals other than those explicitly specified in the organizational charter; the relation of organizational structures to various types of function and personnel and various styles of decision-making;[14] and the interaction of the organization with its environment, particularly in exchange relationships with other organizations.[15] In all these instances, the mode or level of social science contribution is much the same. It is not that of telling the practitioner how he should go about his business, but rather that of helping the practitioner understand the situation within which he is working—in this case, aspects of the question of why organizations behave as they do.

A related contribution is the more specific one of leadership studies. Perhaps the key issue in this field is the relation between formal positions of leadership and informal leadership processes.[16] Other aspects of leadership are best considered in connection with power structure studies, which will be referred to presently, but one issue merits special attention here. This has to do with the various types of leadership and the dimension of permissiveness or nonpermissiveness. We are lacking systematic knowledge about the circumstances in which the more permissive type of leadership (as opposed to more directive leadership) is most likely to achieve a certain set of goals. This is due, in part, to a lack of sufficiently rigorous research studies. Another reason for our lack of systematic knowledge is, in my estimation, a strong ideological investment in the idea of permissive leadership, often resulting in a confusion as to whether we are considering it as a means toward specified task goals or as an end in itself. In any case, although it would be difficult to prove, it appears that the leadership studies that have been done have been a contributing factor in the current trend in community organization toward a more favorable predisposition toward directive leadership.[17]

Power Structure Theory

The theory of power structure is likewise a burgeoning field of investigation, particularly among political scientists and sociologists. It has led to a succession of well-documented conclusions, even though there are still many unanswered questions. One of the first big findings was Hunter's conclusion that the people who wield the power over the flow of community events are not necessarily the same people who occupy the official power positions in the organizational structure, governmental or nongovernmental.[18] But a rush of more specific findings ensued, namely, that the people who wield power in actual specific community issues are not necessarily those who are reputed to be the power figures; that there are various kinds of power, which may be distributed unevenly among so-called power figures; that communities vary considerably in the extent to which the power structures of governmental, economic, educational, and social service arenas are dominated by the same people or are relatively discrete; that power cannot be conceived statically, but that at any given time there is slack in the power system, and also that, over time, it is possible through organization to add important actors to the power system—an example being the relatively recent rise of civil rights leaders as an important voice in the community dialogue.[19]

In no other area of social science contribution has there been such premature generalization by practitioners (and also, in part, by social scientists) and so much ignoring of the fine print. The banal statement "We've got to get the power structure behind this if we intend to get anywhere with it" is perhaps a good example of the possible misunderstandings, misinterpretations, and misapplications of the power-structure findings, when taken at this naïve level of specificity.

Social Stratification

Variation in socioeconomic status has been studied intensively, as have the differences created by such variation in many aspects of living—education, utilization of social services, behavior norms, aspiration level, family living, employment, unemployment, and leisure-time pursuits.[20]

In this field, too, a succession of waves of new knowledge and understanding has emanated from the studies. There was, for example, the early realization that effective social work must be based on an adequate understanding of the total living patterns of people in relation to their position in the socioeconomic hierarchy: middle-class workers must learn how to relate effectively to people of lower socioeconomic status.[21] Then there came a number of research efforts, notably in the fields of delinquency and mental illness, that indicated tremendous differentials in both diagnosis and treatment based on social status differences.[22] More recently, the increasing salience of poverty as a social problem has renewed the interest of both researchers and practitioners in the differences in opportunity structure that social stratification implies, and has focused attention increasingly on the social-structural aspects of such problems as delinquency, unemployment, and dependency, as distinguished from the earlier view, which considered them more or less as aberrations on an otherwise healthy body politic.[23]

Regardless of how one feels about the effectiveness of the total social response to such questions, one is confronted here with a situation in which there has been a richness of relatively competent social science research that has received considerable attention from practitioners.

Community Processes

A number of studies and conceptualizations have been developed concerning processes that have definite relevance to the field of community organization —such as conflict[24] or community reaction to disaster.[25] The relevance of studies such as these to community organization work seems to indicate greater utilization of these types of findings than has apparently been the case so far.

Ecological and Demographic Studies

Numerous studies have been made in the general area of the distribution of people and activities in spatial relation to each other and in the analysis of population structures and rates of change.[26] These have definite relevance to the matter of community and neighborhood analysis in relation to intervention programs of various types. Such studies provide part of the data necessary for informed judgment regarding the differences in possible target neighborhoods, for decisions as to where to intervene, and for decisions as to planning for changing the demographic and ecological configurations of various parts of the city through deliberate policy.

System Theory

System theory has come to be used not only in the analysis of small groups and formal organizations, but also in the analysis of the less cohesive agglomerations called communities, which constitute the area of operations of many community organization workers. Like other approaches to the community, system theory helps in finding an answer to the question "What *is* the community in which I work, and how does my work relate to it?" While system theory affords a means for grasping and analyzing the complex, multistructured network of social relationships involved in the community concept, its principal contribution is perhaps not that of analyzing communities globally so much as of affording conceptual tools with which to uncover and analyze the particular aspects of the larger community whole in which most community work goes on. Putting this another way, few ventures involve, or even purport to involve, the entire community. System analysis helps to locate and understand those particular networks

and constellations that are especially relevant to the venture at hand and to discover and give appropriate consideration to relationships that do not appear on
any formal organizational chart. It is particularly helpful in approaching the
complex "wheels within wheels" characteristic of the many networks and formal
organizational relationships with which the community worker deals, both horizontally, across the structure of the community, and vertically, taking into consideration the relationship of neighborhood to community, to metropolitan region, to state, interstate region, federal, and international organizations and networks.

The increasing importance of these vertical relationships has given added
impetus to the use of system analysis. Two aspects of this are particularly noteworthy. One is the increasing need to cope with the metropolitan area as a
system, even though it does not coincide with any governmental jurisdiction;[27]
and the other is the increase in the activity of federal agencies in providing
finances and program stimulation in municipal affairs.[28]

Structural Aspects of Social Problems

The principal interest of sociologists in social problems is in structural
aspects, rather than in unique situations of individual cases.[29] In a sense, sociologists take the wholesaler's viewpoint of social problems, rather than the re-
tailer's. They ask questions about the larger context within which individuals
come to behave in ways that dominant groups come to define as social problems.
They look for orders of data, not so much at the level of the unique individual
experience—although that level has its own relevance—as at the level of circumstances in which the adaptive behavior of relatively large numbers of individuals takes such forms as are considered to constitute social problems. This is
perhaps best illustrated by the early work of Shaw on delinquency areas, in which
he found that certain neighborhoods in Chicago produced high delinquency rates
regardless of the country of origin of the people who moved into those areas.
There was, in other words, something about the constellation of social processes
in and around the neighborhood that produced delinquent behavior.[30]

In a similar sense, but with a whole variety of concepts and analytical techniques, one can ask about the constellation of social processes that produce
poverty, racial discrimination, slums, and alienation. This mode of analysis, the
most characteristically sociological one, has little direct relevance to those concerned with the problems of specific individuals. But when one begins to look
away from the individual pathology to the context in which that individual and
others behave, such sociological studies become more meaningful. As we all
know, we are actually in the midst of a sizable shift in emphasis, a shift whose
net effect is to place more significance on intervention at the social-structural

level and less relative weight on the possibilities of intervention at the individual level. This is the principal reason for the considerable attention the work of sociologists is receiving today, as contrasted with a decade or two ago.

The Structure of Social Services Within American Society

A related area of research directly relevant to community organization is the study of social services as an integral part of American society, and as modes of behavior that dovetail with important social values and behavior patterns. We are not referring here to the conflict between the residual and the institutional conceptions of social welfare as depicted by Wilensky and Lebeaux, but rather to the type of analysis their book exemplifies—the attempt to depict and analyze the supply and organization of social welfare services in the United States in relation to their integral connections with important values, processes, and behavior patterns in American society.[31] In a sense, this is an extension of the previous point; it involves the consideration not only of social problems as an integral part of American society—trying to understand them as a deeply rooted part of the whole—but also of social welfare services as an integral part of American society, taking their form in relation to other parts of the society, and likewise as a deeply rooted part of the whole. Again, as the "wholesale" approach grows relative to the "retail" approach, the importance of such research grows with it.

Impact-Evaluational Studies

In the past decade, a number of important studies have attempted to assess, through carefully controlled experimental designs, the efficacy, or lack of efficacy, of various types of direct service programs on individual recipients. For the most part, these do not constitute a contribution to behavioral theory. Indeed, most of them are not conceptually related to any specific disciplinary body of knowledge, such as sociology, social psychology, or anthropology. Nevertheless, a number of social scientists have conducted such studies, as have a number of social work researchers.[32] Their importance lies in their affording an alternative method of assessment to the more usual social work type of evaluation based on the following of accepted professional standards. Their relevance to community organization has been, paradoxically, in the generally negative nature of their findings. Hence the findings of such studies have given added impetus to the "wholesale" approach—to looking at the structural aspects of social problems, and to placing greater importance on intervention in the social structure than on intervention solely with the individuals involved.

Specific Community Studies

The number of careful studies of one community or another in one part of the country or another has grown by leaps and bounds in recent decades. Beginning, perhaps, with the two classic studies of Middletown, such studies have afforded analyses of the interconnected life of a large number of communities, and although each one unfortunately remains within the bounds of its own conceptual framework, making rigorous comparability impossible, they nevertheless aggregate to a large fund of intensively researched descriptions of social life in various community settings. They offer case studies, as it were, each with a more or less carefully developed set of analytical categories pointing up the interrelatedness of institutions and activities within American communities; and on this level they afford a rich basis for understanding the setting within which community workers often operate.[33] One should perhaps mention the much smaller number of books that have attempted to organize the rich materials from these studies and from other sources into more or less systematic analyses of American community living.[34]

SOCIAL SCIENCE CONTRIBUTIONS
IN THE AREA OF SOCIAL CHANGE

Let us turn now to the second large area of social science contribution—the area of social change. Before we do so, brief mention should be made of a controversy regarding theoretical orientation that colors social science work in this field. One can choose two alternative foci as points of departure in analyzing society. One is the question of how individual actions actually aggregate to behavior patterns that are more or less interlocked as well as to larger institutional forms that likewise are related in a more or less coherent system of values, roles, behavior patterns, and so on, all of which show remarkable coherence and stability. This theoretical orientation stresses continuity, equilibrium, and system maintenance.[35]

An alternative approach is to note the constant stress and strain, the continual flux and change, the conflict of interest and purpose, and the discontinuity and disorganization. From this view, little is permanent, and the large model of society is not of a system in equilibrium but of a constantly changing set of conditions caused by the constant interplay of shifting forces, interests, and power balances.[36]

This difference in emphasis is noteworthy, not only because it makes more intelligible some of the debates that rage within the social sciences, but also because it has direct relevance for community organization. The current conflict around the question of change strategies—consensus or dissensus, collaboration or contest—is the practical counterpart of these two theoretical points of view, the former emphasizing system maintenance and the latter emphasizing system change.[37]

The observation that systems must change in order to maintain themselves seems so simple as to border on the banal. Yet it helps clarify the theoretical relationship, even if it does not help the practitioner who is asking himself, "Should we give in in order to preserve consensus, or should we fight 'em?"

Generally speaking, social scientists have been concerned primarily with the theoretical difficulties in conceptualizing how systems can change; the relation of values to social change; the question of whether change in some ultimate sense stems primarily from some sector or aspect of society, such as the distribution of economic resources and economic power; or whether technological changes are at the root of most changes in other aspects of society. They have been concerned with change at the macro-level primarily, though, more recently, organizational theory has considered change at the formal organizational level.[38] Most of the emphasis has been on change emerging somehow as a product of social interaction, rather than as the result of deliberate intent on the part of a change agent. There are two exceptions to this statement, both at the macro-level. One is the theory of revolution, and the other is the related theory of social movements. Both of these are pertinent to the situation within which the community organization worker finds himself, namely, that of seeking to influence change under circumstances where others are likewise seeking to influence change, the others being variously potential allies or potential opponents. But revolutionary theory and social movement theory are understandably directed at the level of the total society rather than at the level where practitioners find themselves trying to influence change in the community, and usually in a relatively narrow field.

Purposive Change

The more confined field of purposive change at the community level likewise offers a growing body of research findings and pertinent "principles" derived from social science research, though of course these principles are not in any way integrated into a unified theory.

Three particular areas of concentration seem particularly appropriate for the problem of purposive change at the community level:

1. There is a considerable and growing body of literature regarding resistance to change, particularly to types of change goals desired by a change agent who comes in from outside or who represents a different culture or subculture. There are numerous volumes of field studies by sociologists and anthropologists documenting individual cases of trying to bring about changes such as the introduction of new public health practices, of agricultural production technologies,

or of social interaction patterns.[39] These studies, from different parts of the world, have a much more direct bearing on analogous change attempts within our own society than is usually recognized.

2. A second body of literature is that of carefully researched attempts at community change within our own society. In such instances, the social scientist is not himself seeking to bring about change, but rather is seeking to study the processes that occur as someone else attempts to bring about change. A decade or so ago, there appeared four outstanding examples of this, one being a study of attempts to accomplish specific objectives—such as hospital construction—in a large number of communities in different parts of the country,[40] and the other three being studies by social scientists of communities that were themselves conducting self-studies with a goal of action, principally in the public health field.[41] Others have studied urban renewal programs,[42] housing programs,[43] attempts at mental health education,[44] and so on.

3. A third and closely related body of literature consists of various attempts, large and small, important and unimportant, based on original field research or on secondary sources, to develop models and other conceptualizations of purposive change at various levels of social interaction, including the community level.[45] As indicated earlier, this effort is not tied in, theoretically, with the large body of social change theory on the macro-level. Nevertheless, the body of social change theory of revolution and of social movements is relevant, especially today, when the overlapping social movements of civil rights and antipoverty constitute a dynamic component in the changing community situation.

APPLICATION OF KNOWLEDGE:
A SURVEY OF THE PROFESSIONAL LITERATURE

Let us turn now to the question of how much, and in what ways, these categories of knowledge are being utilized by practitioners. One way of answering the question is to review the articles in the *Social Service Review* and in the *Journal of Social Work* for the five-year period 1961–1965. Taking all articles in the field of community organization (broadly considered to include several articles on social problems and social policy), we can make a tabulation of the social science materials cited and attempt to classify these materials according to the categories discussed earlier. It is interesting to note how the social science materials cited in these journal articles actually correspond to the categories already discussed as being most pertinent and important. In considering these findings, it must be kept in mind that, although this was a rather careful empirical tabulation, no attempt was made to define rigorously the terms involved or to pursue the content of the citations and incorporate the other refinements that would be necessary for this brief empirical check-tabulation to be accepted as a definitive study.

With these reservations, then, there were forty-seven articles sufficiently within the field of community organization to warrant their inclusion in the tabulation. Of these, ten had no references to social science materials, leaving thirty-seven articles on which the following figures are based. Rather than go through the complete tabulation, I shall mention only those categories in which the most frequent social science citations occurred. Then I shall point out some ways in which the pattern seemed surprising.

Below are the topics represented by more than ten citations from the social science literature among these thirty-seven articles:

Organizational theory	20
Models and conceptualizations of purposive social change	18
Social stratification	17
Specific community studies	16
Community setting (a residual, inclusive category)	13
Power structure theory	11

It is not necessary to repeat the designations of categories that received less than ten citations. The reference here is to citations of articles or books from the social sciences that have been classified according to the categories used in this paper. A total of 126 citations fitted into at least one of these categories; on the other hand, 51 citations from the social science literature did not fit credibly into any of the categories used for classification. They were distributed over a multitude of considerations, mostly having to do with idiosyncratic references to some part of the social science literature relevant to a particular point being made but not immediately relevant to community organization.

With all the limitations of such a superficial review, a number of observations seem warranted.

It appears that the considerable body of research findings available on voluntary organizations is virtually neglected in these articles. There were only four citations, three of which were to an early work by Axelrod.[46] There was no reference, for example, to Sills's work on *The Volunteers,* which constituted a highly significant contribution to our understanding of the relation of local organizations to national groups and to the process of recruitment and utilization of volunteers.

Again, in connection with community processes, there was only one reference to Coleman's masterful publication on *Community Conflict.* Is conflict so irrelevant to the present concerns of community organization, and is this summary and analysis of the process, geared to the community level, so unimportant?

It was surprising to note the paucity of references to publications dealing with the structural aspects of social problems.

Another surprise was the lack of a single reference to a work considered by many to be one of the best contributions to our understanding of community action processes: the book by Sower and his associates on the health self-survey in a midwestern county.[47] In this county of 65,000 people, over 700 individuals conducted interviews in 10,000 homes. The interview data on health problems were tabulated, and a report was given to community leaders. It is significant that after this massive accomplishment involving volunteer participation as an educational and motivational process, no action was taken that could be interpreted as an outcome of the study. In addition, it was found by the research team that the 700 people who conducted the interviews (a supposedly educational process) had little understanding of the purposes of the study, the possible uses to which it might be put, or the relevance of the questions they had asked. Yet many people continue to assume that enlisting people in voluntary efforts will help motivate them toward carrying through on implementation, and that it will build up a body of informed citizens to support change. Not so—at least, not in this carefully researched venture. Where else do these hopeful outcomes not apply? It is simply not known. But certainly a book like this must be of greater significance to the field than its complete lack of mention in these articles might indicate.

Among all the articles surveyed, there was not a single reference to either Meyerson and Banfield's study of the Chicago Housing Authority[48] or Banfield's subsequent study of political influence.[49] In these days of increasing federal, state, and municipal governmental expenditures for various types of action programs in local communities, of the increasing importance of political processes and of interaction of the more conventional social work agencies with an increasing number of housing, poverty, urban renewal, mental health, and other local, publicly supported planning-action agencies, one wonders how forty-seven articles could be written in the field of community organization without mentioning these books.

But the importance of the individual omission must not be exaggerated. There were only 177 social science citations in all. My own bibliography of books on the community contains many more than this number, and one could single out any one of them and make a strong case for its inclusion. The sample of citations, in other words, is too small to enable us to extract much significance from the exclusion of any particular work. Nevertheless, the individual omissions mentioned may be considered as representative of a more generalized trend of omission.

CONCLUSIONS

Just as there are styles and changing fashions in community organization practice, there are styles and changing fashions in social research and theory. Two decades ago, the great thing was stratification studies. A decade ago, the great power-structure surge began. And a few years ago, poverty and civil rights began to capture the imagination of many sociologists. Today the big thing is system theory. What will it be tomorrow? To imply that changing research emphases are simply fadism would be overreduction. But social science, like social work, is impervious neither to a certain fadism nor to a certain scanning eye on what topics are fundable from government grants.

More important is the situation regarding the interrelation of substantive findings, conceptual tools, and social science theory. This paper has enumerated some of the areas in which the social sciences have presumably achieved a body of substantive findings arising from fairly careful research—findings that have relevance to community organization. There has been less time to give specific attention to the conceptual tools, as distinguished from findings, that have been developed by social scientists and that can be useful to community organization. Examples are social stratification, power and its numerous subcategories and distinctions, system maintenance and system change, anomie, and so on through a long list. But it is one thing to have a number of relatively disparate, mutually unrelated research findings, however pertinent, and a kit of conceptual tools with which to assess social situations and choose action strategies. It is another thing to be able to organize the concepts and the findings into a consistent body of theory and specific empirical content that will be useful to the practitioner. Kadushin has pointed out a potential danger in the borrowing of concepts and findings from the social sciences: "the danger that the borrowed material will remain an undigested lump in the body politic of social work, interesting but un-integrated and unused."[50] Whether or not this is the case in social work, it is certainly the case in sociology. That is, it seems that sociologists have a lot of relevant findings and useful concepts to offer the community organization prac-titioner, but from the sociologists' own standpoint, as well, they represent "an undigested lump." The digestion process would entail the integration of research findings into a consistent, interrelated body of propositions constituting a broad theory. It is perhaps premature to expect or demand such theoretical elegance. But if one must crawl before he can walk, then too few of us are doing any-thing more than lying on our backs and kicking our legs in the air.

There is a need for a common, integrated core of social science knowledge —no matter how small the base at first—regarding the various aspects of pur-posive change at the community level and sufficiently broad to encompass not only the community organization practitioner and his various agency settings and change goals, but also the change efforts in various sectors of the com-munity, involving housing, economic development, urban renewal, transportation planning, formal education, health planning, and so on. It is quite possible that whatever knowledge social scientists evolve that is important, theoretically integrated, and potentially usable in any of these settings will be so in all of them.

In turning to the question of areas of particular promise for additional research, it should of course be acknowledged that additional research is needed in all the areas discussed earlier as relevant to community organization. But a suggestion or two beyond that can be made.

A number of years ago, Kaufman wrote that "the sociologist has a continuing challenge to work with action leaders in developing and making explicit various alternative designs for the good community and suggesting conditions under which these goals may be realized.[51] This is a challenge that many sociologists refuse to take up. Generally speaking, sociologists tend to shy away from making explicit value statements, preferring to make none at all or to smuggle them into their discourse by quoting someone else or by using some other dodge. Those few who have taken definite value stands regarding the nature of the community tend to be those who "view with alarm" the passing of community values associated with the small, largely preindustrial community.

Few sociologists are willing to work seriously and deliberately in helping to formulate the specifications, including value assumptions, for something called "the good community." Even such practitioners as social workers and city planners devote amazingly little time and intellect to spelling out what a good community would look like if it existed. Call it research, or applied social science, or philosophizing, it does seem desirable that a knowledgeable group of people, including social scientists and social workers, should spend some time probing into areas of agreement and disagreement with respect to a normative approach to the community, to constructing a model, or several alternative models, of "the good community."[52]

Another area warranting further research is that of interorganizational behavior within the community. The current situation in cities seems to be assessed by all in much the same manner, in this one respect at least: that American cities are characterized by an increasing number of planning centers whose spheres of interest and activity overlap each other in many supportive or competing ways. Yet there is little systematic social science knowledge that applies to a situation such as this. It is necessary to know a great deal more about the nature of these planning organizations—housing authorities, health departments, antipoverty organizations, urban renewal authorities, chambers of commerce, health and welfare councils, etc.—and about the behavior of these organizations in interaction with each other and with other environmental forces, such as local politicians, federal grant-in-aid agencies, ethnic group leaders, business interests, civic associations, and the rest. There are some wonderful case studies, but there is no systematic knowledge.[53]

There is much to be desired in what social scientists have to offer to the field of community organization today. The ratio of pontification to verifiable, generalizable knowledge is alarmingly high. It has become increasingly apparent that many social scientists and community organization practitioners share a certain aspiration for community organization practice in social work: that it continue to break free from a narrow agency-oriented conception of the community and from a narrow conception of community organization as being focused on coordinative work with social agencies. These bounds are being broken further asunder each day; and, with all its shortcomings, social science knowledge has been an important element in the process.

NOTES

[1] *An Intercultural Exploration: Universals and Differences in Social Work Values, Functions, and Practice* (New York: Council on Social Work Education, 1967).

[2] Florence R. Kluckhohn, Fred L. Strodtbeck *et al., Variations in Value Orientations* (Evanston, Ill.: Row, Peterson, 1961); Robert S. Lynd and Helen M. Lynd, *Middletown in Transition: A Study in Cultural Conflicts* (New York: Harcourt, Brace, 1937); and Irwin T. Sanders, *Making Good Communities Better,* rev. ed. (Lexington: University of Kentucky Press, 1953), pp. 17ff.

[3] *Ibid.* See also Robin M. Williams, Jr., *American Society: A Sociological Interpretation* (New York: Knopf, 1951); W. Lloyd Warner and Paul S. Lunt, *The Social Life of a Modern Community* (New Haven: Yale University Press, 1941); August B. Hollingshead and Frederick C. Redlich, *Social Class and Mental Illness: A Community Study* (New York: Wiley, 1958).

[4] James S. Coleman, *Community Conflict* (Glencoe, Ill.: Free Press, 1957).

[5] Warner and Lunt, *Social Life of a Modern Community,* contained an early explicit analysis of ethnic group identification and position in "Yankee City." Since then, various aspects of the question have been reported in numerous publications on the topics of nationality groups, Negroes in the United States, and poverty.

[6] Charles R. Wright and Herbert H. Hyman, "Voluntary Association Memberships of American Adults: Evidence from National Sample Surveys," *American Sociological Review,* 23, no. 3 (June 1958): 286–94; and Morris Axelrod, "Urban Structure and Social Participation," *American Sociological Review,* 21 (February 1956): 13–18.

[7] Robert F. Bales and Philip E. Slater, "Role Differentiation in Small Decision-Making Groups," in Talcott Parsons and Robert F. Bales, *Family, Socialization and Interaction Process* (Glencoe, Ill.: Free Press, 1955).

[8] For instance, David L. Sills, *The Volunteers: Means and Ends in a National Organization* (Glencoe, Ill.: Free Press, 1957).

[9] An example is the rapid adoption of the work of Levine and others on exchange among organizations (see n. 15).

[10] See Robert K. Merton *et al., Reader in Bureaucracy* (Glencoe, Ill.: Free Press, 1952).

[11] For example, Robert K. Merton, *Social Theory and Social Structure,* rev. ed. (New York: Free Press, Macmillan, 1957), pp. 195ff; Robert A. Dahl and Charles E. Lindblom, *Politics, Economics, and Welfare: Planning and Politico-Economic Systems Resolved into Basic Social Processes* (New York: Harper, 1953), pp. 247–61.

[12] Fritz J. Roethlisberger and William J. Dickson, *Management and the Worker* (Cambridge: Harvard University Press, 1939); George C. Homans, *The Human Group* (New York: Harcourt, Brace, 1950); and Alvin W. Gouldner, "Organization Analysis," in *Social Science Theory and Social Work Research,* ed. Leonard S. Kogan (New York: National Association of Social Workers, 1960).

[13] Merton, *Social Theory and Social Structure*, p. 199; and Philip Selznick, "An Approach to a Theory of Bureaucracy," *American Sociological Review*, 8 (February 1943): 48.

[14] See, for example, James D. Thompson and Arthur Tuden, "Strategies, Structures, and Processes of Organizational Decision," in James D. Thompson *et al., Comparative Studies in Administration* (Pittsburgh: University of Pittsburgh Press, 1959).

[15] James D. Thompson and William J. McEwen, "Organizational Goals and Environment: Goal-Setting as an Interaction Process," *American Sociological Review*, 23, no. 1 (February 1958); Eugene Litwak and Lydia F. Hylton, "Interorganizational Analysis: A Hypothesis on Coordinating Agencies," *Administrative Science Quarterly*, 6, no. 4 (March 1962); Sol Levine and Paul E. White, "Exchange as a Conceptual Framework for the Study of Interorganizational Relationships," *Administrative Science Quarterly*, 5, no. 4 (March 1961); Sol Levine, Paul E. White, and Benjamin D. Paul, "Community Interorganizational Problems in Providing Medical Care and Social Services," *American Journal of Public Health*, 53, no. 8 (August 1963).

[16] Two rather differing studies indicate the range of this broad field: William F. Whyte, *Street Corner Society: The Social Structure of an Italian Slum* (Chicago: University of Chicago Press, 1943); and Floyd Hunter, *Community Power Structure: A Study of Decision Makers* (Chapel Hill: University of North Carolina Press, 1953).

[17] See, for example, Robert Morris and Martin Rein, "Emerging Patterns in Community Planning," *Social Work Practice, 1963* (New York: Columbia University Press, 1963).

[18] Hunter, *Community Power Structure*.

[19] There is a vast body of literature on the power structure. For bibliographies and for overall depictions, see Charles M. Bonjean and David M. Olson, "Community Leadership: Directions of Research," *Administrative Science Quarterly*, 9, no. 3 (December 1964); and Nelson W. Polsby, *Community Power and Political Theory* (New Haven: Yale University Press, 1963).

[20] For example, Warner and Lunt, *Social Life of a Modern Community;* August B. Hollingshead, *Elmtown's Youth: The Impact of Social Classes on Adolescents* (New York: Wiley, 1949).

[21] Earl L. Koos, *Families in Trouble* (New York: King's Crown Press, 1946).

[22] Hollingshead, *Elmtown's Youth;* Hollingshead and Redlich, *Social Class and Mental Illness;* and Orville R. Gurrslin *et al.,* "Social Class and the Mental Health Movement," in Frank Reissman *et al., Mental Health of the Poor* (New York: Free Press, Macmillan, 1964).

[23] Harry C. Bredemeier, "The Socially Handicapped and the Agencies: A Market Analysis," in Reissman *et al., Mental Health of the Poor.*

[24] Coleman, *Community Conflict* and "Trigger for Community Conflict: The Case of Fluoridation," *Journal of Social Issues*, 17, no. 4 (1961).

[25] See William H. Form and Sigmund Nosow, "Disaster Strikes the Community," *Community in Disaster* (New York: Harper & Row, 1958).

[26] George A. Theodorson, ed., *Studies in Human Ecology* (Evanston, Ill.: Row, Peterson, 1961); Eshref Shevky and Wendell Bell, *Social Area Analysis* (Stanford: Stanford University Press, 1955); and Wendell Bell, "Social Areas: Typology of Urban Neighborhoods," in *Community Structure and Analysis,* ed. Marvin B. Sussman (New York: Crowell, 1959). In addition, there have been numerous administrative and planning studies that have used ecological material as a basis for proposed programs.

[27] See John E. Bebout and Harry C. Bredemeier, "American Cities as Social Systems," *Journal of the American Institute of Planners*, 29, no. 2 (May 1963).

[28] Charles I. Schottland, "Federal Planning for Health and Welfare," in *The Social Welfare Forum, 1963* (New York: Columbia University Press, 1963).

[29] See Robert K. Merton and Robert A. Nisbet, eds., *Contemporary Social Problems* (New York: Harcourt, Brace & World, 1961). Many books of the Chicago school also

relate to the structural aspects of social problems. See Walter C. Reckless, *Vice in Chicago;* Clifford R. Shaw, *Delinquency Areas;* and Clifford R. Shaw and H. D. McKay, *Juvenile Delinquency and Urban Areas* (Chicago: University of Chicago Press, 1933, 1929, and 1927, respectively).

[30] Shaw, *Delinquency Areas.*

[31] Harold L. Wilensky and Charles N. Lebeaux, *Industrial Society and Social Welfare* (New York: Russell Sage Foundation, 1958).

[32] Edwin J. Thomas *et al., In-Service Training and Reduced Workloads* (New York: Russell Sage Foundation, 1960); Henry J. Meyer, Edgar F. Borgatta, and Wyatt C. Jones, *Girls at Vocational High: An Experiment in Social Work Intervention* (New York: Russell Sage Foundation, 1965); Roland L. Warren and Jessie Smith, "Casework Service to Chronically Dependent Multiproblem Families: A Research Demonstration," *Social Service Review,* 37, no. 1 (March 1963).

[33] There is a vast number of such community studies. Among the more important are: Robert S. Lynd and Helen M. Lynd, *Middletown: A Study in Modern American Culture* (New York: Harcourt, Brace, 1929); Lynd and Lynd, *Middletown in Transition;* James West, *Plainville, U.S.A.* (New York: Columbia University Press, 1945); Art Gallaher, Jr., *Plainville Fifteen Years Later* (New York: Columbia University Press, 1961); and Arthur J. Vidich and Joseph Bensman, *Small Town in Mass Society: Class, Power, and Religion in a Rural Community* (Princeton: Princeton University Press, 1958).

[34] Irwin T. Sanders, *The Community: An Introduction to a Social System* (New York: Ronald Press, 1958; 2nd ed., 1966); and Roland L. Warren, *The Community in America* (Chicago: Rand McNally, 1963).

[35] Talcott Parsons, *The Social System* (Glencoe, Ill.: Free Press, 1951).

[36] Ralf Dahrendorf, *Class and Class Conflict in Industrial Society* (Stanford: Stanford University Press, 1959).

[37] Roland L. Warren, *Types of Purposive Social Change at the Community Level,* Brandeis University Paper in Social Welfare no. 11 (Waltham, Mass.: Florence Heller Graduate School for Advanced Studies in Social Welfare, Brandeis University, 1965); reprinted as chap. 1 of this volume.

[38] See Warren G. Bennis, Kenneth B. Benne, and Robert Chin, *The Planning of Change: Readings in the Applied Behavioral Sciences* (New York: Holt, Rinehart & Winston, 1961); and Ronald Lippitt, Jeanne Watson, and Bruce Westley, *The Dynamics of Planned Change: A Comparative Study of Principles and Techniques* (New York: Harcourt, Brace, 1958). Neither of these books restricts itself exclusively to change in formal organizations.

[39] See Benjamin D. Paul, ed., *Health, Culture, and Community: Case Studies of Public Reactions to Health Programs* (New York: Russell Sage Foundation, 1955).

[40] Paul A. Miller, *Community Health Action: A Study of Community Contrast* (East Lansing: Michigan State College Press, 1953).

[41] Solon Kimball and Marion B. Pearsall, *The Talladega Story: A Study in Community Process* (University: University of Alabama Press, 1954); Christopher Sower *et al., Community Involvement: The Webs of Formal and Informal Ties that Make for Action* (Glencoe, Ill.: Free Press, 1957); Floyd Hunter, Ruth Connor Schaffer, and Cecil G. Sheps, *Community Organization: Action and Inaction* (Chapel Hill: University of North Carolina Press, 1956).

[42] Harold Kaplan, *Urban Renewal Politics: Slum Clearance in Newark* (New York: Columbia University Press, 1963); Scott Greer, *Urban Renewal and American Cities* (Indianapolis: Bobbs-Merrill, 1965); and Peter H. Rossi and Robert A. Dentler, *The Politics of Urban Renewal: The Chicago Findings* (New York: Free Press, Macmillan, 1961).

[43] Martin Meyerson and Edward C. Banfield, *Politics, Planning, and the Public Interest* (Glencoe, Ill.: Free Press, 1955).

[44] Elaine Cumming and John Cumming, *Closed Ranks: An Experiment in Mental Health Education* (Cambridge: Harvard University Press, 1957).

[45] Lippitt, Watson, and Westley, *Dynamics of Planned Change;* Bennis, Benne, and Chin, *Planning of Change;* Sower *et al., Community Involvement;* Warren, *Community in America,* chap. 10; and Warren, *Types of Purposive Social Change.*

[46] Axelrod, "Urban Structure and Social Participation."

[47] Sower *et al., Community Involvement.*

[48] Meyerson and Banfield, *Politics, Planning, and the Public Interest.*

[49] Edward C. Banfield, *Political Influence* (New York: Free Press, Macmillan, 1961).

[50] Alfred Kadushin, "The Knowledge Base of Social Work," in *Issues in American Social Work,* ed. Alfred J. Kahn (New York: Columbia University Press, 1959), p. 69.

[51] Harold F. Kaufman, "Toward an Interactional Conception of Community," *Social Forces,* 38, no. 1 (October 1959): 17.

[52] For an attempt to convert this precept into practice, see chap. 15.

[53] See chaps. 10 and 11.

SECTION

C

*Structure and Process
In Urban Planning*

INTRODUCTION

If modern cities had walls, as did many ancient and medieval ones, and if one were to choose a motto or slogan to be chiseled in large letters above their main gates, there would be much to say in favor of making that slogan *E pluribus unum*. For it remains the enduring challenge both to social theorists and to harried practitioners that the modern city is, in still not completely fathomed ways, "one out of many."

Even to speak of "the city" or "the metropolitan community" is to risk reification, the fallacy of assuming that there is some *thing* out there that corresponds to the word we use. A good case could be made for asserting that there is no thing out there to correspond to the term "community"—or, at best, that what is out there is, in the vernacular, a can of worms. Yet planners and community organizers—and at times sociologists—seem to find little difficulty in speaking of the community interest, of planning for the community, of securing community participation, of implementing community goals. Is it not essentially fallacious to convert this can of worms into a unit by the mere verbal magic of calling it a community, and then to treat the word itself as though it represented some virtually tangible thing that has interests, has goals, resists this, supports that, has needs, is planned for, and so on?

The problem is truly enigmatic. The astute reader will recognize in the problem simply another version of a fundamental cleft that runs through contemporary social theory, and indeed has characterized social theory from its inception among the Greeks: what we now call "social system theory" as opposed to what we now call "conflict theory." The terms of the dichotomy are unfortunate, since although they are used to represent opposites, they obviously refer to different things. The theoretical issues are complex, but many of them stem from what appears to be a basic distinction—whether a social group of

129

some type is to be considered as a unity, and from this focus the structure and behavior of this unity are to be examined, or whether a social group is to be considered less as a focal reality than as merely a concept or rubric under which clusters of interaction among individual actors are to be studied from the standpoint of the individual actors. A reductionist would perhaps restate it more simply: Which has primacy, the whole or the parts? And if one must reduce complex issues to their simplest terms, that is perhaps not a bad way to do it.

As quoted in another part of this book, Harold Kaplan concludes, in his study of Metro Toronto, that such a metropolitan government "must be described from the bottom up," by what he terms "actor analysis" as opposed to "system analysis."[1] He indicates that Metro Toronto does not have the coherence as a "collectivity" which would make it justifiable to organize the behavior he is studying from the standpoint of an inclusive social system, and account for it in those terms.

The prudent reader may well ask why he should invest his time in pursuing what seems to be a rather abstract distinction—of great theoretical importance, perhaps, but with few practical implications. Yet the practical relevance is great. It lies in the fact that practice theory in both city planning and community organization simply assumes the system-oriented approach, the perspective of the whole, the view from Olympus, as it were. The planner in each case is seen as operating on behalf of the community, in the public interest, and developing plans that are "best for the community." As indicated in Chapter 4, he may base these plans on rational-technical considerations, putting aside in the planning process the political realities of acceptance and implementation, or he may incorporate these into the planning process as he works with "the community," thus assuring acceptance—or at least enhancing its possibility—but at the expense of rational-technical considerations. The first alternative is that taken by city planners generally, and the second is that taken by social work community organizers. They represent opposite ends of a polarity, as indicated in Chapter 3. But what they have in common is an orientation to the community as a unit; an assumption that there is an entity called the "community," and that in the first instance they are planning for or on behalf of that community and in the second instance are interacting with that community and developing plans to implement its goals.

In each case it is doubtful whether this choice was a deliberate one in relation to the system-theory/conflict-theory polarity, for in each case the choice was made and the basic outlines of the practice theory were developed prior to the current growing interest of practitioners in such theoretical distinctions and

[1] Harold Kaplan, *Urban Political Systems: A Functional Analysis of Metro Toronto* (New York: Columbia University Press, 1967), p. 22.

the way they have been treated in social theory. The choice was much more implicit than explicit.

But of greater importance, the choice resulted in a professional orientation that is daily becoming less relevant to the urban scene in the United States. The result is that planning practitioners are armed with a practice theory that simply does not fit the realities they confront every day in their professional practice, and the validity and applicability of which suffer attrition with each passing year.

The foregoing considerations are not the foundation on which the chapters in this section are based. Quite the opposite; they are conclusions to which these chapters have led me, *ex post facto*. For these chapters, which with one exception follow a strict chronological sequence, represent, as well, a certain logical sequence, beginning with a more or less purely empirical assessment of current developments on the urban scene and then progressing more specifically and conceptually into an analysis of their implications. In the process, it has become clear to me—and I hope it will be equally clear to the reader—that a consideration of purposive change in communities today, and of the decision-making that goes into it, must focus on the interaction of a number of specific and relatively independent centers of activity and decision-making. There is no community planning that encompasses all these planning activities. There is rather the interaction—sometimes cooperative, sometimes contesting—of organizations that plan in their own (mutually overlapping) sectors of interest and in relation to the goals and wishes and needs, not of "the community," but of their respective diverse constituencies.

To say this is not to assert that conflict theory is in any basic sense more valid than system theory. It is merely to acknowledge their different foci and to assert that conflict theory is more relevant to a discussion of purposive change at the community level. At the same time, as individual sectors of community interest and local constituencies come to be organized into certain specific types of organizational framework, system theory may be much more important and relevant in examining behavior within these sectors. In some sectors, such as that encompassed by boards of education, this is quite apparent. In others—for example, the field of mental health—it is much less so.

These chapters have deliberately been left in their original great diversity of form and style and depth. They represent what has been a fluctuation, a swinging back and forth between theory and practice, between conceptual abstraction and concrete application, over a period of approximately five years. It will be noted that certain common threads of discourse weave through two or more of these chapters, and they have not been edited out because they do constitute bridges indicating the flow of thought, and because I prefer to keep the original content of the chapters—which were by no means originally written as part of a master plan—intact. In order that each chapter will remain more or less self-sufficient, the original bibliographical references are maintained. The reappearance of certain references in a number of chapters—such as the repeated reference to Odd Ramsöy—constitutes at least a partial acknowledgment of my intellectual indebtedness.

"The Impact of New Designs of Community Organization" served not only the purpose of fulfilling a request by the National Social Welfare Assembly (since reorganized as the National Assembly for Social Policy and Development) for a summary of current developments and their implication; it also provided me with an occasion for a fresh look at American community organization and planning after two years abroad. The things that stuck out were the proliferation of federal programs, the single-problem approach, coalitions, a plurality of planning centers, and an increasingly crowded and competitive field of agency interaction. The assessment is largely empirical, oriented toward the practitioner and to a certain extent reflecting his terminology. One of the concluding paragraphs begins with the statement: "It is not only the powerful federal impact, but the pluralism of planning centers on federal, state, and local levels that makes it impossible for any one agency to plan as though it alone were intervening in otherwise purely crescive social processes." In a sense, all of the subsequent chapters develop the implications of this statement.

Communities can be looked at as encompassing markets, or quasi markets, in which various types of individuals and organizations seek to maintain themselves and pursue their goals through a series of exchange relationships, some of which are necessary, others optional. In "Concerted Decision-Making in the Community: Some Theoretical Considerations," the analysis of organizations focuses on social service agencies, because of the context of the discourse as a Lindeman Lecture at the National Conference on Social Welfare; but the analysis of an enterprise applies of course to all formal organizations, including business organizations, political parties, trade unions, and so forth. Out of this analysis is derived the concept of concerted decision-making, a process in which decisions that would otherwise be made independently are brought into relation with each other. One should perhaps note in passing that much of what is usually denoted by the somewhat more ambiguous term "planning" is encompassed in this process of relating otherwise independent decisions to each other as they are made. When the existing quasi market—the ongoing processes and procedures of the community—does not allocate resources and rewards in a way that is perceived by pertinent actors as satisfactory, the decision is made to intervene, to concert the otherwise independently made decisions and actions that are adding up to a situation perceived as unsatisfactory in such a way that a more satisfactory outcome results. This is presumably the major rationale for planning.

In any case, it raises three kinds of problems—the problem of deciding which decisions should be concerted and by whom, the problem of calculating (in the absence of a market decision) what combination of resources and rewards will yield the highest payoff, and the problem of assuring that all pertinent actors behave in such a way that the presumed higher payoff will eventuate.

In the course of subsequent investigation of the problems posed by a plurality of planning centers at the community level, it became apparent that this plurality was something other than utter chaos. Indeed, in most American communities of any size, a number of readily identifiable types of organizations are set up to engage in concerted decision-making in the respective sectors of activity for which they are legitimated to make decisions. As one goes from city to city, one encounters the same types of organizations with remarkable regularity. This regularity itself underlines the point that community structure is not merely the adventitious resultant of purely local interaction, but reflects characteristics that derive from commonalities of institutional structure across the national society. The result is that despite differences among cities in many details, concerted decision-making functions are parceled out with remarkable regularity to substantially the same organizational *dramatis personae,* and insofar as deliberate decisions are made and implemented at the community level to influence the course of events, this is done largely in and around such legitimated community decision organizations. Examples are the board of education, the city planning commission, the health and welfare council. Each of them is a center of planning, yet, as indicated earlier, their spheres of interest often overlap.

Since such organizations are of central importance in influencing the course of events at the community level through concerted decision-making, it is surprising that so relatively little is known about them as organizations—how they differ from each other, how the individual planning of one meshes or fails to mesh with the others', how and to what extent they engage in concerted decision-making or bring their respective activities into coordination by a vigorously contested interaction process.

"Planning Among the Giants: The Interaction of Community Decision Organizations" is directed at developing these concepts and indicating some areas of needed research. The editors of the journal in which it was first published wanted the title changed to omit the words "Planning Among the Giants." Perhaps it was too colorful. In any case, the original title is restored here, precisely for its color in an otherwise rather intellectually demanding problem context.

"The Interorganizational Field as a Focus for Investigation" adds to the development of the concept of community decision organizations, setting up a heuristic model of the investment by community people in a number of organizations each designed to seek to maximize certain values or objectives, not all of which can be maximized simultaneously. Putting this another way, the contemporary American solution for the problem of community resource allocation is not to centralize the decision-making in one overall organization with authority to allocate resources and rewards and to adjust these allocations in a rational relationship to preestablished priorities; rather it is to distribute these goals and objectives to a number of community decision organizations, to invest them with differing amounts of resources, and to charge them with furthering their respective bundles of presumably desirable objectives. From that point on, priorities are set in a drama, rather than in a planning process. As each community decision organization seeks to apply its resources more or less effectively toward accomplishing its designated objectives, there ensues an interactional process, part cooperation, part contest, out of which the resolutions of their somewhat diverse objectives are aggregated. If the solution of the problem of determining community priorities is thus left to a struggle among large community decision organizations, then the question arises whether the outcome of that struggle might yield a higher payoff for a given community over the whole range of its preference scales under certain circumstances than under others.

In the course of the analysis, it becomes apparent that if progress is to be made in understanding concerted decision-making, some consideration must be given to the contexts in which it occurs. These can be classified as social choice, coalitional, federative, and unitary decision-making contexts, and it can be hypothesized that much of the behavior of the parties engaged in concerted decision-making may be attributable to the type of context in which it takes place.

At this point it should be mentioned that each of these last-discussed chapters was written as a preliminary step in formulating a research project that would seek to add to our remarkably inadequate fund of knowledge regarding the interaction of community decision organizations—the more remarkable because of their central role in community-level decision-making. Since the Model Cities program was being legislated at about this time, and because of its broad scope of pertinence to various sectors of community concern, I decided to study the interaction of a select group of community decision organizations in a number of cities in connection with the development of the Model Cities program in those cities. Many of the suggestions for needed research in these two chapters anticipate this rather extensive research project, as do some of the ideas in the subsequent two chapters.

Under what circumstances do organizations concert their decisions? The chapter on "The Concerting of Decisions as a Variable in Organizational Interaction" considers this question and presents a number of propositions concerning organizational interaction. A number of these propositions seem fairly obvious when stated, yet they have not been stated explicitly in the existing literature. One is that organizations enter voluntarily into concerted decision-making processes only under circumstances conducive to the preservation or expansion of their respective domains, or when trade-off inducements are offered. The chapter deals in several places with the important point that it is not usually organizations as totalities that interact, but rather parts of organizations. It explores and seeks to clarify the circumstances under which organizations concert their decisions and the circumstances under which they do not, and indicates that these variables apply whether or not the issue happens to be one on which they agree on their conception of the desired outcome. It indicates likewise that episodes of cooperation between organizations can escalate and then gradually decline, just as episodes of contest do.

"The Interrelationship of Community Decision Organizations" is more empirical and practice-oriented, having been originally prepared for a meeting of executives of antipoverty community action agencies, united funds, and health and welfare planning councils of the largest American cities. Their organizations dramatize the overlap among community decision organizations; and the community action agencies in particular have been involved in a varied history of cooperation and contest. Since this meeting was focused on collaborative or coordinative planning, it seemed appropriate to indicate some of the meanings applied to the term "coordination"—often left undefined on the assumption that everyone understands what it means. The Model Cities research project was beginning to indicate to the research staff, at least, that the meaning is not so apparent.

In this chapter an attempt is made to delineate schematically the relation of issue outcome agreement or disagreement to intensity of interaction. From this is derived a theoretical description of an action episode, one of the units of analysis in the Model Cities study. It is an episode in which interaction around a particular issue moves from potential cooperation or contest to active cooperation or contest and back again with the subsiding of the interaction.

It will be recalled that the preceding chapter deals in part with the circumstances under which this process occurs. In a sense, this chapter is an attempt to apply to a specific practical setting the theoretical materials developed in the preceding three chapters. This is especially noticeable in the direct application to the interagency setting of the suggested changes for "optimizing the mix," as presented at the end of Chapter 11.

As the preliminary data from the first stage of the Model Cities research began to come in, we began to develop the first preliminary findings regarding the behaviors of the various types of community decision organizations studied. These are yet to be analyzed in relation to an analytical strategy built into this project's methodology—a strategy, incidentally, designed to test some of the more or less didactic statements made in various chapters of this section, especially Chapter 12. In addition to these preliminary, more or less descriptive results, two developments stood out strongly. One was the extent to which the interaction among community decision organizations, with which the study is primarily concerned, was eclipsed by the growth of resident participation and the struggle for power and control of the program vis-à-vis city hall. The other relates more directly to the conceptual development represented by these various chapters, and to a finding that underlies some of the statements made at the beginning of this introduction: the planner's role must be redefined by substituting a model of the planning process in which any individual planner is not a consultant to the entire planning system, but to one of the parties thereto. In Model Cities, as in other programs, there are many planners, many conflicting points of view, many mutually incompatible claims to representing the community interest. These incompatibilities are sifted and reconciled, and a modus vivendi is developed not through the detached deliberations of some body of professional arbiters of the community's welfare, but in a hard struggle with high stakes in a process that is essentially—for want of a better word—political. The process is much more adequately captured by actor analysis than by system analysis, much more validly conceived as a struggle of parties than as the behavior of some unified whole.

8

THE IMPACT OF NEW DESIGNS
OF COMMUNITY ORGANIZATION

In considering the impact of new designs of community organization, I shall first comment briefly on some of the changes at the community level that are associated with these new designs and then raise some basic questions regarding citizen involvement and planned change in the community.

CHANGES AT THE COMMUNITY LEVEL

Let us begin with the change that perhaps seems most dramatic, most challenging, and, from certain standpoints, most threatening. This is the huge input of funds and program development from the federal government. Why is it so important?

First, it offers help, both in funds and in stimulation, to communities that are engulfed by the multiplicity and complexity of problems, many of which stem from sources beyond their control, such as the sweep of automation, the gradual reconversion of defense activities, and the growth of population in areas surrounding the central cities.

Second, federal inputs usually come tied to specific program areas, with consequent limitations on their use and the necessity of tailoring community programs to these specialized federal requirements.

Third, the problem areas in most cases turn out to be extremely complex, even though topically confined. This sets up a dynamic impetus to expand out

Reprinted by permission from *Child Welfare,* 44, no. 9 (November 1965). Originally pre-sented at the annual meeting of the National Social Welfare Assembly, November 1964.

from the core problem to encompass other, closely related ones. And since broad community conditions affect them all, each program is like a stone thrown into a pool—setting up waves spreading toward the perimeter and encountering waves from other programs.

Fourth, though not new to this decade, the number and magnitude of federal programs have increased to the extent that the change is almost qualitative in nature.

Fifth, increasingly these federal programs call for a community plan, or for extensive citizen participation, or for some other community organization component.

Sixth, the range and volume of these programs is so great that few, if any, conventional community welfare councils are able to incorporate them into a centralized and coordinated kind of comprehensive planning.

Seventh, the promise of federal funds constitutes a stimulus not only for the development of a program, but also for a competitive scramble for agency position with respect to the new program. The existing balance of community organization forces is vigorously agitated while the kind of organization that is to receive the funds and carry out the program is being decided. At the same time, the ferment created by the new activities continues to have important side effects.

A number of other changes are occurring, in more or less close association with this huge input of federal funds and stimulation. Thus, even before the delinquency and poverty programs—ever since World War II, in fact—there has been a growing organization of attention and effort around specific community problems, each of which has broad ramifications. What seems to be emerging is the realization that, under current urban conditions, the balanced, administered approach to problems like housing, juvenile delinquency, services for the aging, school dropouts, and mental health is something that cannot be attained by any one agency under any one roof. Rather, specific *ad hoc* attacks on these and other problems have come to dominate the health and welfare scene. As mentioned earlier, though, each of these problem areas has aspects that overlap with others, providing a constant need to look toward collaboration for mutual goals and the avoidance of mutually incompatible programs.

A closely related characteristic of the present scene is the development of *ad hoc* coalitions of agencies and organizations in relation to some of these specific problem areas. Often these are formed outside the community welfare council, in a variety of relationships to it. Each is, in some ways, a little council of its own, circumscribed by its specific problem area; limited, presumably, in time; and performing some, but not all, of the usual council functions. Each constitutes a potential threat to the council's ability to achieve a modicum of coordination in the health and welfare field, and each develops a degree of autonomy that can become a block to joint efforts.

Thus, at the very time when the need for coordinated, comprehensive planning in such fields as housing, urban renewal, and social welfare is being widely voiced, the problem is compounding itself through the appearance of the newer planning coalitions mentioned above. It is increasingly apparent that unified, centralized planning, whether or not desirable, is becoming more and more irrelevant to the current urban scene. A plurality of planning centers, each constituting a powerful coalition, becomes a challenge to conventional concepts of planning.

Meantime, another fundamental change is occurring. We have reached the point where the overlap of interest and activities emanating from specific agencies or specific coalitions is creating an increasingly competitive situation, with one agency's activities being much more basically affected by another agency's decisions and activities than was previously the case.

To oversimplify, we can think of an earlier stage when the client need for various kinds of service was very great and the number of agencies offering services rather small and spotty. The possibility of saturation of the client population was relatively remote. Each agency did what it could, and there was need for all. This is an exaggeration, since councils of social agencies have for decades been trying to avoid duplication of agency services. Nevertheless, the current picture is drastically different. The earlier stage could perhaps be visualized as individual agencies fishing in a placid brook, with relatively little competition or interference with each other. Now the brook has become agitated, various agencies and coalitions are interested in the same fish, lines get tangled, some agencies get the hook, others find difficulty casting in their lines—in short, an exciting turmoil! The need for coordination grows, but at the same time, the difficulties of coordination multiply.[1]

I have admittedly oversimplified the background to the current new designs of community organization, which can be broken down into five rough categories: federal programs, the single-problem approach, coalitions, a plurality of planning centers, and a more crowded field of agency interaction. In the light of these developments, several basic questions occur regarding the relation of these new designs to citizen involvement.

CITIZEN INVOLVEMENT

Like love, citizen involvement is a many-splendored thing. And like love, citizen involvement calls forth certain sweet, tender feelings as well as certain gnawing implications that the relationship never runs smooth. One more parallel: love of the wrong kind with the wrong person can involve a host of circumstances for which we reserve some of the culture's most negative terms— incest, prostitution, homosexuality, adultery. The term "citizen involvement" may offer similar problems of clarity of definition and appropriateness of application.

How vastly different are the implications of citizen involvement if one is talking about citizens at the board-member or policy-making level; citizens volunteering their services through agencies either to help clients or to raise funds; participation in neighborhood organizations dealing with local neighborhood improvement; the organization of clients to feed back into the agency's policy-making procedures; or the organization of protest and conflict groups. One must, in order to speak meaningfully in this field, be clear regarding the segment of the population that is involved, the purposes that presumably are to be accomplished, and the relationship of the citizens to the agency or coalition.

Each of these would require more extensive comments than could be given here. But let me cite a most significant article by James Q. Wilson, in which he points out that it is difficult to obtain the support of indigenous lower-class residents of renewal areas.[2] Although he does not elaborate on this point, it is apparent that citizen involvement in such neighborhoods is not for the purpose of a bottom-upward kind of goal definition and planning for execution, but, on the contrary, an attempt to gain their acquiescence to the changes that are to take place. These changes may have important positive value for the community as a whole, but, for the residents themselves, they may simply imply forcible eviction from one's own dwelling and the destruction of one's own home neighborhood.[3] According to Wilson:

> Planning with people assumes on the part of the people involved a willingness and a capacity to engage in a collaborative search for the common good. The willingness is obviously almost never present when the persons involved will be severely penalized by having their homes and neighborhoods destroyed by wholesale clearance. . . . But what is less obvious is that it may not be present, even when such clearance is not envisaged, because of important class differences in the capacity to organize for community-wide goals.[4]

In an earlier passage, he is more explicit on these differences. Speaking of the low-income sections that are to be renewed, he writes:

> Such people are more likely to have a limited time-perspective, a greater difficulty in abstracting from concrete experience, an unfamiliarity with and lack of confidence in citywide institutions, a preoccupation with the personal and the immediate, and few (if any) attachments to organizations of any kind, with the possible exception of churches.[5]

He thus concludes that, although some degree of citizen participation and involvement on the citywide level is relatively easy to obtain, the problems of citizen involvement on the neighborhood level in renewal areas in a "planning-with" relationship are highly complex.

Professor Wilson is more realistic and perhaps more forthright than some of the rest of us in tackling this hot potato, and it is unfortunate that space limits a more thorough depiction of his analysis. Suffice it to say that his article dramatizes the importance of being clear on whether "involvement" is to be in goal-setting or in goal-receiving; whether it is honestly to broaden the basis of decision-making or merely to get people to jump through the proper hoops; and whether it is for the purpose of policy-making, program development, legitimation, general acceptance, client cooperation, or whatever.

Aside from the instrumental purposes of citizen involvement—to get support, cooperation, or money, and the like—there seem to be two important value considerations. The first is to make social organizations sensitive to broad constituencies—in a sense, the democratic concept of popular accountability. The second is to afford opportunities for creative growth through participation in community activities, a matter of individual enrichment and the good life. We often confuse these two, and we often blandly assume that we are motivated by one or the other or both when it is apparent to a detached observer that our overriding purpose is to secure acquiescence to a preconceived program.

RELATION OF INDIVIDUAL AGENCIES TO A COALITION

My second basic question has to do with the relation of the individual agency to a coalition of agencies. I need only remind you that when it comes to tackling some broad problem, agencies often show a tenacious unwillingness to adapt their own programs to the presumably needed modifications, apparently preferring to continue their own comfortable, tried-and-true kind of program that is admittedly fragmentary and that may be highly ineffective. In addition, competition that involves seeking to protect or expand the agency's domain often looms larger than what the community might expect.

Thus, when Walter B. Miller studied a delinquency-prevention program in a northeastern metropolitan setting, he found the agency behavior so obviously conflicting and ineffective that it could be accounted for only by realizing that "for the great majority of organized institutions which maintain programs directed at juvenile delinquency, the adoption of operating procedures and philosophies which would be effective in reducing juvenile crime would, in fact, pose severe threats to the viability of the institution.[6]

The agency-coalition problem is one of understanding the relation of agency function to the functioning of the more inclusive unit, the coalition. The coalition's goals are more inclusive than the agencies', and they are different from them. The coalition's function may be a comprehensive approach to juvenile delinquency, although the individual agencies may be performing specific functions with various degrees of relevancy to preventing juvenile delinquency.

If these agency functions in aggregate had constituted an effective approach, the coalition would be unnecessary. But the individual approach is fragmented, ineffective, at times self-contradictory. This does not indicate that the agencies themselves are in difficulty. Indeed, the greater their ineffectiveness, the more persuasive may be their appeal for more funds to do the job, for expansion, and for other prerequisites to individual agency well-being. The coalition, however, may face a responsibility that individual agencies usually do not—the responsibility of making an appreciable impact on juvenile delinquency. Once such a responsibility is assumed, with its accompanying mandate to work for a rational, intermeshing, effective approach, changes are usually called for that threaten the domain, and sometimes the existence, of individual agencies.

We need to know more about how to relate agency goals to coalition goals —how to promote goal-attainment on the more inclusive level of the coalition. Eventually, we must have the knowledge that will enable us to make the optimum rational mix between agency survival needs and goal attainment by the coalition. Amitai Etzioni has made an incisive analysis of the relation of organization requirements to the performance of announced goals.[7]

In a highly important but largely ignored book, Odd Ramsöy has attempted a systematic investigation of the relation of groups to more inclusive groups through the simultaneous analysis of the functions of the sub-system and of the more inclusive system.[8]

We are only at the beginning of a systematic attempt to expand organizational theory to include these complex levels of interorganization function and exchange.[9] When we know more about these things and have a better conceptual framework within which to analyze them, we shall perhaps cease flailing away at individual agencies for "resisting" broad community actions and shall cease asking the agencies to risk their own existence, or the professional status of their executive staffs, or their body of donor supporters, or their necessary body of service recipients, for an unknown payoff to the community that may spell disaster to themselves.

LOCAL RESPONSIBILITY FOR CHANGE

My third basic question relates to the issue of local responsibility for change. Is it true that social welfare organizations generally are principally concerned with maintaining society's equilibrium rather than instituting change? Many social scientists have come to this conclusion. The principal emphasis is on giving services to those whom present conditions and circumstances put at a disadvantage rather than on making basic changes in those conditions and circumstances. Joint planning takes place characteristically in noncontroversial areas. Where the need is such as to challenge present institutional and power arrangements, the concern tends to become extruded into largely single-purpose organizations that further a "cause" more or less militantly or are torn between doing so and remaining "respectable."[10]

Savilla M. Simons raised the question at the National Conference on Social Welfare:

> Where have we social workers been that we have allowed inherited poverty to develop in the wealthiest nation of the world? How have we allowed a caste system to develop in this land of the free? . . .
>
> . . . Except for the neighborhood agencies and some new pilot projects, we are alienated not only because our offices are not accessible to the most deprived, but also psychologically and culturally. . . . In an age of conformity we have been conformists.[11]

It is questionable whether the profession of social work has as much impact regarding major institutional change today as it did in the old days of fighting for minimum wages, tenement house laws, child labor laws, and the rest. Perhaps a few random observations on this assertion are in order.

First, it is widely realized that many of the problems that arise at the community level come from forces that are not subject to community control and that require state, regional, and federal action. But having said this, we are still faced with the problem of developing methods through which the wishes of communities may be defined and expressed as distinguished from those of the state, regional, or national bodies with their relatively rigid programs for grants-in-aid to which community programs must be tailored.

Second, if local influence is to be brought to bear in effective ways on state and national policies, it is difficult to see how this can be accomplished without deep involvement in the political process. If agencies cannot become directly involved because of their essential equilibrium-maintenance function and because of the threat to their tax-immunity privileges, then it seems obvious that they must develop a closer relation to local politicians who can become so involved. The role of citizens on agency boards is crucial in this regard.

Third, it is questionable whether changes of the kind required can be effected by community welfare councils, largely because of the essentially conservative nature of their function. Generally speaking, centralized planning can

occur only under conditions of basic consensus on goals—or at least on objectives
—or under conditions where such goals and objectives are considered comparatively unimportant by the powerful groups in the community.

What are the alternatives to conventional health and welfare planning
where value consensus is not obtainable and where the issues are not innocuous
but highly controversial? Two of the most important alternatives come to mind.
The first is that of engaging in the political process, a process of negotiation
among contending forces, where competitive strength and adroitness of tactics
yield the highest payoff. The second is that of engaging in conflict. There are a
number of issues—for example, racial segregation, birth control, fluoridation,
and medicare—in which "planning" has been inadequate and in which the
conflict aspects of the situation have left many agencies in a dilemma regarding
whether to enter the conflict or remain as bystanders. Merely to mention such
a list—and it could be extended—is to indicate both the dilemma regarding
change through conflict and the fact that some agencies actually do engage in
such activities.

ORGANIZATIONAL CHANGE

My fourth basic question has to do with change in relation to the structure
and functions of existing health and welfare agencies. Many agencies will have
to change drastically if they are to be able to continue to exist in the face of
such changes as were listed earlier. Some will be unable to do so, quite aside
from the question of initiating change on their own account.

How do organizations provide for their own change? If change is not the
unusual but the normal, how can agencies so structure themselves as to undergo
change with the least waste motion, the greatest effectiveness, and the greatest
survival value? New concepts of organizational structure—not as something to
be modified only in periods of grave crisis, but as something pliable, constantly
in flux, but maintaining continuity—will be appropriate for the decades ahead.
From agency executives, leadership, in the sense of restructuring, will be called
for in addition to the usual administrative skills.[12] Much will depend on the
willingness of citizen board members to take a flexible approach to community
needs—even on their insistence that the agency do so.

Perhaps most agencies will be unable to effect such continuous flexibility
and change without aid from outside consultants who can help them through
successive sequences of change episodes, as Lippitt et al. have described.[13] Likewise, such works as The Planning of Change offer executives and policy-makers
an opportunity to benefit from what is known—from what little is known, one
must admit—about planning for change.[14]

NATURE OF THE PLANNING PROCESS

My fifth basic question relates to the nature of the planning process. We are entering a phase in which numerous planning centers will be planning for change in certain parts of their communities' structure. As indicated earlier, the planning function in the health and welfare field has spilled over the narrow confines of the conventional health and welfare council. As Charles I. Schottland said at the National Conference on Social Welfare in 1963:

> In spite of the 500 or more welfare councils which have engaged millions of citizens in cooperative community efforts, any analysis of where we stand today in the changing life of the American city raises serious questions about the ability of our traditional vehicles for social planning to cope with the kinds of problems we face and the impact of dozens of Federal programs upon them.[15]

It is not only the powerful federal impact but the pluralism of planning centers on federal, state, and local levels that makes it impossible for any one agency to plan as though it alone were intervening in otherwise purely crescive social processes. If there is to be any degree of coordination among these various planning centers, even on the local level, it will occur less through a rational process in line with conventional concepts of planning than as a process of negotiation and bargaining and exchange among planning bodies, with politics, writ large and small, playing an important part in the final determination. Under such circumstances, survival and success and, let us hope, community betterment will go to those who are flexible and creative, who have a close ear for important constituencies, and who are adroit in the rugged process of political interaction.

Unfortunately, we seem to have few models for this kind of pluralistic planning *cum* politics. On the one hand, we seem to have a planning model that involves the rational adaptation of means to ends, but unfortunately in a social vacuum, conjuring up visions of the dust-gathering report or the ivory-towered master planner. On the other, we have some important chunks of practice theory about planning as a social process, about motivation, participation, and the like, mixed with large chunks of value assumptions.

Neither of these models has been systematically tested, though both have been followed on numerous occasions. The latter, more akin to the humanistic predispositions of the American social worker than the former, unfortunately contains no method for injecting rationality into the decision-making process. Interestingly, it is almost purely a political model, leaving the decision about rationality to the process of negotiated assent—thus providing that if the final planning decisions are less than logically convincing, they may be at least psychologically acceptable. Our two most widely used models of planning, there-fore, call up either the complaint "It may be rational, but you can have it!" or the empty satisfaction of "It may not be rational, but it's ours, all ours!"[16]

Perhaps we should insist on something better. What that something is, I do not know. I do feel, though, that Braybrooke and Lindblom are on the right track. They have developed a method for calculation that, unfortunately, they hide under a bushel by giving it the odious name "disjointed incremental-ism."[17] Nevertheless, their book represents a milestone in that it presents one of the best attempts to deal with the rational aspects of planning as a social process.

In this process, the planner can assume neither omniscience nor omnipo-tence, but has to be in there pitching, trying to be coolly calculating, but making an occasional mistake; trying to have his way, but occasionally having to compromise; trying to make tentative formulations of next steps in a situation that is changing drastically, in part at least as a result of the planning activities of other constellations in the community, but also as a result of the unanticipated side effects of his own activities.

It may be an uncertain path, but it is the path we will all have to follow if citizen volunteers and professional staffs want to keep up with the new designs that are changing the face of American communities and of American community organization.

NOTES

[1] An excellent analysis of this progression of organizations toward a "turbulent environment" has been given by F. E. Emery and E. L. Trist in "The Causal Texture of Organizational Environments," *Human Relations*, 18 (1965): 21–32.

[2] James Q. Wilson, "Planning and Politics: Citizen Participation in Urban Renewal," *Journal of the American Institute of Planners*, 29 (1963): 242–49.

[3] See, for instance, Marc Fried, "Grieving for a Lost Home," in *The Urban Con-dition: People and Policy in the Metropolis*, ed. Leonard J. Duhl (New York: Basic Books, 1963), pp. 151–71.

[4] Wilson, "Planning and Politics," p. 247.

[5] *Ibid.*, p. 245.

[6] Walter B. Miller, "Inter-Institutional Conflict as a Major Impediment to Delin-quency Prevention," *Human Organization*, 17, no. 3 (1958): 20.

[7] Amitai Etzioni, "Two Approaches to Organizational Analysis: A Critique and a Suggestion," *Administrative Science Quarterly*, 5 (1960): 257–78.

[8] See Odd Ramsöy, *Social Groups as System and Subsystem* (New York: Free Press, Macmillan, 1963).

[9] For a ground-breaking study, see Sol Levine and Paul E. White, "Exchange as a Conceptual Framework for the Study of Interorganizational Relationships," *Administrative Science Quarterly*, 5 (1961): 583–601.

[10] See Martin Rein and Robert Morris, "Goals, Structures, and Strategies for Community Change," in *Social Work Practice, 1962* (New York: Columbia University Press, 1962), pp. 127–45.

[11] Savilla M. Simons, "Social Change Implications for Policy and Practice Re: Deterioration of the Inner City—A First Step Toward Defining a Small Area Approach" (paper presented at the National Conference on Social Welfare, Los Angeles, May 1964), p. 5.

[12] Philip Selznick, *Leadership in Administration: A Sociological Interpretation* (Evanston, Ill.: Row, Peterson, 1957).

[13] Ronald Lippitt, Jeanne Watson, and Bruce Westley, *The Dynamics of Planned Change: A Comparative Study of Principles and Techniques* (New York: Harcourt, Brace, 1958).

[14] Warren G. Bennis, Kenneth D. Benne, and Robert Chin, eds., *The Planning of Change: Readings in the Applied Behavioral Sciences* (New York: Holt, Rinehart & Winston, 1961).

[15] Charles I. Schottland, "Federal Planning for Health and Welfare," in *The Social Welfare Forum, 1963* (New York: Columbia University Press, 1963), pp. 116–17.

[16] See chap. 4.

[17] David Braybrooke and Charles E. Lindblom, *A Strategy of Decision: Policy Evaluation as a Social Process* (New York: Free Press, Macmillan, 1963).

9

CONCERTED DECISION-MAKING
IN THE COMMUNITY:
SOME THEORETICAL CONSIDERATIONS

When Max Weber turned his attention to the city as an object of sociological investigation, he took as his point of departure a type of social life that was characterized by a market.[1] In this market, a variety of possible purchasers and the availability of a variety of wares made possible an impersonal type of exchange in which people could satisfy their individual needs in optimal fashion. Buyer and seller could engage in transactions in which price would fluctuate to reconcile demand and supply.

It is interesting to conceive of the city in this way—as a colossal exchange mechanism through which needs are expressed and efforts are made to satisfy them. Insofar as some article or some service is not available within the household, one can go to the market, as it were, and procure it.

Over the decades and centuries, it seems, more and more things have been made available in the market which formerly were products of the immediate household. In an analysis of the changing functions of the American family, William F. Ogburn documented the wide variety of goods and services that have become available on a commercial basis—for a price—in the market.[2] It is little wonder that Simmel, in seeking to capture the spirit of the metropolis, asserted, "All things float with equal specific gravity in the constantly moving stream of money."[3]

But it is obvious that the market, in any narrowly literal sense, does not always operate to distribute resources and rewards in optimal fashion. Where this is the case, several courses are open.

Reprinted by permission from *The Social Welfare Forum, 1965* (New York: Columbia University Press, 1965). Presented as the Lindeman Memorial Lecture, National Conference on Social Welfare, Atlantic City, May 1965.

1. Restrictions may be placed on producers, limiting some aspects of their freedom to pursue their individual profit.

2. Certain functions can be performed outside of the profit sector, and money raised to pay for them through taxes.

3. Voluntary associations, supported largely by gifts, may be formed to distribute certain goods or services on some basis other than the payment by the customer of the going price in the free market.

4. One can, further, attempt to plan in concerted fashion for the optimum distribution of goods and services in relation to need, rather than leaving this adjustment to the exigencies of the market. This would seem to be precisely the function of the activity called community organization, in its conventional form. In a widely held conception, community organization is viewed as a process of bringing about and maintaining a progressively more effective adjustment between social welfare resources and social welfare needs. Obviously, if this function were performed satisfactorily in the open market of demand and supply, such community organization activities would not be necessary.

As a matter of fact, Simmel is highly misleading in his pithy statement on money as a common denominator; for there are many important types of goods and services that are best distributed on some other basis than the price that individual consumers can and will pay for them in a free market. In such areas as police and fire protection, education, highways, probation services, vocational training programs, costs of medical care, and family casework services, price as the resultant of demand and supply in a free market is largely irrelevant.

THE COMMUNITY AS A QUASI MARKET

We can see, then, that if the concept of the city as a great market for the allocation of resources and rewards is to be useful in trying to understand the disposition of needs and services, it cannot be the pure market model of the classical price theorists. This model is too narrow, since it excludes much relevant activity from the profit sector of community activities, and is almost completely irrelevant to the governmental and voluntary associational sectors.

This paper is an attempt to review some of the aspects of the community context in which resources and rewards do get allocated on a basis other than the operation of the free market and price as the determiner of purchases and sales. It will become apparent that our allocational techniques are considered to be generally poor, and that in many cases some type of concerted decision-making has to be instituted in order to assure that resources and rewards are allocated more favorably than would otherwise be the case.

Such deliberate concerted allocation is often termed "planning." From this viewpoint, planning can be seen as a process of concerted decision-making in situations where the resultant of individual decision-making has not operated to produce a satisfactory allocation of resources and rewards.

In considering this question, the concept of the community as a market is helpful, though of course not in the narrow sense of the classical economists. In recognizing that classical market theory is largely irrelevant to great sectors of public life, we have perhaps thrown out the baby with the bath water, failing to recognize that the community is still, in an important sense, a colossal distributive market, even though classical market theory does not apply to much that occurs. Unfortunately, there is no neat substitute for classical market theory, but it is possible to delineate some of the aspects in which the community nevertheless functions as a market—or rather, as a quasi market. And it is possible to draw some implications from this analysis for concerted decision-making, or planning.

Terms like the gift market, the client market, or the research market are more than mere figures of speech. For demand, supply, competition, and other aspects of conventional markets are present in all segments of community activity. Is it possible to outline some characteristics of a market theory that would include all of these aspects of the community but which would permit analysis of important differences between different sectors or settings of local activity? One can do so by making central use of a concept of *enterprise,* that is, of an organizational activity designed to achieve certain goals. The concepts of financers, acceptors, exchange, and survival needs are also useful. The concept of enterprise is broad enough to include not only the usual private profit undertaking, but also such projects as governmental offices and voluntary associations. Needless to say, most activities in the health and welfare field are conducted by one of these three types of enterprise. What do they have in common?

In the first place, they come into being through an *entrepreneurial function.* Someone has to develop the idea, define the venture's goals, gain the necessary support for it, and gather together capital, labor, experts, and management, having made some type of previous assessment of the market. Regardless of the setting, *financers* must be found. In government, this may involve political activity leading to legislation and financial appropriations. In private enterprise, it involves finding investors. In voluntary associations, it means finding people who will pay dues or give money for the enterprise. In today's community context, this last often occurs within the framework of the council-fund setup.

There must also be customers, clients, recipients, or whatever they are to be called. They are, in a sense, the consumers of the product. Let us call them *acceptors.* A club must find and keep members, a social agency clients, a hospital patients, a school pupils, a store customers, and so on. Note that some of these acceptors themselves pay for the services they receive. In other cases, they pay in part; in still others, they do not pay at all. In any case, the enterprise must find and maintain acceptors, or it will be unable to stay in operation.

In order to accomplish its goals, an enterprise must enter into certain *exchange* transactions. Some of the principal exchanges are with acceptors. Goods or services are offered in exchange for dues, fees, or purchase prices. But the exchange may not be of a monetary nature. The social agency client, for example, may pay no fee, but simply offer himself as an acceptor in exchange for agency services, with the money coming from taxes or gifts. This role is far from inconsequential. But it is important to note that many health and welfare enterprises do not have to sell their product in any literal sense. They only have to find people who will accept it without payment, provided that the enterprises can finance themselves from other sources. In this they differ from a store, for example, or from an individual lawyer charging his client a fee for the complete cost of his services.

Enterprises enter into exchange relationships with each other, as well. In these exchanges, money may pass in one direction in return for some other resource, but this does not invariably occur. In interenterprise transactions, including those between social welfare agencies, a long list of things may be exchanged, in varying proportions: services to the enterprise's internal structure; services improving the enterprise's position in its environment; money; prestige; access to financers, acceptors, personnel, or other important actors; access to new rewards; legal waivers; free advertising; endorsement; political power; promissory notes (psychological, legal, or other "redeemable" obligations); release from debts, both monetary and nonmonetary. This is only a partial list of the types of things that may be exchanged between enterprises.[4]

Finally, in this brief listing of the characteristics of enterprises, there are certain *preconditions for survival* and means of measuring success. These are often conceptualized as task accomplishment needs and organizational maintenance needs. The relationship of the two is complex. To oversimplfy somewhat, we can say that every enterprise must meet minimal maintenance needs or disintegrate. Task accomplishment, or the fulfillment of the explicit goals of the enterprise, may contribute toward the filling of maintenance needs, but this is not invariably the case—especially in the short run. Indeed, sometimes the maintenance needs of the enterprise operate to vitiate task accomplishment.

This relationship is analyzed by Thorstein Veblen in connection with businessmen and production. "Addiction to a strict and unremitting valuation of all things in terms of price and profit leaves [businessmen], by settled habit, unfit to appreciate those technological facts and values that can be formulated only in terms of tangible mechanical performance." He goes on to assert: "They are unremittingly engaged in a routine of acquisition, in which they habitually reach their ends by a shrewd restriction of output; and yet they continue to be entrusted with the community's industrial welfare, which calls for maximum production."[5]

It is interesting to note that a precondition for classical market optimization of utility is free competition. But since, as Veblen noted, higher profits for the individual enterprise can in certain circumstances be achieved by limiting competition and restricting output, there has been a constant struggle among producers to limit competition and control the supply of goods and services, through trusts, cartels, mergers, and other devices, and a constant response through government to limit such activities in the interests of preserving a modicum of competition.

But in the nonprofit sectors of the community, the opposite is true. In the case of both public and voluntary agencies, lack of competition, in the form of avoiding duplication of services, is declared to be in the public interest, and professional norms call for various devices through which competition is minimized. The result resembles a free market much less than it does a territory cut up by industrial cartels, with each enterprise agreeing with others regarding clear boundaries of the kinds of clients that "belong" to each enterprise, and under what circumstances exchange of acceptors, in the form of client referrals, will take place. Through welfare planning councils, a cartel is in effect formed which not only thus establishes domains, allocates acceptors, and delineates trade areas, but also exerts extreme pressure against the emergence of new competitors.[6]

A pivotal need of any enterprise is for financers. The competition among enterprises in the community for financers takes place either:

(a) in the grim price market battle for the customer's or investor's dollar, or

(b) in the gift market—either the free gift market of available donors or the organized gift-allocation system called the United Fund—or

(c) in the struggle for tax dollars focused so often in the budget committee hearing of some legislative body.

Generally speaking, given a modicum of entrepreneurial and managerial ability, personnel can be recruited, goods and services can be produced, acceptors can be found, and appropriate interagency transactions can be made—provided the financing continues. In the last analysis, the financing will continue if the private investor is given a profit, or if the enterprise can compete favorably in budget hearings where the ultimate arbiter is votes in the legislature and beyond it within some broad voting constituency, or in the interplay of competing demands within the budget committee of the United Fund.

In each of these ultimate sources of decision the financial survival or non-survival of the enterprise is only indirectly related to the effective and efficient performance of its explicit functions. The business enterprise may reduce production, rather than increase it, in order to make a profit. Or it may, as in the case of television, be able to make a profit, but by means that many consider to fall short of maximization of utility. A mental health clinic may be able to maintain itself and expand its domain by catering to middle-class rather than lower-class acceptors. It may be easier this way to recruit and maintain professional staff; it may be easier to show a large demand among acceptors; it may be easier to show results of a type that will satisfy budget committees. A program designed to enhance the opportunities of the poor may be able to meet its survival needs without really benefiting the lower half of its target population. Indeed, the costs of carrying benefits to this lower half may be so great, the technologies for this purpose may be so inadequate, and it may be so difficult and costly to recruit acceptors that the enterprise may find it well-nigh impossible to survive if it devotes a major share of its resources to this group.[7]

It has been over a decade now since Etzioni made his trenchant analysis of the relation of goal attainment to the other needs of a given organization. He indicated impatience with behavioral science studies of various kinds of enterprises—mental institutions, custodial institutions, large planning organizations, and so on—which invariably produce findings that organizational goals are often displaced in favor of system-maintenance activities. "What counts," he asserted, "is a balanced distribution of resources among the various organizational needs, not maximal satisfaction of any one activity, even of goal activities."[8]

Given a choice between attaining its goals and meeting its survival needs, an enterprise will usually do the latter. This applies to business, government offices, and voluntary organizations as well. The choice is often implicit in the discrepancy between the kinds of things an enterprise has to do in order to survive and enhance its position and the kinds of things it has to do in order to serve its proclaimed goals. The two are not the same, whether in the private, the governmental, or the voluntary sector of community activities. Perhaps in the future, behavioral science investigators will give more attention to the situational context within which enterprises can meet their survival and maintenance needs and at the same time function effectively either individually or in concert.

On a broader level, the interrelated network of enterprises of all three types—profit, governmental, and voluntary—may in aggregate function in a way that is less than optimal. For example, the allocational process in the United States functions in a way that leaves 34.6 million people with an income below the poverty level, and resources are so allocated that migratory workers necessary for harvesting many perishable crops receive an average annual income of $868.[9] Further, there has been mounting evidence that the largest benefits from the total of public programs, rather than going to the most disadvantaged segments of the population, are drained off into the middle-income groups. Martin Rein has recently asserted that an "iron law of social welfare" operates so that those who most need help in American society do not get it. He musters specific supporting data from the fields of medical care, welfare, child care, education and housing, and mental health to support this claim.[10]

Thus the aggregate behavior of individual enterprises does not result automatically in an allocation of resources and rewards that is accepted as satisfactory. Nor is there any applicable theory of pure market economics that would assure that it would do so.

But certain types of adjustment are nevertheless possible on national, state, and local levels. One adjustment occurs through the competitive struggle within the three major sectors for access to the resources that individual enterprises need for survival and prosperity. The fortunes of enterprises do wax and wain on the basis of criteria that are not valid indicators of their task accomplishment; but these criteria are not wholly irrelevant to task accomplishment, and financers and acceptors may respond accordingly.

Another kind of adjustment may occur where discrepancies go beyond a certain threshold. In such cases, new enterprises may emerge in either the private profit, governmental, or voluntary agency sector whose explicit goals are to meet the needs. Thus, in a very broad sense, a certain clumsy and incomplete market adjustment does take place.

Commenting on this process, Russell L. Ackoff and Britton Harris observe: "Communities have been unconsciously adaptive in an inefficient way because of short-term, short-lived, and complicated objectives pursued by their private components."[11] They ask whether the conscious adaptation of metropolitan communities cannot be raised to a much higher level of efficiency.

A number of studies offer partial but promising cues to the dynamics of this adjustment process. Robert A. Dahl and Charles E. Lindblom have explored such basic sociopolitical processes as the price system, hierarchy, polyarchy, and bargaining.[12] In much less global terms, James D. Thompson and William J. McEwen have explored the processes of competition, bargaining, cooptation, and coalition.[13] John E. Bebout and Harry C. Bredemeier have analyzed the processes according to which units or systems adapt to one another in ways that may constitute integrative problems on the larger system level. Their four processes are coercive mechanisms, bargaining mechanisms, legal-bureaucratic mechanisms, and identification or solidarity mechanisms.[14] James D. Thompson and Arthur Tuden examine the appropriateness, in different organizational contexts, of a number of strategies and structures for decision-making.[15] Jacob Marschak gives an analysis of various types of group classifications based on their ordering of interests with respect to each other, dividing such groups into coalitions, foundations, and teams.[16]

CONCERTED DECISION-MAKING

But there is another way through which unwelcome discrepancies between actual and desired resource and reward allocations can be modified at the community level. This is through concerted decision-making. In this process, the individual enterprises continue as profit enterprises or voluntary or public agencies, but certain aspects of decision-making are pooled. What earlier were individual enterprise decisions now become inclusive decisions. And a certain part of action that formerly was carried out in relation to the goals of the individual enterprises is now carried out in relation to goals established for the aggregate of enterprises, whether at city hall, or in the chamber of commerce, or in the welfare council, or within some ad hoc coalition designed to implement a federally sponsored program. The assumption is that the interests of the community will be better served through this joint decision-making process than by decisions made independently by each individual enterprise. Such concerted decisions may be arrived at on the basis of consensus among all the enterprises, or on some other basis. They may reflect the wishes of all the enterprises or they may in various degrees be imposed on some or all of them.

One should of course note that concerted decision-making occurs not only in relation to independent enterprises operating in the community; it also occurs very typically within formal organizations, where decision-making is allocated to various positions in the hierarchy of authority, according to some criterion that specifies what kinds of decisions are appropriate at each level. Authority exists within the organization to enforce the decisions made at each level.

Typically, there is no such clear-cut hierarchy of authority in the community, even though there are informal power structures, and even though certain segments of the community, like municipal government, may be formally organized on a hierarchical basis. The authority for enforcing decisions is not built into an organizational structure, but is problematical. We shall return to this matter in a few moments.

Now, much concerted decision-making is based on the assumption that certain inclusive goals should take priority over the goals of the individual enterprises, in cases where these diverge. In addition, there may be inclusive goals that can be pursued which, though not opposed to the individual unit goals, could not be realized, or at least were not being realized, by the unconcerted action of individual enterprises. Thus a part of the *raison d'être* of concerted planning is to make possible the setting and accomplishment of aggregate goals that would not be set and accomplished individually. Another part is to assure that in certain cases of conflict between individual and inclusive goals, the latter will be given priority.

But points of view and interests often clash. Certainly, we all know of examples of just such conflicts—cases in which an individual agency protests that the coalition is making the wrong decision, is not operating in the true interests of the larger community, while the dominant powers in the coalition argue that the agency is merely pursuing its own selfish interests in preference to those of the more inclusive community.

Thus, one important aspect of concerted decision-making is the relation of the interests of the individual enterprises to those of the coalition. It is helpful here to make use of one of Parsons' pattern variables, the dimension of self-orientation versus collectivity orientation.[17] A somewhat similar distinction is made by Banfield between private-regarding and public-regarding postures of individuals in the exercise of power in public issues.[18]

A second important consideration in concerted decision-making is the time dimension. Under certain circumstances, individual enterprises make short-run decisions that seem to move in the direction of a specific goal, but in the aggregate miss the goal because they simply do not add up over time. Their aggregate effect in the long run is different from the short-run effects. The most vivid example I can think of is the building of a new pool for Negroes in a community in the deep South, which equaled in elegance the pool for the whites. It was considered a definite step forward by a number of whites who were concerned about discrimination, but who felt that full integration, though desirable, was only a remote possibility, and meantime the providing of separate but equal facilities was a definite step forward. In the short run, it represented a definite advance in opportunities for the Negroes of that community. But in the long run, it served to perpetuate segregation.

Referring to government planning, John D. Millett makes the relationship seem perfectly simple: "Long-range planning," he writes, "gives meaning to short-range efforts. The year-by-year program is simply a phase of realizing ultimate objectives."[19] Yet it should be apparent that short-range decisions will not realize ultimate objectives unless they are so concerted as to do so. Even in planning bodies specially set up for inclusive decision-making, the pressure for decisions that neglect the long-run goals is often great. In describing the experience of the Chicago Housing Authority, Meyerson and Banfield observed that "planning was never an emergency and the problems of the day were always emergencies. Try as they might, the top staff never managed to insulate themselves from the pressures of the day long enough to think systematically about fundamentals."[20]

Concerted decision-making may thus be conceived to have a short-run–long-run dimension as well as a dimension from self-orientation to collectivity orientation.

THE DECISION TO CONCERT

Three major assumptions underlie concerted decision-making.

The first assumption is that the aggregate activity of individual enterprises does not satisfactorily distribute resources and rewards, and that a preferable situation can be brought about by concerting some decisions. Thus individual families may be concerned with their own future economic security, but there is a larger question of the ratio of national savings to estimated national expenditures for the aged. Individual construction companies are concerned about building housing that will return them a profit, but there is a larger question of the availability of housing for so-and-so many millions of people at prices they can afford. An individual agency may be concerned with certain custodial or therapeutic services for juvenile delinquents, but there is a larger question of the complex pattern of forces within which delinquent behavior is generated and sustained.

In each case, concerted decision-making may operate to facilitate the goal attainment of the individual enterprise, on its own terms, through certain types of coordinated action, or it may operate to provide a basis for more inclusive goal-setting and a redisposition of these enterprises in order to pursue the more inclusive goals. In sum, concerted decision-making may facilitate goal attainment for the individual enterprise or it may facilitate the attainment of more inclusive goals. Especially in pursuing inclusive goals, it may redistribute costs or benefits among individual enterprises.

As mentioned earlier, inclusive goals and concerted measures to implement them may conflict with the goals of the individual enterprise. Yet even when this happens, matters continue to be referred to the inclusive group for decision, in the expectation that a greater aggregate benefit will accrue than if each enterprise were left to its own devices. Why does this occur?

Although space is limited, perhaps we can indicate a few of the principal reasons why concerted decision-making is coming to be considered increasingly appropriate.

1. The spheres of interest, or domains, of enterprises are tending increasingly to grow and to overlap. As an example, traditional casework and group-work agencies, as well as community planning agencies, find themselves increasingly in competition with each other with respect to presumed domain in such fields as delinquency and poverty. They also find their domains being invaded by corresponding efforts on the part of housing, urban renewal, and mental health groups, and other kinds of focus for major planning efforts.

2. There is growing awareness that social choices often mean rejections, and that hence a particular proposal cannot be considered adequately without assessing some of the viable alternatives to that proposal. This is a point that the less industrially developed countries have long since had to realize.

As Herbert Simon puts it:

It is not always recognized . . . that there is absolutely no scientific basis for the construction of so-called "standards of desirable service" or "standards of minimum adequate service" for a particular function, until it is known what this service will cost, what resources are available for financing it, and what curtailment in other services or in private expenditures would be required by an increase in that particular service.[21]

In the past community planning bodies have often merely split up the pie in the same old way, innovating only with what new funds were available over and above this usual allocation. As they now cast an entrepreneurial eye on how existing funds might be reallocated to maximize outcomes, the curtain rises on a new and dramatic encounter between individual enterprise decision-making and concerted decision-making.

3. A much more mundane reason for the advance in concerted decision-making is the increasing realization that fragmented approaches are not effective. There is nothing new about this thought. What is new is the sense of urgency at the mounting problems, and the growing willingness to concert decision-making, even though strong opposition from individual enterprises may arise.

4. Finally, there appears to be an increase in the number of problem areas in which the market does not distribute community facilities optimally, either as to need or as to ability to pay. This is usually taken as an argument to take certain decisions out of the profit-enterprise sector and establish them on a voluntary nonprofit basis or as a tax-supported governmental activity. But, of course, this only begs the question, for it assumes that if this is done, resources and rewards will be allocated more satisfactorily. Much of the preceding discussion indicates that when decisions are taken out of the private profit market, they are still in a market, as it were, a quasi market, in which not only private enterprises but also voluntary nonprofit associations and governmental agencies seek to pursue their own goals and to prosper and thrive as individual enterprises. This is true even of enterprises that are specifically developed for concerted decision-making. There still remains the problem of concerting the efforts of the concerting bodies themselves.

And of course there still remains the problem of deciding upon specific criteria for taking a decision out of the market and subordinating it to inclusive goals. Although one may acknowledge that a certain state of affairs in the community is less than 100 percent satisfactory, there is no guarantee that one can actually improve the situation by intervening. Imperfections in the market cannot *ipso facto* be considered a mandate for concerted decision-making. In this connection, it is interesting to note that various Communist countries are now deliberately experimenting with decentralized decision-making in certain sectors, expecting that less concerted decision-making may lead to more satisfactory allocation of resources and rewards.

Hence, to intervene or not to intervene—that remains the question. And we have little systematic knowledge as to when intervention through concerted planning promises a greater payoff than less inclusive decision-making.

CALCULATING ALTERNATIVE PAYOFFS

But there also remains a different kind of problem, which is raised by the second assumption on which concerted decision-making is based.

The second assumption is that an adequate technology exists for calculating the promised greater benefits of concerted decision-making. In classical price theory, the automatic adjustment of demand and supply, with price fluctuating accordingly, constitutes a mechanism that it is claimed will maximize the distribution of resources and rewards. But if this market function is not adequately performed, and if therefore deliberate interventions are to be made for a more satisfactory aggregate outcome through concerted decision-making, how is the greater benefit to be calculated?

Although space does not permit an exhaustive treatment of this subject of calculation techniques, let us consider a few of the principal possibilities. All of these, in one way or another, constitute guides for calculation which presumably may distribute resources and rewards more satisfactorily than the market.

1. *Welfare economics* is the attempt by economists to adduce a general welfare function by rational argument, on the basis of which a concept of the general welfare is derived from individual preference scales. Quite obviously, the difficulty here is in making logically the vital jump from individual preference to general welfare. But it also makes extremely high demands regarding the completeness of knowledge necessary for decisions.[22]

2. A related technique for calculation is *cost-benefit analysis:* the costs of a proposal are calculated, and a calculation is made of the benefits that accrue from the proposal. The technique pursues not only the question of whether the benefits outweigh the costs, but the question of who benefits and who pays the costs, and whether special provisions are to be made for a redistribution of benefits or of costs. In this technique, the attempt is made to assess the benefits and costs in terms of monetary value so that different kinds of costs and benefits can be weighed against each other on the same scale. In effect, this technique supersedes the market in the distributive function, but retains a price equivalent as a common denominator for the assessment of comparative values. A classic work in this field is John V. Krutilla and Otto Eckstein's book, *Multiple Purpose River Development.*[23] In the field of social welfare, an important contribution has been made by Kenneth H. Ives, in a paper on cost-benefit analysis in health and welfare.[24]

3. In the field of community organization for health and welfare, there is a growing body of systems for *priorities planning.* Such calculation techniques seek to give numerical evaluations to any given proposal or program on the basis of such dimensions as "number affected" or "intensity of need." Those who are familiar with these techniques are aware of their definite limitations,

but there seems to be growing agreement that they are better than nothing, if only as a guide to assessment rather than a determiner thereof. Some of their weaknesses have recently been pointed out by Samuel Mencher.[25]

4. A widely known technique for allocating resources and rewards is that of the *budgeting process*. While this process is often conceived as a relatively dry and uninteresting juggling of accounts, few administrators are unaware of its vital function in the distribution of resources and rewards on a concerted basis. In much concerted decision-making, competition in the marketplace is transformed into competition at the budget hearings. Aaron Wildavsky has made an excellent analysis of the various processes through which federal budgets are developed and approved.[26] He makes it quite clear that budgeting is a major process of policy formation, and he studies inductively the procedures according to which competing requests become reconciled to political realities.

Budgeting provides, strictly speaking, only a process for decision-making, not a rationale for calculation. Yet Simon claims:

> The budget, first of all, forces a simultaneous consideration of all the competing claims for support. Second, the budget transports upward in the administrative hierarchy the decisions as to fund allocation to a point where competing values must be weighed, and where functional identifications will not lead to a faulty weighting of values.[27]

5. Budgeting is simply a vehicle through which decisions are made which involve weighing alternatives according to a series of relevant assesment factors. But a rational weighing of alternatives may involve a degree of omniscience that it is unrealistic to expect. While completely rational decision-making would call for a knowledge of preferences under all conceivable circumstances, most decisions can be made without such ideal prerequisites, involving only a limited range of relevant knowledge that actually is obtainable. Taking the preferable choices from a limited set of alternatives about which one has obtained sufficient knowledge to make considered judgments, even though that knowledge is incomplete, is a frequent practice in decision-making. This practice has been called "satisficing."[28]

6. A rapidly growing basis for calculation under conditions of uncertainty is that of *game theory*. Game theory is a method for calculation of optimum moves in situations where two or more parties are involved in a struggle for scarce resources. It has developed most specifically in connection with contests in which there are only two parties and where one can gain only at the expense of the other—the so-called two-person zero-sum games. In the less well-elaborated n-person games, attention has been focused principally on circumstances in which individual gain can be maximized by joining coalitions, thus

restoring some features of the zero-sum, two-person games. Thus far, developments in game theory as a calculation technique have been highly abstract and delimited in their application. Like welfare economics, game theory has tended to make extreme demands on the knowledge of alternatives of action, and strategies do not make allowance for the input of new unanticipated knowledge. Further, game theory is at its weakest in the so-called cooperative solution games, where individual parties may benefit more, either in aggregate or individually, by cooperative action. Certainly, such situations are not irrelevant, and more recent effort in game theory has given them increasing attention, though with as yet disappointing results.[29]

There are other available rationales for calculation, but perhaps enough has been presented to indicate that of the two major functions performed by classical market theory, only one is assured by the concerting of decision-making. That is the distributive function of allocating resources and rewards. There still remains the task of developing an adequate substitute for the other function of classical price theory: to provide a rationale for calculation in inclusive decision-making which would correspond to the price-theory rationale for calculation by individual enterprises where conditions of the true market exist.

THE CONTROL OF IMPLEMENTATION

A third assumption underlying concerted decision-making is that the behavior of constituent enterprises can be controlled so that it conforms to the behavior called for by the resulting decisions. Even in formal organizations where hierarchical control is so distributed as to assure this compliance with concerted goals, there often occurs a pursuing of departmental or divisional goals at the expense of more inclusive goals.

The problem is more complicated when one is trying to concert decision-making among relatively distinct enterprises that retain a large measure of independence. This is the usual situation in planning at the community level.

Nevertheless, the model of organizational control is suggestive of some basic considerations. Ackoff and Harris have given a four-step outline of the prerequisites involved:

1. Formulating objectives and developing measures of system and subsystem performance.
2. Measuring performance relative to system objectives and determining when it is significantly below an acceptable level.
3. Selecting corrective or directive action.
4. Implementing the decision.[30]

The performance of such functions by the relatively weak federations that are set up for inclusive decision-making in various sectors of the community is extremely difficult, because of the relative independence of the enterprises involved. Yet, if concerted decision-making cannot be enforced, of what use is it? "The problem of centrally planned change is essentially a problem of power," Wilson asserts. "There must be—whatever else exists—some actor who can carry into effect ends that have been arrived at by some method other than the registration of an equilibrium among contending interest groups."[31]

Precisely such control is necessary to the extent that the alleged benefits from concerted decision-making are to be obtained.

We can approach this control problem in concerted decision-making as a problem of the simultaneous relations of an inclusive system to one or more subsystems. We are interested primarily in the goal-setting and goal-attaining processes on the two system levels, but in order to understand them fully, we must consider other aspects of the relationship between the inclusive system and the subsystems. Unfortunately, there are not many carefully conceptualized analyses of this type of relationship available. Odd Ramsöy, a Norwegian sociologist, has made the most extensive analysis that we have so far. In his important book on *Social Groups as System and Subsystem*,[32] he explores the problem, leaning heavily on Parsonian formulations. He points out that: "A major strain in inclusive social systems occurs when subsystem adaptive concerns dominate the concern for integration in the inclusive system."[33] But he also asserts that certain more inclusive stable structures may exist, which have complex implications for the individual actors within them. "When the individual participant orients his action to a narrow and to a broader circle of actors, both of which are his membership groups, a complex system frame of reference aggregates the differentiated orientations of many participants in diverse social situations, into system structure and processes on two levels."[34] Or, in our terminology, the individual within an enterprise may orient his behavior to the goals of the individual enterprise or to those of the inclusive system. This dual orientation applies in American communities as it does in Highland Burma, which was the context from which Ramsöy drew his conclusion. Certainly, this has relevance for the agency official, let us say, who is urged to take some action on the part of some inclusive community planning body, an action that he may feel is not in the best interests of his agency as an individual enterprise.

This problem of the conflict between the interests of the enterprise and those of the more inclusive system, as experienced by the harried agency executive, is illuminated by some observations made by Philip Selznick in his study of the Tennessee Valley Authority. He approached this problem from the standpoint of organizational commitments. "A *commitment* in social action is an enforced line of action; it refers to decision dictated by the force of circumstance with the result that the free or scientific adjustment of means and ends is effectively limited."[35] Obviously, therefore, the ability of an enterprise to function in a planning coalition is limited by its commitments. These commitments are of many types, including its own organizational imperatives, the viewpoints and interests of its personnel, the established patterns of behavior it has followed in the past, the normative restraints on behavior in the surrounding environment, and the special goals and problems of those to whom authority is delegated.[36]

A related problem in inclusive decision-making is that of the respective constituencies of the individual enterprise and the inclusive planning system. "A constituency," says Selznick, "is a group, formally outside a given organization, to which the latter (or an element within it) has a special commitment."[37] Now the constituency of an individual governmental or voluntary agency, let us say, is not usually identical with the constituency of a more inclusive planning system. The relationship between the two constituencies, particularly in regard to the distribution of power relevant to agency survival, may be a crucial factor in determining the extent to which specific agency goals, or more inclusive goals, are given primacy by the agency.

Even if the individual agency official should prefer the more inclusive goals of the planning system, he is not always free to pursue them. What Morton A. Kaplan asserts for actors on the international scene has cogency on the interagency scene within the local community:

> One reason the international system is not a political system stems from the fact that, within the personality systems of decision makers, their role in the international system is subordinate to their role in the national actor system. Moreover, to the extent that this is not true of a particular decision maker, he is likely to be replaced in office.[38]

Although Herbert Simon's orientation is that of the formal organization rather than the problem of concerted planning among organizations, he puts his finger on one key point in this situation. "Loyalty to the larger group will result," he concludes, "when loyalty to that group is rewarded even in conflict with loyalty to the smaller group."[39] This is a realistic note to which I shall return in a moment.

Where this situation does not prevail, much may depend on whether the agency official views the other agency or agencies with whom cooperation is urged as friendly or hostile, as Selznick points out:

> If an official is hostile to the organization with which cooperation is proposed, he will consider the possibility that the joint program will serve to strengthen that organization through: (1) the precedents to be established, which may be difficult to overcome at a later date; (2) the

possible influence of that organization upon his own rank and file;
(3) the extent to which funds allocated to him may leave his control
in the course of the joint activity; (4) the danger that public credit
may be shared, or that the two organizations will become confused in
the public mind; (5) the possibility that access to client publics, not
previously available, will now be afforded to the cooperating organizations; and (6) the establishment of an actual machinery (personnel,
facilities, reciprocal commitments) which might become intrenched.
If the attitude is friendly rather than hostile, and especially if there is
interest in actually building the cooperating organization, then precisely
these considerations will strengthen the case for cooperation. But if
the official is organizationally self-conscious, he will not ignore them.[40]

In the light of the foregoing, we can conclude that if concerted decision-
making at the community level is to be effective, the control problem must be
so handled that inclusive-system considerations will prevail over individual-
enterprise considerations, when the two conflict. Obviously, this problem cannot
be solved by moralistic admonitions to individual agencies about the general
welfare, or by platitudinous complaints about "agency resistance to community-
wide programs."

Ramsöy confronts this problem on an abstract level by considering the
relation of self-orientation and collectivity orientation. Where conflicts exist,
each subsystem, in pursuing its own subsystem-oriented goals, will claim that it
is *really* acting on behalf of the true interests of the more inclusive system—that
it is *really* collectivity-oriented. He points out how difficult and subjective such
issues become, but seems unable to escape them.[41] In my estimation, such considerations of subjective motivation are largely irrelevant to the analysis at hand.
Much more relevant is the question of exploring the possibilities for changing
the structure of interenterprise behavior in a direction that tends toward convergence of goal attainment of the inclusive system and the fulfillment of
maintenance needs of the subsystem, or individual enterprise.

We are here at the borderline of validated knowledge, or perhaps we have
already overstepped it. But a number of observations may nevertheless be
hazarded.

It is perhaps superfluous to state that the behavior of individual enterprises
must be changed, or new ones created, if any steps are to be taken in the direction of implementing concerted planning. An exception might be the joint
creation of a new agency whose operation, alongside that of existing agencies,
is expected to attain the inclusive-system goals. I would be inclined to speculate,
though, that even such a new agency would willy-nilly have deep impacts on
existing agencies. The question is only whether these are, as far as possible, to

be planned or merely haphazard, and whether they are to be concerted with respect to inclusive-system goals.

One way of observing the change in the interagency field is through an analysis of changes in interagency exchange; for it is probably justifiable to assume that to the extent that enterprise behavior changes, these changes will be reflected in transactions among agencies.

Implied in the above is the possible need for a greater centralization of the process of allocating resources and rewards among enterprises, so that they can both survive and contribute more effectively to the attainment of inclusive goals.

Presumably, convergence of agency survival needs and inclusive-system goal attainment can be furthered by two methods. Let us call them the stick and the carrot.

The "stick" method is to restructure the controls operating on individual enterprises so that they must more directly pursue inclusive goals in order to meet their survival needs as enterprises. As indicated earlier, this would suggest a closer correspondence between actual task accomplishment and the survival prerequisites of the agency. The ability to attract the donor's dollar with a tearful appeal or to sway the budget committee of the United Fund or the legislature does not necessarily coincide with demonstrated task accomplishment. Hence, bringing these two into closer alignment may be effective, particularly in those cases where there is relatively little conflict between the stated goals of the agency and those of the inclusive system. Further development and application of evaluative research are needed here.

The "carrot" method would pay particular attention to the realistic commitments and survival needs and constituency relationships of individual enterprises as the inclusive goals are developed. It would seek to avoid pushing unwilling agencies through closed doors, and would concentrate on opening the doors that would make it possible for agencies to cooperate without endangering their own survival.

In either case, a change in the structure of the field of interenterprise behavior suggests itself. The system of sanctions—or rewards and punishments, as it were—within which the individual enterprise operates must be modified. It must be modified, as Simon suggests, in a way that rewards compliant behavior more than noncompliant behavior. This rewarding of behavior does not mean testimonial dinners, medals, or other such largely epiphenomenal sanctions, but rather must penetrate to the heart of the matter: the system of entrepreneurs, financers, acceptors, exchange relationships, and task and maintenance functions that comprise the dimensions of the individual enterprise. The sanction system, as it applies to these factors, must be modified if inclusive planning is to be viable.

In some or all of the instances in which concerted planning is proposed, there will of course be many who think the costs are too great. This is a matter of public policy to which this paper does not address itself.

Implied in what has been said so far is the fact that the inclusive decision-making system, whether it be a council or an ad hoc coalition of some sort, itself constitutes an enterprise, with its own system of entrepreneurs, financers, acceptors, exchange relationships, and task and maintenance functions. In inclusive planning among organizations, the nature of this enterprise is customarily extremely weak, with a minimum of authority, a high salience of self-orientation among participating enterprises, and a consequent difficulty in agreeing upon or in pursuing any goals that are not in accord with the self-regarding interests of all of the members, or at least of the most powerful ones.

As this situation changes, as the inclusive organization grows in strength in relation to its members, it begins to take on the characteristics of a formal organization. To the extent that it does so, the organizational model for concerted decision-making, as developed in administrative theory, becomes increasingly relevant.

It has not been the purpose of this paper to develop pat solutions to the problems of concerted decision-making at the community level, but rather to explore some of the theoretical considerations that surround its basic assumptions. One can but hope that in a decade's time we will know a great deal more about the criteria that make concerted decision-making appropriate and feasible at the community level, about the methods by which we can make calculations that will yield a higher aggregate utility than the market, and about the relationships that exist and the processes that take place between individual enterprises and more inclusive planning systems at the community level.

We need such knowledge if we are to concern ourselves seriously with a problem that was very close to the thinking of the man in whose name this lecture has been presented. Over four decades ago, Eduard C. Lindeman wrote:

> When an institution functions primarily to enhance its own welfare and growth, it is certain in the end to jeopardize the interests of the community as a whole. This presents one of the chief problems of democracy. How can we secure efficient institutions which will at the same time contribute to the welfare of the community?[42]

Much of this paper has been abstract and perhaps has seemed remote from the day-to-day problems of our modern communities. As a behavioral scientist I can but affirm my faith that in the long run such abstract and detached investigations contribute to the knowledge base within which more effective action can be taken on behalf of widely desired goals. And in the absence of more convincing proof of this faith than can as yet be mustered, I can only be grateful that a profession that cannot escape the day-to-day problems of a hectic and troubled world is willing to give such endeavors the benefit of the doubt.

NOTES

[1] Max Weber, *The City,* trans. and ed. Don Martindale and Gertrud Neuwirth, 2nd ed. (New York: Collier Books, 1962).

[2] William F. Ogburn, *Recent Social Trends* (New York: McGraw-Hill, 1933), chap. 13.

[3] Kurt Wolff, ed. and trans., *The Sociology of Georg Simmel* (Glencoe, Ill.: Free Press, 1950), chap. 4.

[4] In their pioneer study, Sol Levine and Paul E. White consider clients, resources, and services as three types of exchange elements. This typology is helpful, but perhaps would have to be modified in order to accommodate adequately the full range of resources that enter into interenterprise exchange transactions. See their "Exchange as a Conceptual Framework for the Study of Interorganizational Relationships," *Administrative Science Quarterly,* 5, no. 4 (March 1961).

[5] Thorstein Veblen, *The Engineers and the Price System* (New York: Viking Press, 1921), pp. 40–41.

[6] For the application of the cartel concept to the activities of a certain type of enterprise—churches—see Peter L. Berger, "A Market Model for the Analysis of Ecumenicity," *Social Research,* 30, no. 1 (Spring 1963).

[7] See Harry C. Bredemeier, "The Socially Handicapped and the Agencies: A Market Analysis," in *The Mental Health of the Poor,* ed. Frank Reissman, Jerome Cohen, and Arthur Pearl (New York: Free Press, Macmillan, 1964). Bredemeier's analysis is a highly significant contribution to an understanding of the basic processes involved.

[8] Amitai Etzioni, "Two Approaches to Organizational Analysis: A Critique and a Suggestion," *Administrative Science Quarterly,* 5, no. 2 (November 1960), p. 262.

[9] The sources for these figures are the Office of Economic Opportunity and the Senate Subcommittee on Migratory Labor, respectively. See the *New York Times,* May 3 and April 17, 1965.

[10] Martin Rein, "The Strange Case of Public Dependency," *Trans-action,* 2, no. 3 (March–April 1965): 21–22.

[11] Russell L. Ackoff and Britton Harris, "Planning, Operations Research, and Metropolitan Systems," in American Institute of Planners, *A Report of the Newark Proceedings, Newark, N.J., August 16–20, 1964,* p. 95.

[12] Robert A. Dahl and Charles E. Lindblom, *Politics, Economics, and Welfare: Planning and Politico-Economic Systems Resolved into Basic Social Processes* (New York: Harper, 1953).

[13] James D. Thompson and William J. McEwen, "Organizational Goals and Environment: Goal-Setting as an Interaction Process," *American Sociological Review,* 23, no. 1 (February 1958).

[14] John E. Bebout and Harry C. Bredemeier, "American Cities as Social Systems," *Journal of the American Institute of Planners,* 29, no. 2 (May 1963).

[15] James D. Thompson and Arthur Tuden, "Strategies, Structures, and Processes of Organizational Decision," in James D. Thompson *et al., Comparative Studies in Administration* (Pittsburgh: University of Pittsburgh Press, 1959), chap. 12.

[16] Jacob Marschak, "Towards an Economic Theory of Organization and Information," in *Decision Processes,* ed. R. M. Thrall, C. H. Coombs, and R. L. Davis (New York: Wiley, 1954).

[17] See Talcott Parsons, *The Social System*, 2nd ed. (New York: Free Press, Macmillan, 1964), p. 60.

[18] Edward C. Banfield, *Political Influence* (New York: Free Press, Macmillan, 1961), p. 315.

[19] John D. Millett, *The Process and Organization of Government Planning* (New York: Columbia University Press, 1947), p. 51.

[20] Martin Meyerson and Edward C. Banfield, *Politics, Planning, and the Public Interest: The Case of Public Housing in Chicago* (Glencoe, Ill.: Free Press, 1955), p. 277.

[21] Herbert A. Simon, *Administrative Behavior: A Study of Decision-Making Processes in Administrative Organization*, 2nd ed. (New York: Macmillan, 1961), pp. 212–13.

[22] Jerome Rothenberg's *The Measurement of Social Welfare* (Englewood Cliffs, N.J.: Prentice-Hall, 1961) analyzes many welfare economics theories and contributes one of its own.

[23] See John V. Krutilla and Otto Eckstein, *Multiple Purpose River Development: Studies in Applied Economic Analysis* (Baltimore: Johns Hopkins Press, 1958).

[24] See Kenneth H. Ives, "Costs-Benefits Analysis: Its Theory and Components—with Applications to the Health and Welfare Fields," (unpublished manuscript, 1964).

[25] See Samuel Mencher, "Current Priority-Planning," *Social Work*, 9, no. 3 (July 1964).

[26] See Aaron Wildavsky, *The Politics of the Budgetary Process* (Boston: Little, Brown, 1964).

[27] Simon, *Administrative Behavior*, p. 214.

[28] "Examples of satisficing criteria that are familiar enough to businessmen, if unfamiliar to most economists, are 'share of market,' 'adequate profit,' 'fair price'" (*ibid.*, p. xxv). A somewhat similar analysis is given by Charles E. Lindblom, in "The Science of 'Muddling Through,'" *Public Administration Review*, 19, no. 1 (1959), and by David Braybrooke and Charles E. Lindblom, in *A Strategy of Decision: Policy Evaluation as a Social Process* (New York: Free Press, Macmillan, 1963).

[29] An excellent selection of contributions to game theory may be found in Martin Shubik, ed., *Game Theory and Related Approaches to Social Behavior: Selections* (New York: Wiley, 1964).

[30] Ackoff and Harris, "Planning, Operations Research, and Metropolitan Systems," p. 94.

[31] James Q. Wilson, "An Overview of Theories of Planned Change," in *Centrally Planned Change: Prospects and Concepts,* ed. Robert Morris (New York: National Association of Social Workers, 1964), p. 17.

[32] Odd Ramsöy, *Social Groups as System and Subsystem* (New York: Free Press, Macmillan, 1963).

[33] *Ibid.*, p. 197.

[34] *Ibid.*, p. 140.

[35] Philip Selznick, *TVA and the Grass Roots: A Study in the Sociology of Formal Organization* (Berkeley: University of California Press, 1949), p. 255.

[36] *Ibid.*, pp. 255–59.

[37] *Ibid.*, p. 145.

[38] Morton A. Kaplan, *System and Process in International Politics* (New York: Wiley, 1957), pp. 19–20.

[39] Simon, *Administrative Behavior*, p. 217.

[40] Selznick, *TVA and the Grass Roots*, p. 166.

[41] Ramsöy, *Social Groups as System and Subsystem*, pp. 189–90.

[42] Eduard C. Lindeman, *The Community: An Introduction to the Study of Community Leadership and Organization* (New York: Association Press, 1921), p. 23.

10

PLANNING AMONG THE GIANTS:
THE INTERACTION OF COMMUNITY
DECISION ORGANIZATIONS

It is a commonplace that unified economic, physical, and social planning at the community level is a will-o'-the-wisp whose possibility for realization, if it was ever present, is rapidly diminishing. Rather, the situation in all but the smallest cities can be characterized as follows: There is a large and increasing number of organizations at the city or metropolitan level, each of which is more or less legitimated for program planning or operation in some particular sector of the community's interest. Almost without exception, these community decision organizations[1] receive a large portion of their funding from agencies of the federal government, from which they also receive varying amounts of program stimulation. While they have different fields of emphasis and activity, the pursuit of these fields often involves them in various types of relationship with one another. Sometimes these relationships are cooperative, as when a housing authority and an urban renewal authority and a united community service agency may collaborate in planning for a particular type of service to low-income people. At other times (or even simultaneously) they may compete for a major say in decisions which affect them all, for funds, or for clout in the mayor's office.

Indeed, as one goes from city to city, one sees with remarkable consistency the same general types of community decision organizations, however they may

Reprinted from *Social Service Review*, 41, no. 3 (September 1967), by permission of the University of Chicago Press. Copyright © 1967 by the University of Chicago Press. Originally published as "The Interaction of Community Decision Organizations: Some Basic Concepts and Needed Research." Notes have been renumbered.

vary in details of organization or program. There are the city planning commissions, the urban renewal authorities, the local poverty organizations, the chambers of commerce, united community services, united funds, housing authorities, welfare departments, health departments, industrial development corporations, and so on. Although many of these organizations confine their activities to the city limits, others encompass roughly the metropolitan area. The aggregate of their activity governs, to a large extent, the amount of conscious, coordinated direction given to the affairs of the community.

Yet such organizations do not constitute the sole influence on decision-making at the community level. On the one hand, they themselves are subject to various types of social, political, and economic pressures, and, although many of them are set up autonomously, presumably to apply rational, deliberate effort toward accomplishing their stated goals, they are not immune to the pressures of the marketplace. On the other hand, many decisions which they are presumably legitimated to make are actually made under other auspices at quiet meetings between the mayor and a few business leaders or other members of one or another top power structure. Or they are hammered out inside and around the city council, in a bargaining process with Washington, or in various combinations of such settings.

The behavior of these community decision organizations is seldom neatly confined to the community arena, whether this is considered roughly as the central city or as the metropolitan area. On various types of projects, it has been observed that the interaction of these organizations is only a part of a larger process of interaction concerning any particular project. Other agencies and organizations at a less inclusive level of the community, such as neighborhood organizations or direct-service agencies, or organizations at a more inclusive level, such as agencies of the state or federal government, are also involved. In the complex, multileveled interaction surrounding the development of most community projects, there does not appear to be a distinct field of interaction at the community level which is clearly distinguishable from the total process of multilevel, mixed-level interaction. Nevertheless, there is little doubt that such community decision organizations, in their interaction, play a large role in the multicentered decision-making (and decision-avoiding) processes that characterize most American cities. There is some indication that large cities have a greater number of such relatively autonomous legitimated community decision organizations than do the smaller ones.

There is every indication that this situation, in which interrelated concerns of the city or metropolitan area are largely—though not exclusively—determined through the interaction of such major community decision organizations, will characterize the predictable future. This opinion is held by many agency executives who differ as to the desirability of having such a large number of relatively autonomous organizations, each planning as a separate entity, or the desirability of setting up a superagency or some other mechanism for concerted planning efforts and programs.

To summarize, insofar as deliberate, rational control is brought to bear on the process of social change at the city or metropolitan level, it is done largely through a number of community decision organizations, each of which is legitimated to speak for the community in some substantive area of community interests. A number of such organizations can be found in much the same form throughout the large cities of the United States. These organizations form only a part of the forces influencing change, other forces being the mayor's office, the city council, the political parties, and various groups or coalitions of businessmen, politicians, ethnic-group leaders, religious leaders, and so on. Further, in the development of specific community projects, these organizations may be engaged with neighborhood organizations and parties, as well as with those from state and federal levels. Nevertheless, planned developments at the community level usually take place under the rubric of one or more of the community decision organizations.

PREVIOUS RESEARCH ON COMMUNITY DECISION ORGANIZATIONS

In view of the importance of community decision organizations in comprehensive and coordinated planning and the presence of more or less the same types and combinations of them in different cities, the paucity of systematic research on their behavior is surprising. Once one considers the presence of roughly the same types of organizations in various cities, a dozen interesting and researchable questions arise regarding the differences in the structure and behavior of any one type of organization in various cities—urban renewal authorities, chambers of commerce, or welfare departments—and their relation to a number of environmental variables. Likewise, the development of a systematic body of knowledge concerning the behavior of these organizations with respect to each other, as they go about planning or operating programs in fields which often overlap, seems desirable.

The existing social science knowledge base for understanding the behavior of community decision organizations consists principally of intensive case studies of particular organizations, conducted mainly by sociologists, and studies and conceptualizations from the burgeoning field of organizational and administrative theory, in which research is widely interdisciplinary.

Selznick's early study of the Tennessee Valley Authority[2] was particularly fruitful, especially in its development and elaboration of the concepts of goal displacement, organizational commitment, cooptation, and constituency. Meyerson and Banfield's study of the Chicago Housing Authority[3] documented the complexity of the political process in which that organization was involved and revealed the manner in which the formal planning operation was overwhelmed by the interests and behavior of various actors in the community other than the Authority. John R. Seeley and his associates made an intensive study of the operation of the community chest in Indianapolis,[4] in which they gathered comparative data from other cities. They analyzed community chest behavior in relation to a number of variables and made interesting comparisons with the local Red Cross organization and with the hospital fund campaign. Sills studied the recruitment, training, and utilization of volunteers by the National Foundation for Infantile Paralysis.[5] He was able to relate much of that organization's behavior to its structure as a corporate type, as distinguished from a federative type. Paul M. Harrison studied the process through which national officials of the American Baptist Convention acquired power over local church organizations, even though the decentralized organization ascribed them little legitimate authority.[6] Peter H. Rossi and Robert A. Dentler made an intensive study of urban renewal in the Hyde Park–Kenwood district of Chicago,[7] with particular emphasis on the interaction of a voluntary neighborhood association, the University of Chicago, the Chicago Community Conservation Board, the City Council, and a number of other organizations and agencies. More recently Scott Greer, in an extensive study of the operation of urban renewal programs in various American cities, related them to governmental units at the local, state, and federal levels, and analyzed some of the dynamics of the contexts in which they operate,[8] and Harold Kaplan made an interesting study of the urban renewal program in Newark.[9] Interestingly enough, the most impressive study of the structure of decision-making conducted in a sufficiently rigorous manner to permit quantitative analysis of the variables is Paul A. Miller's study *Community Health Action,* published in 1953.[10]

While few studies from the organizational literature deal with community decision organizations as such, a number of organizational studies and conceptualizations have direct relevance to possible future research in this field. Amitai Etzioni, Richard L. Simpson and William H. Gulley, and Jacob Marschak[11] give varied typologies for classifying types of organizations. William A. Rushing, Jerald Hage, Peter M. Blau, and Eugene Litwak[12] all attempt to specify and in preliminary fashion to operationalize a number of variables of presumed importance in accounting for various aspects of organizational behavior. From the wide literature on conceptualizations of organizational decision-making, those by William J. Gore, James D. Thompson and Arthur Tuden, and Herbert A. Simon[13] can be taken as useful analytical schemes that lend themselves to empirical research in behavior of community decision organizations. Gladys M. Kammerer has made an interesting study of city managers, in which she was able to operationalize Gore's three types of decision-making.[14]

A question of increasing importance is that of the circumstances under which organizations display innovative behavior, as opposed to routine or adaptive behavior, to follow a distinction developed by Gore.[15] A literature on organizational innovation is growing, from which the contributions of Simon, Wilson, and Thompson[16] are particularly pertinent for research on community decision organizations.

Likewise, there are a number of pertinent studies and articles on the relation of organizations to their general environment, although most of them do not address themselves to this specific type of organization.[17] There is also a growing body of possibly relevant literature on the specific relations of various organizations to each other.[18]

VARIABLES FOR POSSIBLE STUDY

In connection with preliminary interviews in three eastern cities, I made a more intensive study in Boston, exploring a number of variables that I believe may prove of some importance in accounting for differences in behavior of community decision organizations. The operation of these variables was investigated in connection with the development of three projects in Boston, all of which involved federal funding, but which otherwise were chosen to give a variety of settings and contexts. One was the development of the plans for renewing Boston's waterfront. Another was the development and final approval of the plan for Housing Authority contracts with private owners of multi-unit housing for blocks of their apartments to be rented to low-income tenants, with the difference in rental paid by the Authority—"instant housing." The third was the development of the Columbia Point project, through which Tufts University Medical School undertook, with funds from the Office of Economic Opportunity, to develop a comprehensive program of medical services for residents of an isolated public housing project and to utilize these health services as a focus for the organization of residents.

Input and Output Constituencies

In analysis of the structure of large community decision organizations in relation to their environments, the distinction between input and output constituencies was found useful.[19] "Input constituency" is conceived of as those other organizations or actors acknowledged by the organization as supporting, financing, promoting, providing program material, or making decisions regarding the functioning of an organization. In other terms, it is the group of parties to which the organization acknowledges a responsibility in determining its policy and program. "Output constituency" is conceived of as those other organizations or actors acknowledged by an organization as being the appropriate targets of the organization's activity.*

One preliminary result of the use of this conceptualization has been to suggest the importance of the relationship between the input constituency and the output constituency. As an example, the recipients of social services are not usually members of the input constituencies of the social service agencies, but community-action programs involving the participation of the poor, tenants' councils, and organizations of relief recipients are examples of the effort to gain recognition as part of the input constituency of poverty organizations, housing authorities, and welfare departments, respectively.

A second preliminary outcome from this conceptualization is the suggested hypothesis that organization policy and program are more sensitive to the interests of the input constituency than to those of the output constituency.

A third preliminary implication is that the nature of the interaction between two or more organizations will be determined—in part—by their respective presence or absence in each other's input or output constituencies.

Organizational Structures and Leadership Types

Any analysis of organizational behavior, to be complete, must account for the impact of personality as well as situational variables. Preliminary study in the three cities indicated that the possibly vast difference in the behavior of an organization and the behavior of other organizations toward it can be attributed in part to differences in style of behavior on the part of the top leader, usually, though not always, the principal staff executive. This is particularly evident in intercity comparisons. Preliminary study indicates that a classification of leadership styles into charismatic, bureaucratic, and collegial appears to capture many of the differences that the interview data have revealed.

The concept of charismatic leadership is substantially, though not completely, an inventory of the characteristics described by Max Weber.[20] The emphasis here is on personal innovativeness and ad hoc structuring of specific projects, rather than on following normal channels, either in interorganizational procedures or in intraorganizational procedures.

The concept of bureaucratic leadership likewise follows Weber's general description, but with some minor modifications. Emphasis is placed on following formal channels, both within the organization and outside of it; on decision-

---

* Obviously, there are other organizations and actors that affect or are affected by an organization which are not part of its output or input constituency. These relationships are treated in two ways: first, as side effects, insofar as the behavior is not deliberately related to them; second, as various interorganizational interaction processes, for which a typology is presently being developed.

making according to rules, policies, and precedents; and on the hierarchical organization of decision-making following the organization's structure.

The concept of collegial leadership receives its description and rationale less from Weber than from the human relations and group dynamics literature, but also from the literature of community organization in social work. The two principal elements, as I conceive them, are flexibility in the decision-making process and greater initiative coming from subordinates at any point in the administrative hierarchy.

Two questions from these considerations suggest more extensive research. One has to do with whether the specific structure and setting of certain organizations encourages one type of leadership rather than another. A number of considerations, for example, might suggest that public welfare departments would be more congenial to bureaucratic leadership; antipoverty boards and urban renewal authorities might be more amenable to charismatic leadership; and community welfare councils, hospital councils, and church federations might be more amenable to collegial leadership. Even if this preliminary hypothesis is proved valid, it is nevertheless quite obvious that there are also variations based on the particular style of the incumbent leaders, and that these, as well as the structural variables, may have important effects on organizational behavior. Hence, one must differentiate the structural aspects of these leadership styles from the personality aspects of individual leaders.

Innovativeness in Community Decision Organizations

A related question is that of innovativeness in organizations. The past five years have been characterized by widespread expression of the need for creative, innovative solutions to urban problems and by disillusionment with routine methods, particularly in the social planning field. For example, the antipoverty program initially was committed to innovation, and it apparently based much of its operating policy on the conclusion that existing organizations in its field, particularly the community welfare councils, were unable to innovate sufficiently to bring about system change, as distinguished from system maintenance, through customary, largely palliative, modes of service. The Office of Economic Opportunity, structurally, operationally, and in the personal style of its director, showed many of the characteristics of charismatic leadership. In its encouragement of innovativeness in the local community; in its impatience with normal operating procedures and channels and with the mere expansion of existing services by alleged unimaginative local organizations; in its encouragement of setting up new, flexible organizations and of keeping them flexible; and in its emphasis on getting things done and on "the man with the idea," it seemingly has demanded a charismatic type of structure with charismatic types of leaders relatively unencumbered by the constraints of bureaucratic routine or by the slow process of consensus-seeking among peers which characterizes the collegial style.

Many meaningful and researchable questions are raised by such a concep-tualization. One such question has to do with whether the local community action programs, from the administrative point of view (as distinguished from the controverted and highly volatile aspect of the participation of the poor in policy-making), followed the course of most new innovative structures—namely, development toward routinization and bureaucratization, or what Weber de-scribed as "the routinization of charisma."[21] Unfortunately, space does not permit a fuller elaboration of the interesting research questions related to the above analysis, but it is hoped that enough has been said to indicate the relevance and significance of a systematic study of leadership styles in community decision organizations.

A Typology of Explicit Functions

A variable which preliminary investigation indicates may be useful in studying the behavior of community decision organizations is that of the explicit functions which the organization is expected to perform and legitimated to per-form. Presumably, the constraints on an organization's behavior will be somewhat different if it is designed primarily for joint planning among a number of member agencies than they will be if it has to maintain an operating program of its own. For example, a hospital council conceived as an organization to pro-mote joint services (common laundry, common purchases) for its member institutions will experience different constraints than it would if it were legiti-mated by its member institutions and others for broad health-planning functions in the community.

Other Aspects of Organizational Behavior

In this preliminary study, it was found that decisions were being made in four different contexts and that the nature of the context appeared to influence the type of interaction that took place in the decision-making. These contexts varied from that of units within a formal, hierarchically structured organization at the one extreme to the loose sort of individualistic pursuit of goals by various independent persons or organizations without any formal structure for decision-making. These four contexts, extending from unitary through federative and coalitional to "social choice" contexts, are described in detail in another report.[22]

In conclusion, it might be well to indicate, in the briefest fashion, other important aspects of the problem, to be developed more fully in other papers.

There are two levels for studying the interaction of organizations. The first concentrates on the individual organization. This field has been treated so far in two interrelated ways. From the point of view, as it were, of the individual organization, one may consider that organization's own behavior in relation to the configuration of its environment, or one may examine the nature of exchange transactions between organizations. These approaches take as their focus the individual organization in its interaction with other organizations.

The second level deals not with individual organizational behavior in the interaction process, but with the field in which the interaction takes place. Community decision organizations themselves are a response to a situation described by Karl Mannheim, who stated that "the increasing *density of events* (*Dichtigkeit des Geschehens*) makes the possibility of a natural balance through competition or through mutual adaptation more and more hopeless."[23] More recently, F. E. Emery and E. L. Trist have analyzed what they call the causal texture of organizational environments and pointed out that under contemporary conditions, in which the environment is characterized as a turbulent field, "individual organizations, however large, cannot expect to adapt successfully simply through their own direct actions."[24] Such considerations give rise to the desirability of studying the interactional field within which community decision organizations interact, as a level of analysis quite distinct from that of the action of any individual organization.

As in other analogous fields, there are the alternatives of studying "relationships" as a more or less steady state of the system and, on the other hand, studying interactional behavior as it flows through time in response to changing situations. They are not mutually exclusive. The second, however, seems particularly attractive in that it lends itself to a type of flow study, with both practical and theoretical implications—for example, the study of the interaction of community decision organizations in the process of the development of specific federally sponsored programs.

A number of questions immediately arise. What differences in the interactional field in various cities account for the differential utilization and implementation of available federal grant-in-aid programs? What variables appear to be related to the specific locus which a program is given in various cities— which body is chosen as the local public authority for urban renewal programs, or as the community action agency for antipoverty programs? What differences do these loci make in program development and operation? Under what circumstances and for what purposes are project decisions made largely within the normal operating procedures of the organizations themselves, and under what circumstances are they made in other settings—at the bankers' club, at city hall, etc.? What circumstances are associated with program innovativeness? Do coordination among organizations and innovativeness and quality of program vary in inverse relationship to each other, as some bits of theory from analogous settings might suggest?

Finally, what of the public welfare? Are there researchable forms into which questions can be put regarding the type of interorganizational structure that would maximize utility for the community as a whole? Must these questions, loaded as they are with hidden assumptions and value postulates, remain in the field of armchair debate, or are there ways of setting reasonable criteria for a healthy situation regarding the interrelation of organizations in a given community? Are there methods of calculation—welfare economics, cost-benefit analysis, game theory, simulation—which can make significant contributions to the question?

Given a plurality of community decision organizations, each legitimated to speak on behalf of some segment of the community's welfare, but whose interests overlap and whose goals cannot all be simultaneously maximized, what are the relevant criteria that will help improve the mix? This question, like the others immediately preceding it, will have to wait for treatment elsewhere. Meantime, it is hoped that a case has been made for further research on the interaction of community decision organizations.

NOTES

[1] We had originally approached this study thinking of "planning" organizations, but it soon became apparent that the usual ambiguity around the term "planning" applied here as well, and, even more importantly, that "planning," regardless of definition, was one of the variables, rather than a differentia, of these organizations. What seemed important was not the extent to which they fitted some definition of planning but whether or not they were legitimated to speak for or represent the community in some aspect of its interests, whether this be schools, land use, industrial base, health care, vertical mobility for the poor, low-cost housing, or whatever. The term "community decision organization" was coined by James J. Callahan, Jr., a doctoral candidate at Brandeis University.

[2] Philip Selznick, *TVA and the Grass Roots: A Study in the Sociology of Formal Organization* (Berkeley: University of California Press, 1949).

[3] Martin Meyerson and Edward C. Banfield, *Politics, Planning, and the Public Interest: The Case of Public Housing in Chicago* (Glencoe, Ill.: Free Press, 1955).

[4] John R. Seeley et al., *Community Chest: A Case Study in Philanthropy* (Toronto: University of Toronto Press, 1957).

[5] David L. Sills, *The Volunteers: Means and Ends in a National Organization* (Glencoe, Ill.: Free Press, 1957).

[6] Paul M. Harrison, *Authority and Power in the Free Church Tradition: A Social Case Study of the American Baptist Convention* (Princeton: Princeton University Press, 1959).

[7] Peter H. Rossi and Robert A. Dentler, *The Politics of Urban Renewal: The Chicago Findings* (New York: Free Press, Macmillan, 1961).

[8] Scott Greer, *Urban Renewal and American Cities: The Dilemma of Democratic Intervention* (Indianapolis: Bobbs-Merrill, 1965).

[9] Harold Kaplan, *Urban Renewal Politics: Slum Clearance in Newark* (New York: Columbia University Press, 1963).

[10] Paul A. Miller, *Community Health Action* (East Lansing: Michigan State University Press, 1953).

[11] Amitai Etzioni, *A Comparative Analysis of Complex Organizations: On Power, Involvement and Their Correlates* (New York: Free Press, Macmillan, 1961); Richard L. Simpson and William H. Gulley, "Goals, Environmental Pressures, and Organizational Characteristics," *American Sociological Review*, 27 (June 1962): 344–51; Jacob Marschak,

"Towards an Economic Theory of Organization and Information," in *Decision Processes,* ed. Robert McDowell Thrall, C. H. Combs, and R. L. Davis (New York: Wiley, 1954).

[12] William A. Rushing, "Organizational Rules and Surveillance: Propositions in Comparative Organizational Analysis," *Administrative Science Quarterly,* 10 (March 1966): 423–43; Jerald Hage, "An Axiomatic Theory of Organizations," *Administrative Science Quarterly,* 10 (December 1965): 289–320; Peter M. Blau, "The Comparative Study of Organizations," *Industrial and Labor Relations Review,* 18 (April 1965): 323–38; Eugene Litwak, "Models of Bureaucracies Which Permit Conflict," *American Journal of Sociology,* 67 (September 1961): 177–84.

[13] William J. Gore, "Decision-Making Research: Some Prospects and Limitations," in *Concepts and Issues in Administrative Behavior,* ed. Sydney Mailick and Edward H. Van Ness (Englewood Cliffs, N.J.: Prentice-Hall, 1962); James D. Thompson and Arthur Tuden, "Strategies, Structures, and Processes of Organizational Decision," in James D. Thompson *et al., Comparative Studies in Administration* (Pittsburgh: University of Pittsburgh Press, 1959); Herbert A. Simon, *Administrative Behavior: A Study of Decision-Making Processes in Administrative Organization,* 2d ed. (New York: Free Press, Macmillan, 1965).

[14] Gladys M. Kammerer, "Role Diversity of City Managers," *Administrative Science Quarterly,* 8 (March 1964): 421–42.

[15] Gore, "Decision-Making Research."

[16] Herbert A. Simon, "The Decision-Maker as Innovator," in *Concepts and Issues in Administrative Behavior,* ed. Mailick and Van Ness; James Q. Wilson, "Innovation in Organization: Notes Toward a Theory," in *Approaches to Organizational Design,* ed. James D. Thompson (Pittsburgh: University of Pittsburgh Press, 1966); Victor A. Thompson, "Bureaucracy and Innovation," *Administrative Science Quarterly,* 10 (June 1965): 1–20.

[17] For example, Simpson and Gulley, "Goals, Environmental Pressures, and Organizational Characteristics"; James D. Thompson and William J. McEwen, "Organizational Goals and Environment: Goal-Setting as an Interaction Process," *American Sociological Review,* 23 (February 1958): 23–31; William R. Dill, "The Impact of Environment on Organizational Development," in *Concepts and Issues in Administrative Behavior,* ed. Mailick and Van Ness; Eugene Litwak and Lydia F. Hylton, "Interorganizational Analysis: A Hypothesis on Co-ordinating Agencies," *Administrative Science Quarterly,* 6 (March 1962): 395–420; James D. Thompson, "Organizations and Output Transactions," *American Journal of Sociology,* 68 (November 1962): 309–24.

[18] For example, Sol Levine and Paul E. White, "Exchange as a Conceptual Framework for the Study of Interorganizational Relationships," *Administrative Science Quarterly,* 5 (March 1961): 583–601; Sol Levine, Paul E. White, and Benjamin D. Paul, "Community Interorganizational Problems in Providing Medical Care and Social Services," *American Journal of Public Health,* 53 (August 1963): 1183–95; and William M. Evan, "The Organization Set: Toward a Theory of Interorganizational Relations," in *Approaches to Organizational Design,* ed. Thompson.

[19] These concepts are modifications of Evan's "input set" and "output set"; see Evan, "Organization Set."

[20] Max Weber, *The Theory of Social and Economic Organization,* trans. A. M. Henderson and Talcott Parsons (New York: Oxford University Press, 1947).

[21] *Ibid.,* pp. 263ff.

[22] Roland L. Warren, "The Interorganizational Field as a Focus for Investigation," *Administrative Science Quarterly,* 12, no. 3 (December 1967): 396–419 (and chap. 11 of this volume).

[23] Karl Mannheim, *Man and Society in an Age of Reconstruction: Studies in Modern Social Structure* (New York: Harcourt, Brace & World, 1951), p. 157.

[24] F. E. Emery and E. L. Trist, "The Causal Texture of Organizational Environments," *Human Relations,* 18 (February 1965): 28.

11

THE INTERORGANIZATIONAL FIELD
AS A FOCUS FOR INVESTIGATION

There is a growing literature of research and conceptualization on the relation of organizational behavior to various aspects of the environment and, more specifically, on the interaction of specific organizations, especially on exchanges that occur among them.[1] This paper attempts to indicate the need for research focusing deliberately on the field within which organizations interact.[2] It depicts the American metropolitan community as a special instance for interorganizational field analysis and presents a simplified conceptual model for the analysis of this field. It then raises some questions about further research to determine specific modes of organizational interaction in the community field, and also about possible changes that might increase the overall usefulness of interorganizational decision-making.

CONCEPT OF INTERORGANIZATIONAL FIELD

The concept of interorganizational field is based on the observation that the interaction between two organizations is affected, in part at least, by the nature of the organizational pattern or network within which they find themselves. For example, the interaction between two department stores of a given size will be somewhat different if they are the only two department stores in a medium-sized city from what it would be if they constituted two out of twenty department stores of approximately the same size in a metropolis.

Reprinted by permission from *Administrative Science Quarterly*, 12, no. 3 (December 1967): 396–419. Notes have been renumbered.

Karl Mannheim has taken, as a central condition in his consideration of social planning, the concept of "density of events." Using the example of the traffic light, which becomes necessary only after the density of traffic reaches a certain point, he says: "This simple illustration enables us to see precisely how the increasing *density of events* (*Dichtigkeit des Geschehens*) makes the possibility of a natural balance through competition or through mutual adaptation more and more hopeless."[3]

The density of events, even among the same type of actors, increasingly focuses attention on the structure of their interaction, but it may, in addition, relate different types of actors in new modes of interaction. Thus a local department store and a local bank, which formerly interacted in terms of exchanges involving loans and repayments, or deposits and withdrawals, now may find themselves interacting with other units in a larger group setting up an industrial development corporation or attempting to influence the course of urban renewal in the downtown area.

Elsewhere, Mannheim uses the concept of "field structure" for a situation in which various parties interact in such a way that their mutual influence tends to exceed the borders of structured institutional and organizational channels. He adds: "Whenever society, instead of expanding in concentric circles, develops new spheres of action which traverse the boundaries of the concrete groups, we speak of a field structure."[4] One need not reify this field structure into an entity independent of the behavior of its constituent parts in order to concede the importance of studying it as a more inclusive level than that of the exchange behavior of an individual organization with other actors in its environment.

Emery and Trist made the point that "the environmental contexts in which organizations exist are themselves changing, at an increasing rate, and towards increasing complexity."[5] With such change, the environmental contexts themselves become an important subject for analysis. "In a general way it may be said that to think in terms of systems seems the most appropriate conceptual response so far available when the phenomena under study—at any level and in any domain—display the character of being organized, and when understanding the nature of the interdependencies constitutes the research task."[6] But can the environmental field in which organizations interact be considered to be organized, and if so, what can be said about such environmental organization systematically?

Emery and Trist answered the first question affirmatively and developed a typology of four environmental "textures," extending from the placid, randomized environment to the turbulent field environment. They analyzed these in terms of strategy, tactics, and operations; the complexity of actors in the field and their similarity or dissimilarity; and the types of behavior necessary for organizational survival in each case. The turbulent field had, in addition to the increased complexity of interorganizational relationships characteristic of the third stage, a new emergent in that "the dynamic properties arise not simply from the interaction of the component organizations, but also from the field itself. The 'ground' is in motion."[7] In these circumstances, "individual organizations, however large, cannot expect to adapt successfully simply through their own direct actions."[8]

COMMUNITY DECISION ORGANIZATIONS

An exploratory project on the interrelationship of community-level* planning organizations in three cities—Philadelphia, Detroit, and Boston—considered organizations such as community welfare councils, urban renewal authorities, antipoverty organizations, housing authorities, chambers of commerce, federations of churches, municipal health and welfare departments, boards of education, and so on.† It became apparent that the term "planning," in addition to its ambiguity and current semantic explosiveness, did not accurately distinguish these organizations from others. But all the organizations mentioned purported to—and in varying degrees were legitimated to—represent the interests of the community in some segment of broad community concern; therefore the term "community decision organizations" (CDOs) was adopted.[9]

Such organizations constitute the means through which the community attempts to concert certain decisions and activities. Presumably a higher aggregate utility is attainable through joint decision-making and action within the respective CDOs than if decisions within each field of concern were left to what Banfield calls "social choice."[10] Most cities today have many and varied CDOs. Many of them receive strong financial support and program stimulus from the federal government or other extracommunity sources, and their spheres of activity, although differentially defined, overlap in various relationships.[11]

It has often been observed that communities do not have a single organizational structure, but rather are constituted of many formal structures (includ-

* The term "community level" is used here loosely to denote both the city itself and the metropolitan area. Community decision organizations included in the present analysis may have either of these domain boundaries. The distinction between the two, though extremely important in many contexts, is not important here. Furthermore, although the present analysis confines itself to interaction among organizations at this community level, the vertical relations to organizational systems outside of the community, as, for example, the federal government, should not be overlooked. The term "community level" does not imply a discretely identifiable level, except for purposes of analysis. One of the aspects of the turbulence within which community decision organizations interact is the fluid admixture of organizations from all levels, both more inclusive than the community, such as state and federal, and less inclusive than the community, such as neighborhood organizations.

† Fieldwork in Philadelphia and Detroit was extremely limited, being confined to a limited number of interviews with leaders of such community decision organizations, principally for the purpose of qualitive comparison with the more intensive exploratory fieldwork conducted in Boston.

ing that of the municipal government) as well as interaction patterns through which locality-relevant decisions are made. The process through which this occurs is bewilderingly complex. Norton Long has sought to capture it as an ecology of games "in the local territorial system [which] accomplishes unplanned but largely functional results,"[12] and Banfield has treated the process as an elaborate system of "political influence."[13] Greer sums it up as follows:

> The over-all polity is, however, a sum of efforts ranging from those of neighborhood improvement associations to the negotiations between the central city mayor and the plenipotentiaries of powerful organizations. In the absence of a central arena and polity, the public decisions are made in response to the politically potent demands of a fragmented electorate and the professional concerns of the political managerial elite. They suffice to accomplish a minimal ordering.[14]

But the perennial question is whether that minimal ordering is an optimal ordering, and if not, how an optimal ordering may be achieved. The time when the community welfare council could aspire to be *the* instrument of the community for social planning has long since passed, as the texture of the organizational environment has become complicated by the multiplicity of organizations exercising a planning function in this field. A recent trend toward closer collaboration between physical planners and social planners in the urban field is apparent in the professional literature and behavior of each. Earlier attempts, such as the Syracuse and Onondaga County Post-War Planning Council, to bring the existing CDOs into one organization for centralized decision-making have largely been abandoned. A newer trend is the function of mayors—and their development coordinators—as a locus not only for some integrated centralized decision-making, but also as a decision-making resource when the conflict of CDO interests threatens an impasse.

CHARACTERISTICS OF INTERORGANIZATIONAL FIELD

It is of little interest to investigate the interorganizational field in which the activities of one CDO—say the health department—can be carried on with little relation to those of another, such as the chamber of commerce or the metropolitan transit authority. Alan Altshuler has concluded:

> The most distinguishing feature of the bureaucratization of society in recent generations has perhaps been the extent to which planning at the level of governments and large private organizations has gradually become more and more systematized. The proliferation of specialized

research and planning staffs in large bureaucracies of all kinds is symptomatic of this trend. Planning becomes "political" only when the efforts of some men and organizations to plan come into conflict with those of others.[15]

Eugene Litwak and Lydia F. Hylton distinguish interorganizational analysis from intraorganizational analysis by "(1) the operation of social behavior under conditions of partial conflict and (2) the stress on factors which derive equally from all units of interaction rather than being differentially weighted by authority structure."[16]

In getting at some of the other distinguishing characteristics of interorganizational interaction, Burton R. Clark considers three patterns of concerting influence. The first is the organizational or bureaucratic pattern. At the other extreme is that "found in political arenas characterized by a formal decentralization of authority, and therefore to be understood by a theory of political influence,"[17] such as Banfield's. Between the two are patterns of confederative organization or organizational alliance which "converge with and become somewhat a part of political influence, in that they are the result of efforts to co-ordinate autonomous agencies, to unite effort *without* the authority of formal hierarchy and employee status. They are somewhat different in that they develop away from formal political arenas and often escape the constraints of political accountability."[18] He contrasts such interorganizational patterns with bureaucratic (intraorganizational) ones, as indicated in Table 11–1.[19]

INCLUSIVE CONTEXTS FOR DECISION-MAKING

A preliminary study in Boston analyzing the highly complex context in which community decision organizations operate indicated that decisions were being made in the most varied organizational contexts, and that the difference in contexts seemed to be related to the behavior of the CDOs in the interaction process. Four such contexts were discernible and may be of general applicability in examining organizational and interorganizational behavior.

The context typology distinguishes between the ways in which organizational units interact in the decision-making process as these are influenced by their relationships to an inclusive decision-making structure. The four types of context are: (1) unitary, (2) federative, (3) coalitional, and (4) social choice.

These are distinguished from each other on the basis of a number of dimensions: (1) relation of units to an inclusive goal, (2) locus of inclusive decision making, (3) locus of authority, (4) structural provision for division of labor, (5) commitment to a leadership subsystem, and (6) prescribed collectivity

Table 11-1

BUREAUCRATIC AND INTERORGANIZATIONAL PATTERNS
AS DEPICTED BY CLARK

	Bureaucratic Patterns	Interorganizational Patterns
Authority and supervision	Inherent in the office	Less through formal structure and more shared by specific agreement
Accountability	Accountability up the line, supervision down the line	Looser accountability and supervision; provided by general agreement, limited in scope and in time
Standards of work	Explication, formalization, universal application	Less formal and more indirect; often through manipulating resources and incentives in a large market or economy of organizations
Personnel assignment	Periodic review of performance, replacement or reassignment when appropriate	Other methods of strengthening weak sectors, including supplying resources
Research and development	Usually provided for in organizational chart	Subsidizing private innovative groups by major agencies, facilitating dissemination of innovations to the field

orientation of units. These dimensions all vary in ordinal fashion, in the same direction from one extreme (the unitary context) to the other (the social-choice context).

The *unitary context* is exemplified by a city health department or transportation authority. The units (divisions, bureaus, and so on) are deliberately organized for the achievement of inclusive goals. Decision-making, as to policy and program, takes place at the top of the structure and final authority over the units rests there. The units are structured in a division of labor for the achievement of the inclusive goals. Norms call for a high commitment to following the orders of a leadership subsystem.[20] The units are expected to orient their behavior toward the well-being of the inclusive organization, rather than toward their own respective subgoals.*

The *federative context* for inclusive decision-making is exemplified by a council of social agencies (to a lesser extent by the newer type of community welfare council) or by a council of churches. The units (member organizations, rather than integral departments) have their individual goals, but there is some formal organization for the accomplishment of inclusive goals, and there is

* Organizational literature is replete with exceptions to this statement; that is, examples of departments or other units within organizaions which develop and pursue their own goals even when these are at variance with the goals of the inclusive organization. Nevertheless, the unitary organization is specifically designed to avoid this, regardless of the extent to which it may fail.

formal staff structure for this purpose. Decision-making is focused in a specific part of the inclusive structure, but it is in effect subject to ratification by the units. Authority remains at the unit (member) level, with the exception of some administrative prerogatives, which are delegated by the units to a formal staff. The units are structured autonomously, but they may agree to a division of labor that may affect their structure without making them departments of an inclusive organization, as in the unitary context. The norms are for moderate commitment of the member units to the inclusive leadership subsystem, but considerable unit autonomy is tolerated and expected. A moderate degree of collectivity orientation—consideration of the well-being of the inclusive organization—is expected.

The *coalitional context* for inclusive decision-making is exemplified by a group of organizations cooperating more or less closely to attain some desired objective, such as persuading a new industry to locate in the community or developing a federally sponsored project. Each organization has its own set of goals, but collaborates informally and on an ad hoc basis where some of its goals are similar to those of other organizations in the group. There is no formal organization or staff for inclusive decision-making. Rather, decision-making takes place at the level of the units themselves, as they interact with each other. Also, the coalition itself has no authority, the authority for its behavior resting with the units. The units are autonomously structured to pursue their own various purposes, but they may agree to ad hoc division of labor in order to accomplish their inclusive goal. Such division of labor ordinarily involves a minimum of restructuring of the cooperating units. There are no norms of commitment to an inclusive leadership, but there are general norms that govern the interaction of the unit leaders involved. There is only a minimal prescription of collectivity-orientation by the units, it being understood that the units are concerned primarily with their own goals, and only secondarily with the loose interactional structure in which they happen to be collaborating.

The *social-choice context* for inclusive decision-making is exemplified by the autonomous behavior of a number of organizations and individuals in the community as they relate themselves and their behavior to any particular issue which concerns more than one of them—as, for example, the issue of medicare or of housing desegregation, or highway location.[21] They do not necessarily share any inclusive goals, and indeed, their goals with respect to the issue may be discordant. There is no formal inclusive structure within which the units make their decisions; rather, decisions are made at the level of the units themselves, many of which may be inclusive organizations of a unitary, federative, or coalitional type. Likewise, authority rests at the unit level. There is no formally structured provision for division of labor within an inclusive context, each unit pursuing its own goals and organizing itself for that purpose as it deems appropriate. There is no expected commitment to a leadership system other than that of the individual units.* Finally, there is little or no prescribed collectivity orientation of units, the units being highly self-oriented as they pursue their goals, and there being no structure to whose well-being such collectivity orientation would be addressed.†

As indicated, there is a progression in these four types of context from that in which various units are integrally organized for division of labor and centralized decision-making to that in which there is no identifiable central decision-making body, and the units are related to each other only within a general interactional field, without provision for centralized decision-making or centralized authority. Table 11–2 illustrates the relationships. The four contexts should be understood as points along the various dimensions, rather than as discrete states.

The typology is useful in categorizing CDOs. Poverty agencies, community planning councils, city planning commissions, urban renewal authorities, city health departments, and similar organizations are either unitary or federative. Presumably, the variation in the dimensions analyzed accounts for some of the differences in the behavior of CDOs toward each other. The federation, depending ultimately on the continued assent of its autonomous constituent organizations, is under great constraint to operate on a consensus basis. Since innovations and major system changes are likely to threaten this consensus, it is under constraint to avoid them. On the other hand, coalitions, because their existence is based solely upon a convergence of interests around some particular issue, may engage freely in controversy, but have little persistence beyond the immediate issue. By contrast, unitary organizations show much greater stability and persistence, even in conflict situations.

RELATIONS AMONG CDOs

What of the relation of CDOs to each other? Almost by definition, the context in which two or more CDOs interact cannot take the form of a unitary

---

* In a sense, the power structure may be considered as a leadership subsystem within the community where the social choice is being made. To the extent that a power structure actually centralizes decision-making among the CDOs of a community, it would represent evidence contrary to the statement. But one should not overlook the plurality of power structures found in many large cities. Even in cities with monolithic power structures, these would seem to serve primarily a diffuse function of general policy constraints with an actual centralization of decision-making only occasionally, where the social choice process has resulted in an impasse or an undesirable outcome.

† Although there is no formal inclusive structure, it can still be said that the community is a meaningful focus for collectivity orientation among CDOs. In addition, CDOs often make explicit claim to be representing community welfare or the public interest in pursuing their own goals. The final section of this article discusses the interrelation of CDO goals from the standpoint of a more inclusive community interest.

Table 11-2

TYPES OF INCLUSIVE CONTEXT

Dimension	Type of Context			
	Unitary	Federative	Coalitional	Social choice
Relation of units to an inclusive goal	Units organized for achievement of inclusive goals	Units with disparate goals, but some formal organization for inclusive goals	Units with disparate goals, but informal collaboration for inclusive goals	No inclusive goals
Locus of inclusive decision-making	At top of inclusive structure	At top of inclusive structure, subject to unit ratification	In interaction of units without a formal inclusive structure	Within units
Locus of authority	At top of hierarchy of inclusive structure	Primarily at unit level	Exclusively at unit level	Exclusively at unit level
Structural provisions for division of labor	Units structured for division of labor within inclusive organization	Units structured autonomously; may agree to a division of labor, which may affect their structure	Units structured autonomously; may agree to ad hoc division of labor, without restructuring	No formally structured division of labor within an inclusive context
Commitment to a leadership subsystem	Norms of high commitment	Norms of moderate commitment	Commitment only to unit leaders	Commitment only to unit leaders
Prescribed collectivity orientation of units	High	Moderate	Minimal	Little or none

organization, but frequently takes the form of a federation—as in the case of the various social agencies that unite in a council of social agencies or a federation of municipalities which performs certain minimal functions in a metropolitan area. It may also take the form of a coalition, as in the case of the collaborative efforts of three or four specific organizations to establish some new service or secure passage of a new piece of legislation. Or it may take the form of a social-choice context, with various parties seeking to advance their own goals with whatever outcome the total combination of actions may produce.

The fourfold typology lends itself readily to the wheels-within-wheels phenomenon; for a unitary organization may be a member of a federation which in turn may be a member of a coalition which is acting to some extent in concert in a larger social-choice decision. Other combinations also occur. At whatever level the analysis is being made, however, the dynamics of the structure of the field are pertinent in attempting to assess the interaction processes taking place.

The first two contexts, especially, are of great potential usefulness in studying the behavior of CDOs toward each other. Although a rigorous systematic study has not been made, a cursory examination of the Detroit and Philadelphia settings and a more extensive examination of the Boston setting indicate that the behavior of CDOs is directly related to their position with respect to some of the six inclusive context dimensions just considered. Research is needed to indicate the extent to which various kinds of unitary organizations behave in similar ways under similar conditions in community decisions and to contrast this behavior with that of federations and coalitions. Research is also needed on the characteristic structure of a specific type of CDO, e.g., an urban renewal authority, to determine whether the organization in the various cities approaches the unitary or the federative type of structure, and the accompanying differences, if any, in its interorganizational behavior.

The CDOs that are the subject of this paper are typically unitary or federative organizations. Each has its own legitimated segment of interest and operations which sometimes overlaps that of other CDOs. Occasionally, short-term issues bring the most diverse kinds of CDOs together in their interest in the same issue. But on any particular issue, whether short-term or long-term, an interested CDO might be able to classify all other CDOs into one of the following categories: (1) not involved in the issue, (2) involved in the issue in a manner that supports the first CDO in its pursuit of its goals, and (3) involved in the issue in a manner that hampers the first CDO in its pursuit of its goals.

Many of the CDOs have specific financial and bureaucratic support through a federal grant-in-aid agency, as well as an accompanying set of federal constraints. Each CDO has a local input constituency, consisting of those parties to which it acknowledges a responsibility in determining its policy and program, and an output constituency, consisting of those parties which are acknowledged by the organization as being the appropriate targets of the organization's activity.

MAXIMIZING VALUES IN THE INTERORGANIZATIONAL FIELD

Let us consider the seminal point about partial conflict characterizing the interorganizational field. Litwak and Hylton write:

Values may be theoretically consistent, but limited resources force individuals to choose between them without completely rejecting either choice. (This is one of the classic problems of economics.) Or it may be that a given task requires several specialities, i.e., a division of labor, and limited resources at times of crisis force a choice between them, although all are desirable (for example, the conflicts between the various military services). In such cases organizational independence might be given to the specialties to preserve their essential core despite competition.[22]

They then point out that all societies must have a situation of partial conflict, "because of limited resources for maximizing all values simultaneously."[23]

This important point can be helpful in conceptualizing the nature of the interorganizational field of CDOs. But first, a modification of this statement suggests itself. It may well be, especially in particular situations, that regardless of resources, certain value combinations are compatible only within limits, beyond which one tends to interfere with the other. Wayne Leys, for example, has listed six moral standards: happiness, lawfulness, harmony or consistency, survival, integrity, and loyalty, "any one of which may be in conflict with any other." Each has served as the keystone of a complete ethical system of occidental philosophy, and although Leys does nòt himself choose a *summum bonum* among these values, he states: "But I do propose a rather loose-jointed system, in the sense that sound decision-making will involve successive reviews of the decision from the standpoint of each of these six standards."[24]

Such value conflicts characterize not only the interorganizational field, but also the intraorganizational field. In each case they pose the problem of optimal mix, the determination of the best combination of investment in various values. In the intraorganizational context, this is determined largely by centralized decision-making. In the interorganizational context, decision-making is allowed to form out of the interaction of various organizations. These organizations make various investments in one value or another, from differing pools of resources.

In national planning, Gene Fisher indicates some considerations in program budgeting:

Major allocative decisions involve such questions as, Should more resources be employed in national security in the future, or in national

health programs, or in preservation and development of natural resources, etc. Ideally, the decision makers would like to plan to allocate
resources in the future so that for a given budget, for example, the
estimated marginal return (or utility) in each major area of application would be equal. But this is more easily said than done; and at
the current state of analytical art, no one really knows with any precision how the "grand optimum" might be obtained.[25]

Yet despite this uncertainty, allocations are made annually, rather routinely,
through the budgetary process, which no one claims is optimal, but which
serves as partly an organizational and partly a social-choice means of making the
theoretically impossible decisions.[26]

Within the profit-making organization, the simplest model for the allocation process is that which considers only one value—the maximization of profits
—so that the problem of weighting conflicting values does not arise. Values that
limit profit maximization are considered as constraints, rather than as competitive
values, although other values, such as firm prestige or individual career considerations, do of course affect the allocative process.

The nonprofit organization (whether governmental or nongovernmental)
does not have, even theoretically, this simple criterion for allocational decisions. It is somewhat freer in the sense of not having to show a profit, but
like the profit organizations, it makes decisions which, even though essentially based on intuition and subjective value assumptions, are nevertheless
centralized.

By contrast, the social-choice context puts such allocative decisions into a
competitive arena. Here, social processes are equated with a presumably rational
dialectic, and that which emerges in the free interplay of parties and values and
resources is the agreed-upon solution. Where the solution is not acceptable to
significant parties, there are such recourses as trying to get the city council to
pass a law, or getting the mayor to serve as mediator, or setting up an ad hoc
mechanism for meliorating the unacceptable solution, or, in the last analysis, a
public struggle.

Thus, the community interorganizational field shares with the intraorganizational context the inability to calculate rationally the optimum mix from a field
of competing values, but differs from it in not having a structure for centraliz-
ing decision-making and implementing strategy. While this lack of centralization
is bemoaned in some community social and physical planning quarters, it is not
universally deplored. Banfield, for example, concluded that in the major issues
that he studied in Chicago, this process led to decisions which he himself would
have favored, even though these decisions were made for what he considered the
wrong reasons.[27]

HEURISTIC MODEL OF THE
INTERORGANIZATIONAL FIELD OF CDOs

It may help to summarize by presenting a brief model of interorganizational decision-making in the community arena. Let us conceptualize the situation on an "as if" basis.* It is as if the people of the community, concerned with a number of different kinds of values†—adequate housing, a viable economic base, the rejuvenation of the city's core, adequate transit, an appropriate array of social services, good schools, and so on—had parceled these values out among a number of CDOs, giving to each the responsibility for maximizing its particular value—not absolutely, but in interaction with other CDOs. The CDOs have different, partially overlapping value configurations, with different types and amounts of resources at their disposal. Not all the values can be maximized simultaneously, either because of inadequate resources or because some, like adequate low-cost housing, may conflict with others, like eliminating segregation, when they are pressed beyond certain limits. Furthermore, the people of the community have acknowledged the right of these CDOs to speak for the community in their respective fields (i.e., given them legitimation) and have allocated to them money, personnel, and other resources with which to do it.

Although the joint decision usually satisfies no one completely, it produces a resolution well within the bounds of acceptability for most important parties to the community dialogue. Such changes as are needed occur incrementally through the waxing and waning of the various CDOs (resource reallocation) and through changes in legitimation (shifting domain). When the attempts of the CDOs to press incompatible values result in a crisis, the mayor or some other *deus ex machina* is called in to resolve the immediate dispute and perhaps to reallocate resources.

In the long run, if the people of the community do not like the mix they are getting with their current investment of resources and legitimation, they can simply change the mix, through budget reallocation, through the legal setting up or dissolution of a CDO, through shifts in voluntary donation patterns, through new legislation, and so on. Such shifts may be fairly easy or extremely difficult to bring about. They do not determine the specific decisions that will eventually be made in the interaction of CDOs, but they may influence them. What such shifts do is to change the situation within which the decisions arise. They provide a way for the people of the community to intervene in the

---

* Obviously, it is not being asserted here that deliberate community decisions are made in a unitary context. Quite the contrary. Most of the decisions involved here are made in a social-choice context. Nevertheless, the "as if" approach would seem to have heuristic advantages. See Hans Vaihinger, *The Philosophy of "As If,"* trans. C. K. Ogden (New York: Harcourt, Brace, 1924).

† The term "value" is used here not in the normative sense, but rather in the sense of an object having the capacity to satisfy a desire.

interorganizational field, but then to withdraw as it were and monitor the continuing struggle for value ascendancy among the various CDOs.

Deliberate changes in this field of CDO interaction are likewise influenced by the various possibilities of resource input from outside the community, principally from various federal agencies. The availability of such federal financial support, distributed unevenly among the values represented by the various CDOs, constitutes an important component of the decisional field. Thus, the availability of 50 percent or 80 percent reimbursement for an expanded program of a particular CDO may be important in influencing the local decision as to how local resources are to be allocated.

To summarize briefly, the people of a metropolitan community are not organized for making centralized rational choices among values which cannot be maximized simultaneously. Various values are allocated to specific CDOs for maximization. These CDOs, in turn, are the protagonists in a sort of sociodrama in which the mix gets worked out in some relation to respective resources and skill in their use, and within the framework of the range of acceptability of the composite decision to the large and important sectors of the community.

SATISFICING VERSUS MAXIMIZING

In this process, the excessive pressing of a particular value by any one of the CDOs is made virtually impossible by the conflicting claims of the other CDOs. This can be related to Aristotle's principle of the golden mean, adduced from his observation of the deterioration of a value when pushed in either direction beyond a certain threshold.[28] If our current analysis is valid, there may be a definite relationship between this type of rationalistic approach in ethics and the satisficing behavior described by Herbert Simon, which he exemplifies in terms of "share of market," "adequate profit," and "fair price."[29] Banfield has observed that organizations satisfice instead of maximizing, not because they "lack the wits to maximize," as Simon has suggested, but because they "lack the will."[30] In the present context, they lack the will to maximize any particular value and therefore satisfice, because they are constrained by the fact that maximization of one of their values would jeopardize an acceptable degree of achievement of another value. They thus satisfice in order to keep goal achievement in their respective value clusters within an acceptable set of limits.

Within the intraorganizational context, this process of satisficing occurs as a centralized decision-making process. In the interorganizational field of CDOs, it occurs through the competition of various CDOs to advance their particular values. Their respective satisficing thus makes possible a composite result, which is usually acceptable, though never maximal, and perhaps seldom optimal for the community.

Leys presented an analysis that helps further to explain this satisficing process among a number of competing values sought by competing CDOs in the community. On any particular issue, he says, there will be both partisans and bystanders. Some of the partisans want to press a particular value to a point where it jeopardizes the values of other partisans. The bystanders are not specifically concerned with the issue in dispute, but are concerned that the issue does not result in damaging side effects. Because of the wider variety of values that the bystanders represent, they will commonly enforce a resolution of the immediate controversy, usually to the complete satisfaction of none of the partisans.[31] In this way, the dynamic interaction of CDOs constitutes a series of satisficing resolutions in which values are mixed more or less in keeping with community preferences, as indicated operationally by resource allocations. The outcome is not calculable, given the resource allocations, but it is obviously manipulable through such resource allocations. Mannheim writes:

> If one wishes to interfere in these fields (where conflict and competition are the usual forms of adjustment) without doing violence to the spontaneity of events, a specific kind of regulation is necessary. Regulations which are adapted to the nature of the field structure intervene only at certain points in the course of events. They do not determine the line of action in advance as in custom or administration.[32]

The same can be said of resource allocation.

OPTIMIZING THE MIX

Since the outcome of the interaction of CDOs is not predetermined, but emerges in a social-interaction process within the interorganizational field, the question arises as to whether different structuring of this interactional field might produce a more desirable mix.

What would a more desirable mix mean? It would mean, presumably, that satisficing levels on each value would be higher. Presumably, this could occur in one of two ways: either through a more efficient use of resources, where lack of resources had figured largely in the lower satisficing levels; or in finding ways in which higher satisficing levels on particular values could be found that did not jeopardize satisficing levels on other values. Thus, an improvement of the mix would simply mean an advance in the direction of maximization of some values without jeopardizing other values. Our question then becomes whether aggregate value can be increased through manipulating the interorganizational field.

In his analysis of anomie, Durkheim offers a clue to this problem in referring to the interrelation of roles in a division of labor, the resultant of which is facilitated by a body of clearly understood rules governing the interaction. He states:

> But, on the contrary, if some opaque environment is interposed, then only stimuli of a certain intensity can be communicated from one organ to another. Relations, being rare, are not repeated enough to be determined; each time there ensues new groping. The lines of passage taken by the streams of movement cannot deepen because the streams themselves are too intermittent. If some rules do come to constitute them, they are, however, general and vague, for under these conditions it is only the most general contours of phenomena that can be fixed. The case will be the same if the contiguity, though sufficient, is too recent or has not endured long enough.[33]

The interorganizational field of CDOs would seem to approximate this condition. In many large cities today, large CDOs are all seeking, within a unitary or federative context, to rationalize some aspects of decision-making in their respective legitimated spheres, but interacting in loose coalitional or social-choice contexts in ways which often affect one another adversely or favorably, though with little or no concert, and with few clearly defined norms governing the interaction. The interorganizational field is indeed crowded and turbulent, as Emery and Trist have shown,[34] but Durkheim's comments on an opaque environment are equally pertinent.

It is precisely this condition that leads many urban experts to advocate more centralized planning—in this instance, a more inclusive centralization of the already centralized planning of the respective CDOs. Aside from the feasibility or desirability of such centralization, are there changes in the CDO interorganizational field which might improve joint decision-making? From the foregoing analysis, one way that suggests itself would be to make the interactional field less opaque, so that the respective CDOs would be better able to adapt their behavior to each other in a more deliberate way. They could retain their present relative autonomy, but with more comprehensive knowledge of each other's policies, plans, and programs they could better influence decisions where their respective values reinforced each other, and perhaps even reduce some of the value conflicts.

A number of such changes in the interorganizational field of CDOs could be made:

1. The organization of common data banks and systems for retrieval and analysis, so that disparities are not needlessly caused by the use of different sets of figures and projections as a basis for planning, and

so as to facilitate the examination of the reciprocal side effects of plans of the CDOs.

2. Prompt communication of proposed policy or program changes, so as to facilitate anticipatory adjustment in the behavior of other CDOs.*
3. Specific procedures among CDOs for feedback and incremental reformulation of proposed changes in their respective policies or programs.
4. Specific procedures for feedback or feed-in from output constituencies, so that respective fields of activity can be focused together as they are checked against responses from various significant groups in the community.
5. Procedures to improve the process of resource reallocation among CDOs where the mix is perceived as less than optimal.
6. Procedures for overlapping board and committee members, thus providing important bridging roles for people who are competently familiar with two or more CDOs.
7. Deliberate broadening of the scope of interaction among CDOs to include personnel at different hierarchical levels, where more or less inclusive policy or implementing decisions are made, including the lending of staff members to other CDOs for specific ad hoc collaborative ventures.
8. Deliberate establishment of procedures for joint participation in planning among CDOs in major developments that involve the interests of more than one CDO.
9. Specific provision of methods for central decision-making to break impasses or resolve conflicts among CDOs.

An examination of these suggestions may lead to the premature conclusion that they should be accepted as dicta. Perhaps they should, but this cannot be concluded from the present analysis. The suggestions listed could improve the mix through a more efficient use of resources, or by aiding in the discovery of ways in which higher satisficing levels on particular values could be found without jeopardizing other values. But there is no assurance that gains from increased coordination among CDOs through these suggestions might not be offset by losses in innovativeness, intensity, or quality of· individual CDO programs. There is some indication that excellence in a city's urban renewal program or public school system or transit system is often brought about largely through the passionate commitment of relatively single-minded individuals and/or organizations. Implementation of the suggestions above, while bringing about an improvement in the two ways indicated, might conceivably result in a net loss through the smoothing out of peaks of excellence along with the

* This is unrealistic to expect in zero-sum situations, but probably only a minority of inter-CDO situations are zero-sum.

obvious nadirs of ineptness. In other words, it is a question for empirical determination, rather than logical analysis, to discover whether the gains in raised satisficing levels on the various values involved could actually take place without losses on others.

It is believed that most, if not all, of the suggestions can be made operational for research purposes and that a means for controlling many of the other pertinent variables is available. It is hoped that certain aspects of this question will therefore lend themselves to empirical investigation in the near future.

NOTES

[1] Richard L. Simpson and William H. Gulley, "Goals, Environmental Pressures, and Organizational Characteristics," *American Sociological Review,* 27 (June 1962) ; James D. Thompson and William J. McEwen, "Organizational Goals and Environment: Goal-Setting as an Interaction Process," *American Sociological Review,* 23 (February 1958) ; William R. Dill, "The Impact of Environment on Organizational Development," in *Concepts and Issues in Administrative Behavior,* ed. Sydney Mailick and Edward H. Van Ness (Englewood Cliffs, N.J.: Prentice-Hall, 1962) ; Eugene Litwak and Lydia F. Hylton, "Interorganizational Analysis: A Hypothesis on Coordinating Agencies," *Administrative Science Quarterly,* 6 (March 1962) ; James D. Thompson, "Organizations and Output Transactions," *American Journal of Sociology,* 68 (November 1962) ; Sol Levine and Paul E. White, "Exchange as a Conceptual Framework for the Study of Interorganizational Relationships," *Administrative Science Quarterly,* 5 (March 1961) ; Sol Levine, Paul E. White, and Benjamin D. Paul, "Community Interorganizational Problems in Providing Medical Care and Social Services," *American Journal of Public Health,* 53 (August 1963) ; William M. Evan, "The Organization Set: Toward a Theory of Interorganizational Relations," in *Approaches to Organizational Design,* ed. James D. Thompson (Pittsburgh: University of Pittsburgh Press, 1966) ; Bernard Olshansky, "Planned Change in Interorganizational Relationships" (doctoral dissertation, Florence Heller Graduate School for Advanced Studies in Social Welfare, Brandeis University, June 1961). Other recent publications in this field are cited in the course of this paper.

[2] The term "field" is used here essentially in Lewin's sense: "a totality of coexisting facts which are conceived of as mutually interdependent." See Kurt Lewin, *Field Theory in Social Science: Selected Theoretical Papers* (New York: Harper, 1951), p. 240 and *passim.*

[3] Karl Mannheim, *Man and Society in an Age of Reconstruction: Studies in Modern Social Structure* (New York: Harcourt, Brace, 1951), p. 157.

[4] *Ibid.,* p. 297.

[5] F. E. Emery and E. L. Trist, "The Causal Texture of Organizational Environments," *Human Relations,* 18 (February 1965) : 21.

[6] *Ibid.*

[7] *Ibid.,* p. 26.

[8] *Ibid.,* p. 28.

[9] The term "community decision organization" was suggested by James J. Callahan, Jr., a doctoral candidate at Brandeis University.

[10] Banfield has developed the concept of social choice, as opposed to central decision. "A *social choice* . . . is the accidental by-product of the actions of two or more actors— 'interested parties,' they will be called—who have no common intention and who make

their selections competitively or without regard to each other. In a social choice process, each actor seeks to attain his own ends; the aggregate of all actions—the situation produced by all actions together—constitutes an outcome for the group, but it is an outcome which no one has planned as a 'solution' to a 'problem.' It is a 'resultant' rather than a 'solution.' " See Edward C. Banfield, *Political Influence* (New York: Free Press, Macmillan, 1961), pp. 326–27.

[11] Roland L. Warren, "The Impact of New Designs of Community Organization," *Child Welfare,* 44 (November 1965), and chap. 8 of this volume.

[12] Norton E. Long, "The Local Community as an Ecology of Games," *American Journal of Sociology,* 64 (November 1958): 254.

[13] *Ibid.*

[14] Scott Greer, *The Emerging City: Myth and Reality* (New York: Free Press, Macmillan, 1962), p. 200.

[15] Alan Altshuler, *The City Planning Process: A Political Analysis* (Ithaca, N.Y.: Cornell University, 1965), p. 409.

[16] Litwak and Hylton, "Interorganizational Analysis," p. 398.

[17] Burton R. Clark, "Interorganizational Patterns in Education," *Administrative Science Quarterly,* 10 (September 1965): 233.

[18] *Ibid.*

[19] Adapted from *ibid.,* pp. 234–36.

[20] Ramsöy has made an extensive analysis in largely Parsonian terms of the relation of units that can be considered as subsystems of a more inclusive system. In it, he specifically analyzes the development of a leadership subsystem within the inclusive system which contains the units. See Odd Ramsöy, *Social Groups as System and Subsystem* (New York: Free Press, Macmillan, 1963).

[21] Banfield, *Political Influence.*

[22] Litwak and Hylton, "Interorganizational Analysis," p. 397.

[23] *Ibid.,* p. 399.

[24] Wayne A. R. Leys, "The Value Framework of Decision-Making," in *Concepts and Issues in Administrative Behavior,* ed. Mailick and Van Ness, p. 87.

[25] Gene H. Fisher, "The Role of Cost-Utility Analysis in Program Budgeting," in *Program Budgeting,* ed. David Novick (Washington, D.C.: U.S. Government Printing Office, 1964–1965), p. 35.

[26] Aaron Wildavsky, *The Politics of the Budgetary Process* (Boston: Little, Brown, 1964). The present analysis applies specifically to organizational behavior that is oriented toward the attainment of explicit goals. It allows for the widely acknowledged fact that organizational behavior is frequently oriented toward system maintenance as well as toward goals other than the explicit organizational ones. See Amitai Etzioni, "Two Approaches to Organizational Analysis: A Critique and a Suggestion," *Administrative Science Quarterly,* 5 (September 1960).

[27] Banfield, *Political Influence.*

[28] Aristotle, *Ethics.*

[29] Herbert A. Simon, *Administrative Behavior: A Study of Decision-Making Processes in Administrative Organization* (New York: Free Press, Macmillan, 1965), p. xxv.

[30] Edward C. Banfield, "Ends and Means in Planning," in *Concepts and Issues in Administrative Behavior,* ed. Mailick and Van Ness, p. 78.

[31] Wayne A. R. Leys, *Ethics and Social Policy* (New York: Prentice-Hall, 1941), chaps. 12–14. Coleman treats this phenomenon in somewhat different terms; see James S. Coleman, *Community Conflict* (Glencoe, Ill.: Free Press, 1957).

[32] Mannheim, *Man and Society in an Age of Reconstruction,* p. 297.

[33] Emile Durkheim, *The Division of Labor in Society,* trans. George Simpson (New York: Free Press, Macmillan, 1964), pp. 368–69.

[34] Emery and Trist, "The Causal Texture of Organizational Environments."

12

THE CONCERTING OF DECISIONS
AS A VARIABLE IN
ORGANIZATIONAL INTERACTION

It is important to seek conceptual rubrics under which the wide variety of inter-organizational decision-making contexts and processes can be ordered. The present conceptualization has arisen in connection with a study of interaction among organizations of a specific type, but the formulation has been kept as broad as possible, with the idea that it may apply equally to all formal organizations of whatever type—although I am not sure that this is the case.

What, specifically, is meant by the concept of interorganizational decision-making? Under what circumstances do organizational units engage in this process? How does interorganizational decision-making vary according to the contexts in which it occurs, and on what important dimensions does such variation take place?

The wording of this paper's title suggests two underlying theses as a basis for exploring these questions:* (1) *Interorganizational decision-making is fruit-fully approached through utilization of the concept of concerted decision-making.* (2) *Interorganizational decision-making is only one type of organizational interaction.*

Let us begin, then, by differentiating concerted decision-making from other processes of organizational interaction. At the most elementary level, one

Paper presented at the Conference on Interorganizational Decision Making, Northwestern University, February 1969, and included in *Interorganizational Decision Making,* ed. Roger Chisholm, Matthew Tuite, and Michael Radnor (Chicago: Aldine, forthcoming).
* Seventeen assertions constitute the framework for the development of this paper. As they occur, they are numbered and italicized for ready reference.

organization's activities may affect another organization even though such an effect was not intended and even though the first organization is quite oblivious of the very existence of the other organization. When this relationship is reciprocal, one can speak of interaction, but not social interaction in the strict sense of the term. We need not quibble over terms here; the point I am making is that much of the impact of any organization on others is of this inadvertent type, though such impact may be crucial at times.

Beyond this unintentional one-sided or reciprocal impact are those actions in which the two or more parties deliberately relate their behavior to each other. It is this deliberate relating of one's behavior to that of another that Max Weber takes, incidentally, as the criterion of *social* behavior.[1] When it is engaged in by two or more organizations, we can quite appropriately speak of organizational interaction in the sociological sense. Such organizational interaction constitutes a broad field for study and research.

Within the broad field of organizational interaction is a much narrower field in which the interactional process is not confined to a series of mutual adaptations, but encompasses actions taken in concert toward ends mutually agreed upon: interorganizational decision-making.

This narrower field of interorganizational decision-making can be conceptualized as a part of the general concept of concerted decision-making. (3) *Concerted decision-making is a process in which the individual decisions of two or more units are made on a more inclusive systemic level that includes these units.* The rationale underlying the concerted decision-making is that the process will produce a more satisfactory outcome than would be the case if the units were left to make their own decisions independently.[2] In this paper the concept of concerted decision-making will be used as the basis for analysis of interorganizational decision-making.

A number of questions immediately arise from such a formulation. What is a "more satisfactory" outcome? For whom is the outcome presumed to be more satisfactory?

A number of additional questions concern themselves with the circumstances under which the process occurs:

Must the presumed greater satisfaction apply to all the participating organizational units?

What is the role played by coercion in this process, and how do voluntarily negotiated decisions compare with those that are coerced by third parties or by authority within a more inclusive organizational context?

Do units always concert their decision-making when the potential payoff appears greater? If not, under what circumstances do they concert their decisions and under what circumstances do they make them individually?

How inclusive is the *scope* of decisions that are concerted by a given number of organizational units as contrasted with the decisions made at the unit level?

What differences are there in the contexts within which organizational units concert their decisions, and what implications do these differences in context have for some of the above questions?

Such questions can be approached through a consideration of some important dimensions of concerted decision-making among organizations. Let us start with the question of organizational domain. In a current research project on organizational interaction, I have found it helpful to conceptualize domain in terms of an organization's access to necessary resources. In this conception, organizational domain is the organization's locus in the interorganizational network, including its legitimated right to operate in specific geographic and functional areas and its channels of access to task and maintenance resources. The two important components here are the organization's right to do something, and its access to the resources it needs in order to do it. This conception includes the organization's access to both input and output resources, and as such approximates James D. Thompson's definition.[3] It is broader than Thompson's, in that it includes not only those resources needed for task performance, which Thompson emphasizes, but also those needed for maintenance of the organization itself, such as legitimation, investment capital, personnel, and long-range supporters. We see continued access to such necessary maintenance resources as also constituting an important part of an organization's domain. In short, an organization's domain consists of access to those resources it needs to perform its task functions and to remain viable as a system.[4]

I do not believe that any of the subsequent analysis stands or falls on this particular conception of domain. The term has been elaborated only to indicate how it is used in the assertions to follow. The next such assertion, which we take as axiomatic, at least for purposes of the present analysis, is as follows: (4) *In its interaction with other organizations, an organization acts so as to preserve or expand its domain.* This proposition will be of help as we examine the circumstances under which concerted decision-making takes place; but first, two brief comments: The question arises whether the proposition is an assertion about the way organizations in reality behave or whether it applies to the way they would behave if they were completely rational. Actually, the latter is the case here, but I believe that the presumed rational behavior in this respect corresponds so closely to actual behavior in most interorganizational situations that the statement can be taken for our purposes as applicable to most organizational interaction. The same applies to the next assertion as well, to which we will come shortly. The second comment has to do with the circumstance that in some instances, in order to remain viable, an organization must reduce its domain. For example, an organization that has sought to diversify through producing a particular line of merchandise may discover that its venture is not profitable and may decide to withdraw from this activity, thus reducing part of its domain in order to preserve or enhance the remainder and thus assure its continued viability.

THE DIMENSION OF VOLUNTARISM/COERCION

We can now begin our analysis of a number of dimensions affecting inter-organizational decision-making. If our preceding assertions are valid, then it follows that (5) *organizations enter voluntarily into concerted decision-making processes only under those circumstances that are conducive to a preservation or expansion of their respective domains.* Where this situation does not exist, some degree of inducement or coercion is necessary in order to assure the participation of those organizations that see a net threat to their own domains in the concerted decision-making. The inducement may be some form of compensation to equalize the presumed loss to the organization in some aspect of its domain. If such inducements are not possible, then coercion must be exercised to secure participation. Such coercion may be divided for purposes of analysis into three forms: (*a*) coercion exercised by one of the organizations involved over one of the other organizations involved; (*b*) coercion exercised by a third party over one of the organizations involved; (*c*) coercion arising from authority flow within the same hierarchically structured organization.

The question of the relevance of coercion to the possibility of concerting certain orders of decisions among particular organizations is a crucial one. For on the one hand it is sometimes erroneously asserted that coercive power must always be present to assure that decisions are concerted and that the concerted decisions will be carried out; and on the other hand, unrealistic assumptions are sometimes made about the likelihood of persuading organizations to operate in the alleged public interest when there is neither coercive power nor reasonable assurance that each organization can preserve its domain in the concerting process. To sum up, concerted decision-making can take place where there is no coercive power, but it will take place only among those organizations that fear no loss of their respective domains and only on those issues that pose no threat to them.

(6) *In other instances, concerted decision-making is possible only if trade-off inducements can be offered to assure voluntary participation or if coercive power can be exercised to bring it about.* (7) *Such coercive power may be exercised by one or more of the parties over the other(s), or by a third party, or by legitimated authority within a hierarchical structure of which the organizations are an integral part.*

THE DIMENSION OF DECISION-MAKING CONTEXT

In the preceding paragraphs, an important consideration has been temporarily ignored—the organizational context *within which* one is considering the concerting of decisions by organizational units. At the one extreme, we may be talking about the concerting of decisions among virtually autonomous and mutually independent organizations. But on the other hand we must acknowledge that organizations often join together not merely around a single issue, but in more lasting frameworks through which certain types of decision-making are more or less regularly concerted. And organizational units may be combined in various types of organizational framework in which they are not so much independent organizations joined loosely for decision-making as subunits of a single formal organization, hierarchically organized for decision-making. Concerted decision-making is applicable to all these contexts, and it varies with them on several dimensions to be considered below. (8) *Since the concerting of decisions among organizational units may take place at various levels, it is important to identify the level at which the decisions are being concerted, and the context in which they are being concerted at that level.*

Four types of context have been differentiated and described. (9) *Decision-making contexts vary from the social-choice context through the coalitional and the federative to the unitary context.*[5] These types vary as to the structure of the context in which interorganizational decisions are concerted, from a non-existent structure at one extreme to a tightly integrated structure at the other. Specific dimensions of variation in these decision-making contexts include (*a*) the relation of the organizational units to an inclusive goal, (*b*) locus of inclusive decision-making, (*c*) locus of authority, (*d*) structural provision for division of labor, (*e*) commitment to a leadership subsystem, and (*f*) prescribed collectivity orientation of the organizational units.

The decision-making contexts range from the social-choice context at one extreme, with these six dimensions close to the zero point, through coalitional and federative to unitary contexts, where each of these dimensions has the greatest magnitude.

Organizations interacting in a *social-choice* context, where there is no concerting of decisions, may agree that they have mutual interests in concerting decisions around some particular issue; or, as in the analysis above, a third party may attempt to induce them to concert their decisions around some issue or project in the interests of a more inclusive system. Insofar as they do so voluntarily, they may enter into a *coalition*, under which they retain their autonomy but make decisions and act in concert only insofar as they see such behavior as preserving or enhancing their respective domains. There is little permanent structure, little sense of loyalty to a more inclusive decision-making unit, and no authority that the joint venture can exercise over its participants, and the concerted decision-making lasts only until the issue is resolved or for some other reason one or more of the parties no longer finds it desirable to maintain the decision-making interaction. An example is the campaign waged by a number of local industrial organizations to influence the official action of the city government.

Compared with the coalition, the *federation* is stronger on all of the dimensions mentioned above. Here there is not only a partial concerting of decisions through ad hoc interaction, but also a special organization set up for such concerted decision-making, involving strictly delimited parts of the total decision-making scope of the organizational units involved. And the occasion for the concerted decision-making is less likely to be an ad hoc, episodic issue than to be a continuous interaction around certain issue areas over an extended period of time. But the individual organizational units maintain their autonomy except in the strictly delimited area in which they agree to concert their decisions and actions. An example is the trade association.

In the *unitary* context, on the other hand, the organizational units are not autonomous but are part of a single hierarchical decision-making structure that orders their interaction, including the concerting of decisions.

The fourfold typology consists of four ideal types in the Weberian sense. It is not asserted that organizations in reality always fall neatly into one of these discrete types. They represent merely points on the continuum of dimensions. The typology is useful for analytical purposes, so long as this reservation is kept in mind.

To return for a moment to the dimension of voluntarism or coercion in concerted decision-making among organizational units, it is readily apparent that the concerting of decisions among relatively autonomous units involves the question of whether such units, operating in an otherwise social-choice context, wish to enter into a coalitional or federative context for purposes of concerted decision-making. Unless there is coercion, what we have said about the constraints of domain preservation applies. The coercive power that comes from authority flow within a legitimated hierarchically structured organization represents, of course, the unitary context.

THE DIMENSION OF ISSUE-OUTCOME INTEREST

A group of banking companies may pool its efforts to raise investment capital for a specific venture; a number of community agencies may cooperate to plan an application for a federal grant-in-aid program for their city; a number of organizations may concert their activity in opposition to a certain piece of proposed legislation. All these examples involve converging interests of two or more organizations on an ad hoc issue.

It is also possible for organizations to engage in concerted decision-making when their interests around the specific issue are opposed to each other. This type of occasion is sometimes overlooked when interorganizational decision-making is discussed. But it is apparent that organizations may make concerted decisions in areas where their interests do not coincide, and even where they directly conflict. In such cases, the parties wish a different outcome for the issue involved. They may negotiate as the principal parties to the issue. Or a third party may intervene as mediator, conciliator, or arbitrator; or the third party may be a unit or an official in a superordinate position within a formal organizational hierarchy, as when a dispute between department heads is resolved by the general manager.

(This latter, the unitary context, is admittedly a limiting case, for some may argue that the concept of interorganizational decision-making should not be carried over into the subunits of a single organization. But our approach to decision-making contexts makes this possible, though not necessary, and it is useful to pursue it, if only to indicate its applicability to those theoretical conceptions that consider even a so-called unitary organization to be in essence a coalition of subunits.)[6]

(10) *Concerted decision-making may occur under situations of issue-outcome interest convergence or divergence.* (11) *When issue-outcome interests of two or more organizations converge, their concerted decision-making is likely to be characterized by cooperative processes in the decision-making itself and in seeking to assure the mutually desired issue outcome.* Examples of such a mutually desired outcome would be the setting up of an industrial development corporation, the pooling of efforts in obtaining a government contract involving anticipated profits for the respective firms, and the passage of a particular bill before the state legislature. As can be seen from these examples, convergence of issue-outcome interests does not necessarily imply agreement about all the values or goals involved in the issue, but merely that the organizations want the same outcome of the specific issue. They may desire this for the most varied and apparently contradictory sets of reasons. The criterion here is that they want the issue resolved in the same way.[7]

(12) *When issue-outcome interests of two or more organizations diverge, their concerted decision-making is likely to be characterized by contest processes in the decision-making itself and in seeking to assure the mutually exclusive desired issue outcomes.* The decision-making regarding the disputed issue may or may not involve the intervention of third parties.

For purposes of simplification, no consideration has been given to the frequent cases in which organizations have similar issue-outcome interests in some respects but different interests in other respects. Thus, two or more organizations may have similar interests in forming a consortium to obtain a large government contract, but different interests with respect to the resources to be contributed to the venture and the share of the profits to be extracted from it by each organization. For our analytical purposes, these can be considered separate issues, for as Richard E. Walton points out, the quality of the interaction between organizational units differs as one or the other issue comes to the forefront.[8]

THE DIMENSION OF SALIENCE

In what has just been said, the nature of the concerted decision-making has been related to the respective issue-outcome interests of the participating organizations. For purposes of simplicity we have assumed that concerted decision-making is taking place. However (13): *Whether the situation is one of issue-outcome interest convergence or divergence, concerted decision-making is not assured, but depends on a number of variables that can be subsumed under the concept of salience.*

Let us consider first the case of two organizations with similar issue-outcome interests. One might expect that if they have similar interests in the outcome of a particular issue, say the passage of a particular piece of legislation, they will concert their decision-making regarding the ways in which they might respectively work to bring about the desired outcome. But in fact they may or may not act in this way. What are the important variables here? Let us consider the situation from the standpoint of one of the organizations, Organization A.

First, Organization A may not know that Organization B is also interested in the passage of the legislation. Thus it is apparent that the way in which Organization A scans the interorganizational field in search of opportunities to enhance its resource domain will to a large extent determine whether the process of concerted decision-making takes place.

Second, even if it is aware of Organization B's similar issue-outcome interest, Organization A may decide that the benefits offered by concerting decisions with Organization B regarding support of the legislation may not outweigh the resources that would have to be expended in the process. The issue itself—in this case, the passage of the legislation—may not be important enough to merit the investment of executive time in interorganizational conferences, strategy planning, and so on, and the resources to be expended in influencing the legislature, whatever these may be, could be excessive when compared with the prospective benefits.

Third, it may be that Organization A is simply unable to mobilize its resources to bring them to bear on the issue, even though it may consider the issue important. Because of the press of other matters, or because of its own incapacity to move rapidly and fluidly to enhance its own interests, it misses an opportunity to benefit through concerted decision-making.

Fourth, regardless of how important it may consider the issue, or how capable it may be of mustering resources for it, Organization A may feel that concerting decisions with Organization B will not affect the issue outcome. This may be because it believes either that both organizations are presently working as effectively without concerting their decisions as they might be expected to work if they concerted them, or that the fate of the legislation is pretty well decided in any case, and any additional impact that might be gained through concerted decision-making would not affect it.

Fifth, there may be a spillover to this issue from other episodes of cooperation or contest between' the two organizations. The fact that the two organizations have recently collaborated successfully on a similar matter may predispose them to take advantage of this new opportunity as well. On the other hand, recent interaction episodes in which their interests were opposed may make it less likely that the organizations will seize a given opportunity to collaborate to their mutual advantage.

Sixth, inducements may play a role in the decision to engage in interorganizational decision-making. Such inducements may be positive or negative, and may be offered either by the parties that would be directly involved in the concerted decision-making or by third parties.

In sum, given similar issue-outcome interests, organizations may or may not engage in joint decision-making to promote these interests, and in doing so they will be influenced by such considerations as the above. These considerations apply especially to the voluntary development of coalitions or federations from within the social-choice context. Organizational units within a unitary context are subject in addition to authoritative orders from a superior hierarchical level to concert their decisions, even when they might not otherwise care to do so. Yet even in these unitary contexts, the factor of issue-outcome interest and the six circumstances outlined above may also be applicable.

What is less apparent is the circumstance, mentioned earlier, that concerted decision-making may occur not only in situations of convergence of issue-outcome interest, but also in situations of divergence. In situations of issue-outcome interest divergence, it is likewise problematic whether or not concerted decision-making will take place. The scanning process is relevant in these situations as well, for there are numerous situations in which issue-outcome interests differ and where one of the organizations involved might see a potential payoff to entering into concerted decision-making, on the assumption that through such a process the issue will be resolved more favorably from its point of view than it would otherwise. Aggregately, this is a logical possibility in all but zero-sum situations, and even in zero-sum situations any organization, or even a combination of organizations, may consider it in its own interest to concert the decisions in attempting to resolve the issue.

Thus in issue-outcome difference situations, organizations may or may not concert their decisions, and whether they do depends on much the same considerations as those already given for situations of issue-outcome interest convergence.

These considerations have been discussed under the general rubric of salience, a term subject to ambiguity. As can be seen, it is used here only in the general sense of suggesting that the decision to concert decisions does not occur automatically, but is contingent upon the relative importance of the issue, the possible effect of the joint decision-making on the issue outcome, and so on.

THE DIMENSION OF INCLUSIVENESS
OF ORGANIZATIONAL INVOLVEMENT

(14) *On most issues, organizational interaction involves only a part of the personnel, interests, domain sectors, and resources of the respective organizations.* Only parts of the organizations may be interacting, with most of the other parts of the organizations possibly even oblivious of the very existence of the other organization(s) with which their own are presumably interacting. Likewise, the same organizations may be interacting in a competitive fashion with respect to certain aspects of their domains, and in a cooperative fashion with respect to other aspects, and not at all with respect to still other aspects of their domains.

Thus, if we are to do justice to the complexity of interorganizational decision-making, we must recognize the importance of the dimension of inclusiveness of organizational involvement in interaction in general and in concerted decision-making in particular. There is space here to explore only some of the aspects of the fact that interorganizational decision-making usually involves only parts of the organizations in only parts of their total domains.

We have already touched upon one of these aspects in referring to previous episodes of successful concerted decision-making as a factor in the decision to concert decisions. A successfully concluded and mutually advantageous business transaction between two organizations may become the basis for additional transactions that spread to other types of goods or services. The basis for the interorganizational decision-making may be more than an individual transaction, however, and may take the form of a more permanent collaborative relationship of some sort, as when two governments agree to consult each other before taking action in certain areas, or the organizations may set up even more formal and permanent machinery for concerted decision-making in certain aspects of their domains, as in a trade association.

As can be seen, the dimension of decision-making context is definitely relevant to that of organizational involvement. (15) *Generally, the extent of an organization's involvement in concerted decision-making around a specific issue is small or nonexistent in the social-choice context, larger in the coalitional, still larger in the federative, and largest in the unitary context.*

In another vein, just as concerted decision-making applies both to similar issue-outcome interests and to different issue-outcome interests, the degree of organizational involvement in concerted decision-making may either grow or diminish in both types of issue-outcome interest situation. Increasing involvement in interaction is implied in the concept of conflict escalation. On various levels of social organization, including the formal organizational level, what begins as a relatively minor controversy may escalate to one of major proportions. Part of this process of escalation is the involvement of more and more of the personnel and resources and domain activity of the respective organizations in the conflict process. And as the conflict spreads within the organizations, it may come to involve a larger number of issue areas. It may also spread to include the search for allies, the involvement of third parties in the conflict.[9] Parenthetically, conflict episodes are resolved through victory of one of the parties, through compromise, through the coercion of third parties, and so on. The resolution of the conflict involves a rapid or slow de-escalation that in our terms can be seen in a lesser organizational involvement in the conflict interaction.

All this is widely recognized. What is not so widely recognized is the fact that cooperation also may escalate, may involve more of the respective organizations' personnel and resources and domain areas, may draw third parties into the cooperative process, may eventually reach a peak and then de-escalate, as various of these aspects are no longer involved or become involved less intensively. Thus (16): *The escalation and de-escalation of either cooperative or contest processes is associated with the degree of organizational involvement in interaction on the issue.*

Hence the extent of organizational involvement in concerted decision-making is a variable, and will be great or little, whether in issue-outcome divergence or convergence situations, depending on the anticipated effect of the interaction on each individual organization's resource domain and on the considerations of salience discussed earlier. Escalation and de-escalation of the interaction process, whether of a cooperative or contest nature, can be analyzed in terms of the scope of respective organizational involvement in such aspects as personnel, other resources, and the breadth of the domain sector involved.

(17) *Two organizations may engage simultaneously in different types of cooperative or contest interaction focused on different issues and involving different configurations of personnel, interests, domain sectors, and types of resources applied to the issues.*

The complexity of these situations can be accommodated conceptually so long as we recognize the importance of specific issues or issue areas as foci of organizational interaction, and so long as we recognize that organizations seldom act totally on any issue.

This analysis of concerted decision-making among organizations has emerged in the application of some earlier conceptualizations to a current interorganizational research project in which we are examining the interaction of a specific number of so-called community decision organizations, or CDOs, in nine American cities. The CDOs under study are the board of education, the local urban renewal agency, the poverty agency, the health and welfare council, and the mental health planning agency, if there is one. The purpose of this research is to gain more knowledge of the way in which the interaction of these organizations (and others with similar characteristics) affects the outcome of decisions at the community level.

In devising a model of CDO interaction to guide the development of our methodology, it seemed helpful to make certain interrelated assertions about interorganizational behavior that could then be either precisely or roughly tested in our research. We tried insofar as possible to formulate our assertions about the interaction of these community decision organizations in a way that would be applicable to other types of organizations as well, such as, for example, business firms, trade unions, and national governments. Whether or not they can be so broadly applied is problematic. Indeed, we are not even sure that they apply to the community decision organizations we are studying. We feel sure there will be many revisions as a result of our research. Meantime, we have found them helpful, and it has been helpful also to apply some of them to the topic of the concerting of decisions as a variable in organizational interaction. Suggestions are welcome, particularly regarding pertinent areas of interorganizational decision-making to which this type of analysis seems less applicable or relevant.

NOTES

[1] Max Weber, *Wirtschaft und Gesellschaft*, ed. Johannes Winckelmann (Cologne and Berlin: Kiepenheuer & Witsch, 1964), vol. 1, p. 3 and chap. 1 *passim*.

[2] The concept of concerted decision-making is elaborated in my "Concerted Decision-Making in the Community," in *The Social Welfare Forum, 1965* (New York: Columbia University Press, 1965), and chap. 9 of this volume.

[3] See James D. Thompson, *Organizations in Action: Social Science Bases of Administrative Theory* (New York: McGraw-Hill, 1967), pp. 22ff.

[4] The importance of the viability of the organization as a system, in contrast to the importance of merely one aspect of its functions—task performance—has been emphasized recently by Ephraim Yuchtman and Stanley E. Seashore in "A System Resource Approach to Organizational Effectiveness," *American Sociological Review*, 32, no 6 (December 1967), and in an earlier article by Amitai Etzioni, "Two Approaches to Organizational Analysis: A Critique and a Suggestion," *Administrative Science Quarterly*, 5, no. 2 (September 1960).

[5] For an elaboration of this typology, see my "The Interorganizational Field as a Focus for Investigation," *Administrative Science Quarterly*, 12, no. 3 (December 1967), and chap. 11 of this volume.

[6] See Richard M. Cyert *et al.*, *A Behavioral Theory of the Firm* (Englewood Cliffs, N.J.: Prentice-Hall, 1963), pp. 27ff.

[7] For an analysis of the relationship between issue-outcome interests and action strategies, see my *Types of Purposive Social Change at the Community Level*, Brandeis University Papers in Social Welfare no. 11 (Waltham, Mass.: Florence Heller Graduate School for Advanced Studies in Social Welfare, Brandeis University, 1965), and chap. 1 of this volume.

[8] Richard E. Walton and Robert B. McKersie, "Behavioral Dilemmas in Mixed-Motive Decision Making," *Behavioral Science*, 11, no. 5 (September 1966).

[9] James S. Coleman has documented the process for community conflicts. See his *Community Conflict* (Glencoe, Ill.: Free Press, 1957), pp. 9–14.

13

THE INTERRELATIONSHIP
OF COMMUNITY DECISION
ORGANIZATIONS

It is doubtful that anyone could prescribe a set of recipes for collaborative planning among local organizations like community action agencies* and funds and councils, and I am not going to try. In each city relationships must be worked out which take full account of the unique local situation, including personalities and politics, as well as the larger context within which organizations of this type operate.

CAPs, councils, and funds are community decision organizations, in the sense that they, along with housing authorities, boards of education, health departments, urban renewal authorities, and a number of other organizations are legitimated by the community to engage in planning and to make decisions on the community's behalf in their respective spheres of operation. Some of us have come to use the term "community decision organization" to describe them, or CDO for short.

As they seek to improve relationships with each other, CAPs, funds, and councils, like other CDOs, can do so only within the limitations that are imposed upon them by the federal government, city hall, various power structures, and the poor. It is wholesome and inspirational to talk about collaborative

Paper presented at the Training Project for Community Leadership, Institute for Big Cities, Chicago, February 1968, jointly sponsored by United Community Funds and Councils of America and the Office of Economic Opportunity. Original title: "Strategies for Social Planning at the Community Level."
* These are local antipoverty agencies funded by the Office of Economic Opportunity. I shall designate them by the more popular abbreviation CAP, for community action program.

planning, but a realist will be aware of three underlying truths, whether or not he talks about them.

The first is that organizational planning not only must involve purely technical considerations, but must take into account organizational constraints.

The second is that organizations do have different interests, and while these often overlap in a supportive fashion with those of other organizations, some of them will overlap in competitive fashion.

The third is that an organization cannot be expected voluntarily to accept joint planning goals that will be at its own net expense. Unless these realities are taken into consideration, talk about collaborative planning becomes merely ritualistic.

COORDINATION, INNOVATION, AND RESPONSIVENESS

Turning now to the goals of community planning, I would like to point out that organizational goals and community goals are not necessarily identical. For example, let us take the goal of more efficient planning and delivery of services to the poor. It is one to which, at least in the abstract, CAPs, funds, and councils can all agree (though each must work toward that goal within the limits of its own constraints). At the broader community level, however, a more inclusive set of goals must be taken into consideration. They are goals or objectives that have a bearing on many matters other than service delivery to the poor. They have been, in one way or another, a part of a whole series of programs within larger cities, including the Ford Foundation Gray Areas Program, the program of the President's Committee on Juvenile Delinquency, the program of the Office of Economic Opportunity, and now the program of the Model Cities Administration. These three goals are coordination, innovation, and responsiveness.

Coordination among various CDOs becomes increasingly necessary at the community level because of the existence of a plurality of planning centers whose interests overlap and which compete for scarce resources. We have been telling each other this for a number of years now, but precisely what do we mean by coordination? Let me give a number of meanings that have frequently been applied to the word:

1. A mutual checking out of plans so that two or more organizations may act in full knowledge of each other's intentions.
2. Formal or informal agreements to avoid duplication of services.
3. Joint planning of new programs that go beyond the domain of any single organization.
4. Setting up mechanisms, formal or informal, for settling differences on issues when the interests of the organizations conflict with each other.

There is an additional meaning of coordination, often implied when we use the term. This is coordination in the allocative sense. In this sense, two or more CDOs are coordinated from the community standpoint when the benefit from expenditures for their respective programs yields equal utility to the community, in terms of the value it places on their respective goals. In this conception, coordination assures that the community, with its various goals, is getting the greatest return for its money in terms of its investment in each of the organizations.

Both the funds and the councils have assumed a responsibility for coordination at the community level in just this sense. The funds have been primarily concerned with the allocation of voluntary donations in such a way that presumably they will be optimally distributed among the member agencies in terms of the community's needs and priorities. Likewise, the councils have been concerned with the allocation of agency energies into programs and projects, jointly or separately, where presumably they will yield a higher aggregate return than they would if each member agency were to go it alone.

We do not have space here to explore the various ramifications of *allocative* coordination, as this type of coordination might be called. Let me simply observe that there exists no single allocative body that can bring about such coordination *among* CDOs like the funds, councils, CAPs, or any of the others. They are thus left with the task of trying individually to get the greatest possible amount of resources and support for their respective endeavors in a process that is essentially one of competition rather than allocative planning.

There is a still different meaning of coordination—one that is often overlooked but nevertheless highly relevant. In this meaning, two or more organizations are coordinated to the extent that the behavior of one is modified in accordance with the behavior of the other(s). When two organizations go their own ways in utter disregard of each other, there is no coordination. Coordination occurs as the action of one comes to be based, in part at least, on the action of the other. Obviously, cooperation is one possible form of such coordination, and conflict is another. We do not often think of conflict as a form of coordination; but it is, if we mean by coordination the adaptation of one organization's behavior to that of another. Let us call this meaning of coordination *adaptive* coordination.

I have tried to make clear that allocative coordination is something different from adaptive coordination. In the difference lie some implications for the interrelation of CAPs and funds and councils that will be considered at the end of this paper.

Innovation is another important objective of community-level planning, and one being emphasized by various federal agencies. But what is innovation? Like coordination, the word is subject to varying interpretations. The usual meanings seem to relate to the notion that the needs of the urban poor, for example, will not be adequately met by giving agencies additional resources to do more of what they customarily do. The implications are that even if resources available to the agencies were doubled or trebled, present programs would not really meet the problems.

Much of the thinking behind the Economic Opportunities Act and the program development of the OEO were based on the assumption that the older, well-established agencies in the service delivery system were not capable of adapting to new ways and were poor bets either for the types of innovative program that would be needed or for actually getting out and finding new ways to involve themselves with the poor, as distinguished from predominantly middle-class clients. In addition, there was considerable feeling that the constraints of the voluntary agencies as well as of such public agencies as health and welfare departments were such that they too could not be sufficiently flexible, sensitive, and creative.

To be sure, there is another sense in which the term "innovation" is used. It is used at times to denote an alternative to service programs as the principal means of helping the poor. Thus, when some people talk about the need for innovation they mean that increasing emphasis should be placed on changing the social and physical structure of the environment in which the poor live, in contrast to providing services. Emphasis is thus placed on employment opportunities, on adequate income maintenance provisions, on extensive low-cost housing construction, on school improvement, on attracting private capital into the slum areas, and so on. And of course it is true that as one emphasizes such social strategies for confronting poverty, he moves away from the usual type of services that the more traditional health and welfare agencies—voluntary or governmental—have been accustomed to provide.

As we all know, the antipoverty program's experience with the goal of innovation has been mixed; and as many of us had predicted, the Office of Economic Opportunity itself soon began to settle down into a number of more or less standard programs that it funded in a fairly regular bureaucratic manner. The hectic and relatively fluid situation in which the OEO and the various CAPs have found themselves is probably attributable to the exigencies of congressional action more than to the innovativeness of the organizations themselves.

But is there not an inherent conflict between the goal of coordination and that of innovation? I recently had occasion to conduct a number of interviews with CDO executives in three large cities, and to compare their organizations on a number of matters. It appeared that the executives who were the most task oriented, and, in a sense, the most bold, imaginative, and innovative, were the least interested in coordination. Or, better yet, they understood coordination to mean how you get the other organization to do what you want it to do. Coordination for them was a sort of ecumenical movement in which everyone joined their church. Most of the innovators, in other words, seemed to be passionately devoted to furthering some particular set of goals within the framework of the school system or the urban renewal authority or the health department, as the case might be. They had little interest in how the other CDOs were making out. They were trying to get the most resources they could for their own organizations, and couldn't care less about the optimal allocation of resources and effort *among* the CDOs. Optimal for them meant the most for their own organizations and their obviously worthwhile goals.

On the other hand, the people who were concerned about inter-CDO coordination didn't seem to be terribly innovative. They weren't passionately devoted to one set of goals to the exclusion of others. They tried to secure a balance among many goals. This kind of disposition, I believe, is not conducive to innovation.

There seems to be a basic contradiction between trying to advance some particular goal, on the one hand, and trying to keep all goals in balance, on the other. John Friedmann has made a brilliant analysis that helps explain the incongruity. He distinguishes allocative planning from innovative planning, pointing out their incompatibility. He describes allocative planning as a process of "rational decisions optimizing results for all sub-systems," and then contrasts it with innovative planning, which "seeks to obtain the largest possible amount of resources for its projects, even if this should mean weakening competing organizational purposes." It thus "inevitably ignores large parts of the total value spectrum of the society."[1]

But notice one thing. Within his own organization, the innovative planner must make the most effective use of his own resources; he must plan allocatively. It is in his stance vis-à-vis other organizations that he furthers his own organizational goals at their expense.

As mentioned earlier, at the community level there is no overall allocative planning body. Even the budgeting function of the city government is in only partial control of the resources that are available to the local governmental CDOs—for example, the board of education—and has still less control over an organization like one of the funds and councils, or even the CAP, although that may now soon change.

Let us turn to the third planning goal of the new community programs, that of *responsiveness* to the poor. I use the term "poor" here loosely, since presumably the responsiveness called for is to the organization's clientele, whether or not it be below the poverty level. In the jargon of the trade, the aggregates of parties to whom an organization is responsive is called a constituency.

It helps to divide organizational constituencies into two sections. The one is the *input* constituency, to whom the organization acknowledges a role in the determination of its policies; the other is the *output* constituency, the people whom the organization acknowledges an obligation to serve. Thus, for a manufacturing company, stockholders form the major part of the input constituency, customers form the major part of the output constituency. For a service agency, its governing board or those who appoint or elect it form the major part of its input constituency, and its clients form the major part of its output constituency. In simple English, our community organizations are not customarily responsible to those people whom they are supposed to serve.

Now the interesting—and controversial—part of the CAP structure is that through deliberate policy the OEO has provided that the output constituency of the CAPs should be represented in their input constituency: that those whom they serve should have an official voice in determining their policies. We are all familiar with the complex series of circumstances that the activation of this policy has induced.

And interestingly, the councils too have changed their input constituencies over the past decade or so. Earlier, the input constituency consisted clearly and virtually exclusively of the member agencies. While these still form an important part of the input constituency of the councils, this constituency has been expanded to include representatives of the community at large, people who by virtue of their formal or informal positions are thought to represent the broader interests of the larger community. Putting this more succinctly, they are members of the community power structure.

I wonder if there is doubt in anyone's mind that the future will see the poor represented more strongly on the input constituency of organizations like the CAPs *and* the councils—and yes, eventually, the funds.

If the power of the poor in policy decisions is to increase, then who will represent them? CAP executives are familiar with the difficulties of finding "true" representatives of a segment of the population that is unorganized as a group. Sporadic façades of organizations arise, have their day, and decline. Would-be leaders come onto the scene with personal followings of undetermined size, claiming to represent a broad segment of the poor. A thousand people can perhaps be turned out for a protest demonstration, but maintaining an organization and developing a policy and a program are left in the hands of a few. These are the anomalies that come from recognizing the obligation to give a voice to a segment of the population that is not organized for purposes either of developing its own opinion, or of choosing its own leadership, or of formulating policy positions. But such organization will come; indeed, it has in part already come. The changes over the past five years have been tremendous.

What organization at the community level will "represent" the poor in years to come? I do not mean an organization that will develop services for the poor, or act in an advocacy role on behalf of the poor. I mean an organization consisting of the poor, speaking for themselves through representatives they themselves have designated, in the way the best of the labor unions represent their members and derive their strength and resources from them. There are many related questions here. What organization will represent the power structure or the service agencies or city hall vis-à-vis the poor? What organization will provide a bargaining and negotiating arena within which the interests and proposals of these various groups can be resolved?

Such questions, granted the shifting coalitions and constituencies that form the backdrop for today's local planning efforts, are closely related to another kind of realistic question: What will be the future power base of the CAPs, or the funds, or the councils? From which groups will they be able to get the resources they need to stay in business as organizations and, God willing, to accomplish their goals? To remain viable, each CDO must be able to get the resources it needs. Of course, it may not be important to the community that a particular CDO remain in business, but few organizations willingly opt out. Here is another indication of the difference between community-level goals and organization-level goals.

Coordination, innovation, and responsiveness are thus community-level goals, and hence they are relevant as we discuss not the internal allocational problems within CDOs, but their relationships with each other.

THE INTERRELATIONSHIPS OF CDOs

Let us see what the implications of all this might be for strategies of community planning involving the interrelationship of such CDOs as the CAPs, the funds, and the councils.

As a basis for analysis, let us note that any two CDOs may find that their respective goals and interests in an issue agree or disagree. They may agree in favoring a proposal or in opposing it. Or they may disagree, with one favoring the proposal and the other opposing it. The disagreement may be not only as to whether a certain thing should be done (goal disagreement), but as to which of them should do it (domain disagreement). To repeat, then, they may agree or disagree on the desired outcome of a particular issue.

But as indicated earlier, there is another dimension to their relationship. They may coordinate their actions, each one adjusting its own actions to those of the other, or they may not. They may interact vigorously or go their separate ways, regardless of whether their goals coincide or differ.

Thus (and you might have expected this from a sociologist) we have a four-cell table.

Table 13-1

ISSUE OUTCOME

		Agree	Disagree
INTER-ACTION	High	I. Active Cooperation	II. Active Contest*
	Low	III. Potential Cooperation	IV. Potential Contest

* The term "contest" is employed as a broader concept than that of "conflict," which is reserved for the attempt to harm a contestant or force him from the contest. See Roland L. Warren, *Types of Purposive Social Change at the Community Level*, Brandeis University Papers in Social Welfare no. 11 (Waltham, Mass.: Florence Heller Graduate School for Advanced Studies in Social Welfare, Brandeis University, 1965) and chap. 1 of this volume.

Just to make things more tangible, let us take some illustrations of situations in each box, involving the relations between a CAP and, for example, a council.

I. Active cooperation. They are working jointly on a program involving services to the poor which they both want to see brought about.

II. Active contest. They are locked in a domain struggle regarding who is to engage in planning and program building in a certain area of endeavor, each feeling that it should have the major role. Or the CAP favors some new program or measure that the council opposes.

III. Potential cooperation. They have many interests in common which have never been jointly explored, and many possibilities for collaboration which have not been exploited.

IV. Potential contest. Although there are many points of possible dispute over respective domains, these issues have not come to a head.

Once we look at these different situations systematically, we realize how complex they actually are; but at least we begin to have a way of dealing with the complexities.

For example, we often make certain debatable assumptions regarding collaboration and conflict. Let us make two such assumptions for the moment, and qualify them later. Let us assume (1) that any movement in the direction of box I is desirable, and (2) that any movement away from box II is desirable.

And let us remind ourselves that in dealing with organizations like CAPs and councils, we are considering CDOs that have their own sets of goals, that these goals overlap with those of other CDOs, and where they overlap they may be mutually supportive or mutually exclusive. Also, each CDO is a relatively autonomous organization, despite the constraints that may be placed upon it by the federal government, city hall, various power structures, and the poor. And, to repeat, there is no overall allocative body that can adjust their relationships to each other through deliberate administrative action. Rather, they all compete in the community arena for legitimation, resources, and clientele.

Acting on our first assumption, that active cooperation is preferable to the other three possibilities, how is it possible, under the above circumstances, to increase the scope of active cooperation between two or more CDOs? What we are looking for is a means of heightening the interaction in areas where mutual goals and interests are such that each organization can benefit through closer interaction. A number of means for doing this are available, and to save time let us simply list some of them:

1. Use of common data banks, including population projections and various social indicators, so that both the CAP and the council work from the same set of data as to what the existing situation is and what the future situation is likely to be.
2. Procedures for overlapping board and committee members, thus providing important bridging roles for people who are thus made competently familiar with both organizations.
3. Broadening the scope of interaction to include personnel at different hierarchical levels, including the lending or exchange of staff members for specific ad hoc collaborative ventures.
4. Prompt communication of proposed policy or program changes, so as to facilitate the other organization's adjustment to any proposed change.
5. Specific procedures between the CAPs and the councils for feedback and subsequent reformulation of proposed changes in their respective policies and programs.
6. Through various measures, including some of the above, continuous scanning procedures for specific ad hoc matters in which joint planning will further the program interests of both the CAP and the council.[2]

It will be noticed that all of these means may be useful in moving from potential cooperation to active cooperation. Some of them are also useful in moving from situations of potential contest toward active cooperation, or at least in avoiding active contest.

Let us pass now to the second assumed goal, that of avoiding or moving away from active contest. While some of the devices mentioned above may help avoid active contest, it is doubtful that this is in all cases possible. Differences over both what the organization is trying to accomplish and which organization shall be the one to take on some task may be so great that they become salient and interaction of a contest nature is increased, as each organization seeks to get its way despite the opposition of the other. Keep in mind that this condition arises precisely because there is no overall allocative body with power to prevent this somewhat untidy situation regarding organizations with overlapping goals, interests, resources, and constraints. They do not all fit within a single formal organizational structure. Indeed, this is one of the important and enigmatic characteristics of communities as social entities, as distinct from formal organizations themselves.

Some of the suggestions already made may help to *avoid* active contest. The suggestions regarding *reducing* it are fewer in number, but more complex.

First, specific provision can be made for methods for central decision-making to break impasses or resolve contests among CDOs. This can be done in several ways. For example, with many of the municipal or semimunicipal CDOs, the mayor or development coordinator often is in the position of resolving a conflict and in effect telling both organizations how things are going to be. Similarly, in some communities, depending on the nature of the conflict, a relatively small group of influential people, both official and nonofficial, will resolve such an impasse over an informal and unpublicized lunch, perhaps at the Bankers' Club. The point is that it is a help to have special emergency procedures, as it were, for resolving impasses. And this applies to CAPs, councils, and funds as well as to other CDOs. The alternative may be protracted contest, which prevents effective action and spreads the area of controversy.

Second, efforts can be made to contain the contest. When two CDOs such as a CAP and a council get into an eyeball-to-eyeball situation over a particular issue, it is important to resolve the issue and keep it from spreading to other aspects of their relationship—in terms of our table—to keep these other aspects from slipping away from active cooperation in the direction of active contest.

There seems to be a motion clockwise from active contest through potential contest and potential cooperation toward active cooperation, and a possible motion in the other direction. As a result, active contest on one issue may spread to another issue on which there has been active cooperation and tend to pull it away toward potential cooperation. Or active contest on one issue may spread so that another issue on which there is only potential contest breaks out into active contest. Thus the areas of contest between the two organizations involved must be contained.

But there is also the matter of containing the contest as it tends to spill over into relationships with still other organizations and individuals. James S. Coleman has pointed out that community conflicts tend to spread, involving even parties who would prefer to remain neutral, and involving issues not directly related to the primary issue in contest.[3] E. E. Schattschneider has also treated this matter of the spread of conflict, pointing out that often one of the parties to a conflict finds that his chances of winning will be better if he enlists a wider circle of participants. Thus he seeks allies, and the process of escalation begins.[4] Here again it is important to note the difference between the interests or goals of an organization and those of the larger community. They are not necessarily identical. It may be in an organization's interest to spread the conflict, while it may be in the community's interest to contain it.

Before closing, let us revert briefly to the assumptions that active cooperation between organizations like the CAPs and the funds and the councils should be furthered, and active contest should be avoided. Of course, we can smile piously at each other and affirm both of these propositions. But from the standpoint of the individual organization, if the goal is sufficiently important and the organization is sufficiently confident of winning, it is difficult to persuade it voluntarily to cool it. In terms of its own organizational goals, it may be impossible to make a rational case for anything but contest, with an "I win, you lose" outcome. Why can't we be honest about this, while at the same time acknowledging that not all cases of active contest need to take that form, and acknowledging also the possibility that, from the perspective of a wider set of interests, it may be desirable to contain the contest, and to resolve it with all deliberate speed so that it does not spread?

On the other hand, we can likewise spend more of our effort in setting up kinds of relationships and techniques for communication such as those suggested earlier which may move issues from the area of active contest to potential contest, from potential contest to potential cooperation, and from potential cooperation to active cooperation.

It is not always clear that active cooperation is the most promising path for one or both organizations as they pursue their respective goals. There is some evidence to indicate that organizations that do not depend on other organizations for important resources are less likely to interact with other organizations than those that are dependent.[5] In such circumstances the case for cooperation cannot be made at the organizational level, but has to be made at a more inclusive level. Although each organization might be somewhat constrained by the cooperative relationship in pursuing its goals unreservedly, in the inclusive context the cooperative relationship and its outcomes are more important to other parties than either organization's single-minded pursuit of its own specific goals.

In addition, we are not at all sure that the community's interest always lies in the total exploration of every possible avenue of interorganizational cooperation. The community might be more greatly benefited by equal amounts of energy exerted in the single-minded pursuit of each organization's separate goals. The people whose work we look back upon with admiration often tend to fit more closely the innovative planning model than the allocative one.

Nevertheless, even a realist can hope for and expect that organizations such as CAPs, funds, and councils will actively scan the horizon for opportunities where cooperation promises a high payoff to each organization in accomplishing its own goals. I have tried to indicate some of the possibilities and some of the constraints under which this process can take place.

NOTES

[1] John Friedmann, "Planning as Innovation: The Chilean Case," *Journal of the American Institute of Planners,* 32, no. 4 (July 1966): 195.

[2] These and other suggestions are dealt with more systematically in Roland L. Warren, "The Interorganizational Field as a Focus for Investigation," *Administrative Science Quarterly,* 12, no. 3 (December 1967), and chap. 11 of this volume.

[3] James S. Coleman, *Community Conflict* (Glencoe, Ill.: Free Press, 1957).

[4] E. E. Schattschneider, *The Semisovereign People: A Realist's View of Democracy in America* (New York: Holt, Rinehart & Winston, 1960).

[5] Sol Levine and Paul E. White, "Exchange as a Conceptual Framework for the Study of Interorganizational Relationships," *Administrative Science Quarterly,* 5, no. 4 (March 1961).

14

MODEL CITIES FIRST ROUND: POLITICS, PLANNING, AND PARTICIPATION

One development dominates all others in the planning period of the model cities program. This is the unexpected emergence of the "resident participation" element as a powerful reality that has changed the entire conception of what the planning process would be like and what goals might be accomplished. Other developments of a relatively unanticipated type have likewise taken place, raising issues concerning the structure of power and the nature of decision-making as these are being changed by the rapidly moving sequence of events in American cities. Some of these developments will be considered later, but first and perhaps most important is the escalation of resident participation.

During the time between the first-round planning grant applications and the actual award of model cities supplementary grants to the first few cities (roughly, May 1967 to January 1969), a lively drama of politics, planning, and participation has unfolded in the sixty-three original cities designated for the grants. Since July 1968, the Interorganizational Study Project in the Florence Heller Graduate School for Advanced Studies in Social Welfare at Brandeis University has had field staffs in nine of these cities, gathering systematic data for a study of the interorganizational behavior of a specific cluster of community decision organizations. By "community decision organization" (or CDO) I mean an organization legitimated to carry on planning and/or program activities in some sector of broad community concern.[1] The specific organizations under study are the community action agency of the antipoverty program, the

Reprinted by permission from *Journal of the American Institute of Planners*, 35, no. 4 (July 1969).

local public authority of the urban renewal program, the board of education, the health and welfare council, and the community decision organization for mental health, where there is one. The formal analysis of the relationships explored in the somewhat rigorous design will not be available for some time, since the fieldwork is to continue for two years. Meantime, narrative reports from these cities indicate some patterns of potentially great importance.

The nine cities of the study are Oakland, California; Denver, Colorado; San Antonio, Texas; Detroit, Michigan; Columbus, Ohio; Atlanta, Georgia; Newark, New Jersey; Boston, Massachusetts; and Manchester, New Hampshire. Each of these cities was in the first round designated in November 1967 for planning grants. Seven of the cities range between 375,000 and 650,000 in population, but Detroit was purposely chosen for its much larger size (1,660,000 people in 1965), and Manchester for its smallness (90,000 in 1965). The seven medium-sized cities were selected to represent not only a wide geographic coverage but a wide distribution on thirteen variables thought to be important for the study, such as percent nonwhite and per capita income.

RESIDENT PARTICIPATION:
THE GENIE IN THE BOTTLE

It is already apparent that resident participation, perhaps originally conceived as something that could be contained, like the genie in the bottle, has somehow emerged and grown to impressive proportions, presenting the fateful question of what role this powerful new force on the urban scene will play in future decision-making, and what the consequences will be .

The emergence of resident participation as a dominant issue is by no means a total surprise. There had been the experience with OEO, and with predecessors such as the Ford Foundation Grey Areas Program and the program of the President's Committee on Juvenile Delinquency and Youth Crime. It was quite deliberate that the model cities legislation (Demonstration Cities and Metropolitan Development Act of 1966) provided for "widespread citizen participation in the program," a much milder formulation than the "maximum feasible participation" that the Economic Opportunities Act had provided. The mandated participation was to be appropriately circumscribed with the definite proviso that, unlike the poverty program, the model cities program would remain within the ultimate control and responsibility of the local municipal authority.

Despite the provision for "widespread citizen participation," the genie was to be kept comfortably in the bottle. "The poverty program was for the people," complained one CAA director ruefully. "This one (model cities) is for city hall." There was much evidence to support this assertion. In the first place, it was one of the declared aims of the model cities legislation to strengthen local government's ability to confront local problems in a concerted fashion. The program would for the first time give city hall a tremendous resource for comprehensive, concentrated programming, with the inducement of a grant of 80 percent of nonfederal contributions over and above the massive matching funds available through the existing federal programs, provided such rational planning procedures as costs-benefits analysis and program budgeting were followed.

In the light of subsequent developments, it is interesting to review a series of commentaries on the Demonstration Cities Program which appeared in the *Journal of the American Institute of Planners* in November 1966.[2] In five articles, the authors explored the implications for planners of the new program. The issue of resident participation was given modest attention. James Q. Wilson mentioned citizen participation in connection with its incompatibility with the announced objective of maximum coordination achieved by a "single authority with adequate powers." Bernard J. Frieden pointed out that "the objective of widespread citizen participation may conflict with federal and local pressure for early, visible results," and went on to discuss some of the factors that might be expected to exert pressure in the direction of responsiveness to resident wishes. Marshall Kaplan addressed the question at greater length, his main emphasis being on the difficulties of establishing a viable system for representing the neighborhood as an entity. He asserted that "instead of planning for residents of the city, planners will have to plan with them." But even his comments gave little indication of what the following period was to bring forth—a somber, in many instances acrimonious dispute between resident organizations of growing power and growing demands on the one hand, and city hall and various agencies, governmental and nongovernmental, on the other.

The massive growth of resident participation has by no means been uniform in the nine cities of the Brandeis study, and in this respect these cities appear to reflect the nationwide experience. Yet the nine cities show, with only relatively minor variations, a distinct pattern of development during the planning stage, roughly from the submission of the planning grant applications in May 1967 up through the year 1968.

In virtually all of these cities, the application for a planning grant had been developed by city hall in some relation to a number of citywide agencies: urban renewal, the antipoverty agency, the health and welfare council, and several others. Little or no resident participation went into most of the original planning grant applications, and what little there was took the form of last-minute airing of the substance of the planning grant documents, with little opportunity for meaningful feedback and reformulation. The flurry of interagency activity that preceded the submission of the applications by May 1, 1967, quickly subsided, and in many cities relatively little was accomplished until November, when announcements were made for the first round of model cities. Even after the announcement, a period of a few or many months was to elapse before each particular city received its grant contract for the planning phase. Oakland's contract was not awarded until January 1969, delayed by the inability of city hall and the neighborhood residents to come to a satisfactory agreement regarding their respective prerogatives.

Although many people, of whom I am one, had anticipated vigorous competition among the leading citywide agencies to protect or expand their respective domains, in most of the nine cities the model cities developments during this entire period were dominated by the struggle of neighborhood residents with city hall for various degrees of power or control over the program. The period was characterized chiefly by the relative quiescence of the agencies in comparison with this struggle.

Toward the end of the period, as deadlines for submission of the model cities plan were approached, the agencies reentered the scene in a more active way. Significantly, their role was not that of the giants who would cut up the pie, but rather that of providing expert consultation on the various committees and task forces that were developing component plans in such areas as health, education, social services, housing, and so on. It is anticipated (but *caveat anticipator!*) that the agencies will play an increasingly important role as general plans begin to be cast into implementable forms and concrete program components. But will the agencies' relationship to the planning process ever be the same again?

The admonitions given in late 1966 to agency planners by H. Ralph Taylor, assistant secretary of HUD in charge of the program, already sound like an echo from an earlier historic period:

> New techniques for extensive and inexpensive rehabilitation, experimental approaches to urban taxation, new building systems and materials and construction techniques, flexible building codes and trade practices, a new urban design which can revitalize a slum neighborhood without tearing it down and starting anew, and creative new ways of involving residents in planning and carrying out programs, are all hoped-for innovations.[3]

What makes these words outdated is not their substance, but the underlying implication that somehow the agency planners were to have the initiative in the model cities planning process. In many of the study cities, they have not had it, generally, in the first year and a half of the program since the planning grant applications were submitted. The idea of planners finding "creative new ways of involving residents" must have an especially hollow ring in those cities where resident involvement has developed and escalated as a result not of the innovative initiatives of planners, but rather of the active determination of neighborhood resident organizations to fight their way into a position of greater decision-making power than city administrations wanted to give them.

Yet large community decision organizations such as urban renewal agencies, health and welfare councils, boards of education, and antipoverty agencies appear to have tremendous staying power, and it would be unwise to write them off merely because over a period of months they were eclipsed by other participants in the model cities turmoil. One recalls the earlier efforts of the new antipoverty agencies to bypass existing citywide agencies and to set up their own programs while relating directly to a poverty-laden constituency. The other agencies showed tremendous staying power under this challenge—on the one hand by sitting on the boards of the poverty agencies themselves, on the other hand through securing the contracts through which the poverty agencies became less of a threat than a new source of funding. These other agencies were well ensconced in the power structure, and they often had powerful allies in city hall.

Will these other agencies be successfully contained as the servants of neighborhood groups in the model cities programs, rather than as the principal decision-makers? While they have been somewhat in eclipse, only a foolish man would predict their eventual inability to get back into the key spots in the decision-making structures, or to dominate these in some way. One most likely avenue to such domination of model cities by these powerful community decision organizations is their expertise. While they did not play such a strong role as anticipated in the setting of goals and priorities, they began to come back into the action when it came to drafting the actual plans for supplementary grants. And presumably they will be needed even more directly in their execution. Thus they may eventually come to eclipse the power of city hall on the one hand and the neighborhood residents on the other.

A preliminary scrutiny of the structure of the model cities program committees or task forces in various cities lends credibility to this speculation. Yet two things give pause. One is the undoubtedly greater power that neighborhoods are coming to gain under the model cities program, and the other is a process that might be called "reverse cooptation." For there are indications—not everywhere, but in several of the cities—that some of the very agency experts who are being lent out to model cities are coming to behave less like the agencies' men in the model cities program than like the model cities' men in the agencies. They are coming, in other words, to behave like advocate planners for the neighborhood.

The process is too young and not sufficiently widespread to permit its dimensions and implications to be assessed. One hint from a small number of cities is that a certain selectivity operates in the choice of the experts that the agencies are lending out to the city demonstration agency and to the model neighborhood organization. It may be that the expert who has shown an interest in neighborhood participation, or skills in working with neighborhood people, is more likely to be chosen—and in turn more likely to become coopted into a virtual advocacy-planner role for the neighborhood residents.

In two or three of the cities studied, resident participation has not grown beyond a minimum of power over model cities decisions. In some others, it is considerably more substantive, while in a number of others it has grown to truly impressive proportions.

The growth of resident strength is indicated by the amount of funding available to the various model neighborhood boards for engaging their own planning staffs, responsible to them, rather than depending on planning staff parceled out from the model cities agency or from some of the other community decision organizations. It is also indicated by formal provisions assuring the model neighborhood board specific important prerogatives in the planning and implementational process. And it is indicated operationally by the ability of neighborhood residents to extract concessions from city hall in response to specific, hard-pressed demands.

In the matter of funds for their own staffing, the model neighborhood board in one of the cities in the study was able to get independent funding for its extensive planning and consultational activities from the Office of Economic Opportunity. In two cities, the model neighborhood boards were allotted budgets of $106,000 and $99,000 respectively for the planning period. In many instances, planners and experts from various agencies took part at the behest of more or less autonomous neighborhood planning committees, rather than at the behest of the city administration or the community decision organizations.

Examples of formal prerogatives in decision-making are the veto power over all model neighborhood programs won by the boards in some cities; domination by neighborhood residents over the task forces or planning committees in various substantive areas, and in at least one instance over the board of the model cities agency itself through a guaranteed majority of neighborhood residents on the board; and the expansion of decision-making prerogatives to include a strong voice or even a veto of other types of federally funded program in the model neighborhood.

The narrative reports from many of the cities contain references to hard-fought disputes in which neighborhood organizations were able to wrest one concession after another from the city administration in the contest over prerogatives and procedures. One neighborhood board insisted successfully that the model cities agency be located in the mayor's office rather than as a part of the Department of Development, much further down the chain of command. In another city, a local resident organization was successful in having its own plan for citizen participation substituted for the plan originally proposed by the city administration. As is widely known, Newark was the center of a vicious controversy over the location of the campus of the New Jersey College of Medicine and Dentistry in the model neighborhood. In vigorous negotiations with neighborhood groups, strong concessions were made to the local residents, concessions that involved a greater control in model cities and related programs. And in Oakland a long struggle eventuated in numerous important substantive concessions gained by the West Oakland Planning Committee.

To repeat: in two or three of the nine cities, there was very little indication that neighborhood participation was more than perfunctory. But in the others, various combinations of such items as the above added up to impressive degrees of substantive power, power gained largely not because it was planned by the city administration, but more typically in a vigorous contest with the city administration. As Hans Spiegel and Stephen Mittenthal sum things up: "Neighborhood power and a measure of control, envisioned neither by HUD nor by the cities, gradually began to slip in under a number of negotiating tables."[4]

How can one account for the extent to which the component of resident participation, neatly encompassed in the original legislation and anticipated in the manner of the previously quoted sentence from Assistant Secretary Taylor, took on such unexpected momentum in places like Oakland and Newark, Boston and Detroit? There are several reasons why neighborhood residents have come on strong in these and other cities.

First, there is little doubt that some of the impetus came from the Model Cities Administration itself. In the discussion papers that accompanied the November 1967 announcements of the first round of cities designated for planning grants there were frequent stipulations regarding the spelling out or strengthening of the provisions for resident participation in the model cities planning. Regional HUD officials emphasized in varying degrees to the individual cities the importance of setting up meaningful channels of resident participation. The Model Cities Administration's CDA Letter No. 3 of October 30, 1967, on citizen participation interpreted the original act's provision for "widespread citizen participation in the program" to mean that the city government must be responsible "that whatever organization is adopted provides the means for the model neighborhood's citizens to participate and be fully involved in policy-making, planning and the execution of all program elements," and required that the plan must spell out just how such participation and involvement were to be carried out.

But perhaps more important, though less focused, was the existence of a social dynamic in the disadvantaged neighborhoods of America's cities, a dynamic for neighborhood power and control. This dynamic constitutes a virtual social movement, a movement that was undoubtedly given impetus by the anti-poverty program, though it did not originate with it. It is a movement that is associated with a number of other movements, including the movement for decentralization, for participatory democracy, and, of course, for black power.

In most though not all of the study cities (not Manchester and not San Antonio) there was a growing minority population of Negroes who were gradually coming to be solidified through the civil rights struggle and through their experiences with the antipoverty program. In several instances they had also had experience with the Ford and Delinquency Committee programs. They had begun to develop experience in bargaining with city hall, to sense some of the power (so analogous to Sorel's myth of the general strike) that riots or threats of riots had given them, and to grow in bitterness and militancy toward governmental programs allegedly in their interest but run by whites. It did not take them long to realize that they had tremendous leverage over city hall in the fact that unless their own channels of power and control over the program were satisfactorily established, they could prevent their cities from being awarded a contract. As they began to look over the fine language on resident participation contained in their cities' model cities planning grant applications and recalled that up to that point, at least, they had hardly been consulted in the matter, the struggle for control of the program intensified.

Perhaps these neighborhood leaders had learned a lesson from the antipoverty programs—namely, that in a coalition form of decision-making, such as the Community Action Agency boards, even though it was stipulated that one-third of the membership should come from the poor, they could be out-maneuvered and outvoted by more powerful interests. If their participation in model cities was to be meaningful—if it was to be substantive rather than merely administrative, in Selznick's terms[5]—then they would have to gain much more power than they had had in the antipoverty community action programs.

An additional feature of model cities made the stakes much higher and at the same time favored stronger neighborhood organizations. This was the fact that the model cities coordinated approach was to deal with the same specifically designated model neighborhood across the whole broad range of programming. Individual programs such as urban renewal, education, antipoverty, mental health, and others that had fragmented the disadvantaged areas into numerous geographic districts were now brought together in the same neighborhood with the same boundaries, with provisions for leadership selection, discussion of issues, and representation across the comprehensive range of programming. Hence the stakes were higher for control over this more focused neighborhood effort.

Thus two things converged in these model neighborhoods. One was a neatly thought-out provision for resident participation in the program. The other was a powerful movement for neighborhood control which already had a dynamic of its own immeasurably more powerful than the spurt that could be given it by any governmental program, and presumably impossible of eventual containment by any such governmental program. It was already manifesting itself, quite aside from model cities participation, in various types of neighborhood demands and actions for school decentralization, for neighborhood control over social agencies, police, industry, and jobs.

Viewed with detachment, the resident participation provided for in the model cities program served the function of helping to contain this growing social movement, to give it direction, and to channel it in ways acceptable to the white majority. But, to repeat, the social movement for neighborhood control had its own powerful dynamic, quite aside from provisions in the economic opportunities program or the model cities program.

This being the case, Daniel P. Moynihan's criticism of the earlier anti-poverty effort for its emphasis on social action and participation in policy-making by the poor seems somewhat fragmentary.[6] On the one hand, he seems to argue that too little real power was offered them; on the other hand, too much. But in either case (and of course, both can be true at the same time: too much of this kind, too little of that), it was no longer possible even in 1964 to ignore with impunity the growing awareness of ghetto residents that their neighborhoods were not their own and that they would have to win them by any means available. And even if it had been possible to ignore this gigantic new dynamic on the urban scene in 1964, it is hard to excuse ourselves for ignoring it today, after the experience of the poor with the community action programs. The question is not neighborhood organization or no neighborhood organization. The question is how this powerful social movement will be related to various institutionalized channels for improvement of living conditions in American cities.

Parenthetically, are not the days of single simplistic solutions to ghetto problems already passed? Precisely because the problems are so important, can we still afford to waste our time listening to people who see *the* solution to ghetto problems in more coordinated social services, or in neighborhood action, or in housing, or in jobs alone?

It is perhaps possible to exaggerate the importance of the extent to which the movement for neighborhood power and control has escalated in the first phase of the model cities program. It is still too early to tell whether the trappings of neighborhood power described above will actually play a determining role in decisions made at city hall or in the various community decision organizations. As already mentioned, the large community decision agencies have tremendous staying power, and their innings are yet to come. Likewise, the power of city hall over potential threats to its hegemony has been highly apparent throughout the antipoverty experience and has not yet been fully mobilized in the model cities encounter. It may yet develop that the hard-won gains of power by neighborhood residents will prove to be more apparent than real.

Yet one thing seems certain. If the impressive preliminary gains that model neighborhood residents have made vis-à-vis both city hall and the agencies turn out to have been only chimerical, bitterness and violence will be unleashed sooner or later in the ghettos. Resident participation in some meaningful form is no longer an option open to well-meaning liberal policy-makers. It has become an imperative.

COMMUNITY DECISION ORGANIZATIONS AND MODEL CITIES

The Brandeis Interorganizational Study, as it is called, concentrates on the interaction of a specific cluster of community decision organizations in each of the nine cities I have listed. As mentioned earlier, these particular CDOs participated more or less actively in early 1967, then faded out and later began to become more active in different form as the final planning documents were drawn up.

It is interesting to compare the behavior of these different types of organizations across the nine cities in connection with their model cities participation, even though the comparison is based on narrative, impressionistic data from field research associates in the respective cities.

As expected, the CAAs (antipoverty agencies) were already on the scene with neighborhood organizations of the poor, and both at the city level and at the neighborhood level they attempted to guide or influence or control the model cities program, particularly its resident participation aspects. In a number of cities, they made a bid to take over the resident participation function, succeeding in only one or two cities but playing an important role in several of them. In some instances they were more or less rejected by the neighborhood residents for having allegedly made their peace with city hall. Their predominant impact took the form of the presence in many cities of a group of neighborhood organizations and local leaders who had gained experience in the antipoverty program and could afford an identifiable basis of leadership in the model neighborhoods.

Because model cities is a HUD program, because of the aggressiveness and relative fluidity of the urban renewal agencies in a number of cities, and because the neighborhoods to be chosen were to be such as would be pertinent for renewal programs, it was assumed that urban renewal agencies would play a predominant role in model cities planning and development—even to the extent of preventing the explicitly mandated social components from developing. Was model cities to be, despite all the rhetoric, essentially a "bricks and mortar" program? There were many people who thought this was highly likely.

Yet in only two of the nine cities in the Brandeis study did the urban renewal agency actually play a predominant role during the period under consideration. There appear to be three sources of explanation for this relatively modest activity. One is the influence of federal and regional HUD offices and of the entire federal interdepartmental application review system that was set up; these added up to strong constraints on local procedures that might have converted the model cities programs into primarily a program of the urban renewal type. Another was the growth of neighborhood resident power and neighborhood interest in a wide range of programs. Another was a product of the somewhat balkanized structure of physical planning in many cities, with the various agencies that might have emphasized the physical aspects of planning (city planning commission, housing authority, urban renewal agency, community renewal program, etc.) in different types of organizational relationship to each other—a situation that in aggregate constituted a diffusion, rather than a centralization, of the agency power and interests that represent the predominantly physical planning approach. Parenthetically, the fact that these agencies receive large parts of their budgets from the same federal department, HUD, may seem anomalous only to those who do not realize that HUD itself reflects this loose coalition of substantially autonomous agencies, each with its respective constituency, sources of influence, and cluster of goals.

The boards of education in the various cities responded to model cities approximately as expected. It was assumed that with their independent tax base, their lack of dependence on city hall in most instances, and their independent access to state, federal, and foundation funds in addition to their own local taxing power, they would play a more detached role than the central position of the school system in the model neighborhood configurations would indicate. This assumption was borne out. With only minor exceptions, the boards of education appeared to be standing aloof, going it alone, dragging their feet, and in other ways acting the part of agencies whose bases of support and domain were assured and did not depend on success in the model cities struggle.

The health and welfare councils showed perhaps the greatest intragroup variation of any of the CDO types. At least one of them has been entirely aloof from the entire model cities development. Several of the others were prime movers, particularly at the beginning, when they attempted to interest city hall in taking advantage of the new model cities legislation in late 1966, partly as a result of a nationwide conference called by UCFCA, the national association. Like many of the other agencies, they seemed to be eclipsed, after early participation in developing the original planning grant application, by the contest between city hall and the neighborhood residents. Their reentry into the model cities interaction toward the end of the planning period was in some cases particularly noticeable. And interestingly, they often came back in as consultants rather than as primary participants in their own right.

The choice of mental health organizations for special study along with the other CDOs was a deliberate attempt to observe an area of community interest and concern where no single CDO is usually found planning and carrying out community-wide programs in the sense that the other CDOs do. The participation (or lack of it) by mental health organizations in the nine cities studied indicates dramatically the lack of strong citywide decision organizations in the mental health field, and in their absence the attempt by individual organizations of various types—hospitals, clinics, medical schools, governmental units at different levels—to relate themselves meaningfully to model cities.

The fact that mental health is not mentioned among the detailed areas of interest of the basic legislation but is mentioned in the *Model Cities Program Guide* indicates its marginal nature, in the sense that it is relevant and open to exploitation but not mandated. Hence the extent to which mental health organizations entered the model cities planning system depended at least in part on their interest in participating—that is, their perception of the relevance of mental health programs to the model cities effort—and presumably on their ability to get in if they cared to. There was little interest shown by mental health organizations in some cities, while in others there was interest but an apparent inability to become "relevant," to get into the interorganizational whirl out of which programs were spun off.

The lack of citywide community decision organizations in mental health which can speak with authority for the mental health sector as the other organizations can speak with authority in their respective fields appears to be a definite handicap to mental health organizations in the model cities program. The strategy of setting up catchment areas of 75,000 to 200,000 people for purposes of community mental health centers has had the effect of placing the major organizational thrust at the subcommunity level for cities much larger than 200,000. It would appear that insofar as mental health organizations consider themselves relevant to the problems of the inner city, they are at a disadvantage organizationally for citywide decision-making on fast-moving programs like model cities.

POLITICS, PARTICIPATION, AND
THE CONCEPT OF PLANNING

The fact that the planning process for model cities was characterized by a struggle for control over the program between city hall and the neighborhood residents, with the major citywide agencies waiting on the sidelines, is fraught with implications for those who are interested in community planning. Actually, for many of the first-round cities, this period did constitute the planning period, during which their efforts were supported by planning grants from HUD to complete the outlines of a five-year model neighborhood plan and to complete in detail the plan for the first of these years.

Yet field reports from city after city indicate that the process by which the plan was developed bore little resemblance to conventional models of the planning process. The conception of the planner as centrally engaged in the planning process—setting goals, assessing means and resources, assigning priorities, and selecting courses of action—simply did not hold up. All of these conventional planning functions were performed, but they were performed in an essentially political process in which (a) the planners themselves were not in control or in any position of major direction of the process, and (b) no other single decision-making entity that could be said to "plan" was in central control of the process.

But is this not often the case? How relevant is it to the urban planner's role to consider that somehow he is plugged in close to the decision-making power, if he does not have it himself, and that his task is to operate in terms of aggregate processes, aggregate goals? It is this conventional concept of the planner's role that has led to a decade of debate regarding the political and rational components of planning, and the ways in which they are to be mixed— as though the planner himself controlled the sluice gates.

Whether or not such a conception of the urban planner's role ever corresponded to reality, it certainly did not correspond to the reality of the model cities planning period. For even in those cities where the neighborhood–city hall struggle was not so pronounced, the process took the form of a political adjustment among major community decision organizations, the model that the Brandeis staff had mistakenly anticipated would predominate in all the cities. Here again the process was essentially a competitive political struggle for enhancement of domain and accomplishment of goal-oriented objectives by the respective competing organizations.

In the light of the complex process that took place, it is interesting to reflect on the model cities goal of coordination. In the original *Program Guide* designed to set out the criteria and performance standards for the first round of model cities, coordination was a principal function of the city demonstration agency, the officially designated body for operating the program: "To the maximum extent feasible, it should have the authority to reconcile conflicting plans, goals, programs, priorities and time schedules; to eliminate overlaps; and to link operating programs among contributing agencies."[7]

In most cities, the central model cities staff members were arbiters, adjusters, seeking a way to remain viable by keeping as many of the competing parties as satisfied as possible—while keeping HUD satisfied as well. This process afforded a measure of coordination, more through the competitive interplay of opposing interests than through any controlled process of coordinated allocation. There was little evidence of decisions made in accordance with professional rather than purely partisan considerations. While the overall model cities rationale called for the designing of programs specifically suited to attack the problems as these had been identified in the original planning grant application, there is little indication that this process took precedence over the competitive interplay of interests and objectives of various groups and organizations.

Much has been said of the emerging role of the advocacy planner, and most of this has been directed to the relationship between a planner and a disadvantaged constituency, for which he presumably performs two entirely separable functions (often merged in the concept): providing technical expertise to his constituency and representing the constituency's interests vis-à-vis other groups, such as the agencies or city hall. Quite aside from the fact that these two functions are not necessarily optimized in the person of any individual planner, is there not an additional important consideration here that has been largely ignored? I am referring to the fact that the planners who were active in this essentially political process of decision-making that went into the model cities plans were *all* advocacy planners.

As Lisa R. Peattie asserts:

> Advocate planners take the view that any plan is the embodiment of particular group interests, and therefore they see it as important that any group which has interests at stake in the planning process should have those interests articulated. In effect, they reject both the notion of a single "best" solution and the notion of a general welfare which such a solution might serve. Planning in this view becomes pluralistic and partisan—in a word, overtly political.[8]

Some of the planners in the model cities planning had the model neighborhood residents as their primary constituency. Others, specifically those in the model cities agency staff, had the city administration as their constituency. Still others had other agencies—the urban renewal authority, the board of education, the antipoverty community action program, the health and welfare council, etc. —as their constituencies. They not only supplied technical expertise to their respective agencies; they represented these agencies' interests in the political process of decision-making that determined the shape and form and substance of the model cities plans.

It is interesting to consider the relation of federal agencies to individual cities from the perspective of the foregoing analysis. In the review of early field reports from the nine cities of the Brandeis study, one of the elements receiving explicit attention was the influence of federal agencies in general, and the Model Cities Administration of HUD in particular, in the local model cities planning process. The thing that stood out clearly in the numerous instances of federal intervention in the model cities process was the essential fallacy of considering this intervention in the gross terms of the relation of the federal agency to the individual city. For although the fiction is maintained in the case of model cities that the Model Cities Administration and the HUD regional offices relate directly (and exclusively) to the municipal administration, the sociological reality is that they relate differentially to various interacting groups and organizations within the individual cities.

The federal-city relationship in grant-in-aid programs is highly variable. The influence of any particular federal agency may be allied with a particular agency, such as the antipoverty community action agency or the urban renewal authority. In another case, it may be brought in as an ally of city hall. In still another, it may be operating in alliance with neighborhood residents vis-à-vis city hall or the agencies. In still another, its weight may be brought to bear on the side of this or that faction of residents within the model neighborhood itself. Hence it is useless to cast this relationship in terms of the federal government, or even the federal agency, and the local community. In this political struggle for organizational domain, for decision-making power, and for substantive objectives, the federal agency does not relate to the community as such, but to the individual actors in the situation, either as a potential ally or as a potential opponent who will be drawn in (if possible) by the potential allies and kept out (if possible) by the potential opponents. It thus represents— through legislation, possible grants-in-aid, regulations, and the acts of its official representatives—both a set of constraints within which the local struggle for goal setting, resource allocation, and program formulation and implementation takes place, and a potential ally or opponent to one or another party to the local situation at points of crisis.

In this situation a conception of the community planner (notice the ambiguity of the term and the ease with which it misleads) as an expert helping develop community-wide plans according to some rational interpretation of the public interest does not fit the reality of model cities planning or, one might suspect, the reality of many other planning efforts. Bernard J. Frieden wrote a few years ago:

> Increasingly, planners will be working for special-purpose agencies. The growth of separate planning centers will pose formidable problems of management and coordination. The traditional concept of master planning, with its image of a single program fitting together all the separate pieces of public policy, will be even less applicable in the future than it is today.[9]

The model cities planning experience lends support to this assertion. It suggests a more pertinent conception of the planner as one who provides expertise and representation to a particular constituency within the larger political struggle to shape aggregate plans. To the extent that this is the case, then:

1. The planner must be considered a key actor in the essentially political process of interorganizational decision-making.

2. The planner must be recognized as representing a constituency, rather than merely acting from Olympus in an alleged public interest.

3. The planner's role must be redefined by substituting a model of the planning process in which any individual planner is a consultant not so much to the entire planning system as to one of the parties thereto.

4. The injection of rational-technical considerations by the planner usually occurs in relation to certain of the respective parties to the political decision-making process rather than in relation to the whole process.

5. Rational-technical considerations are an adjunct to the pursuit of socio-politically determined goals both within the respective decision-making organizations and among them.

The implications of this conception might form a useful backdrop against which to review the curriculum of university departments of urban planning and schools that train for social welfare planning, broadly conceived. They might show a broad discrepancy between the reality of the planner's participation in fast-moving, complex programs such as model cities and the more conventional models of the planner's tasks which have survived from an earlier (and simpler?) era.

NOTES

[1] For an elaboration of the concept, see my "The Interaction of Community Decision Organizations: Some Basic Concepts and Needed Research," *Social Service Review*, 41, no. 3 (September 1967), and "The Interorganizational Field as a Focus for Investigation," *Administrative Science Quarterly*, 12, no. 3 (December 1967), chaps. 10 and 11 of this volume.

[2] H. Ralph Taylor and George A. Williams, William L. C. Wheaton, Marshall Kaplan, James Q. Wilson, and Bernard J. Frieden, "Comments on the Demonstration Cities Program," *Journal of the American Institute of Planners*, 32, no. 6 (November 1966).

[3] *Ibid.*, p. 367.

[4] Hans B. C. Spiegel and Stephen D. Mittenthal, *Neighborhood Power and Control: Implications for Urban Planning* (New York: Institute of Urban Environment, Columbia University School of Architecture, 1968), p. 62.

[5] Philip Selznick, *TVA and the Grass Roots: A Study in the Sociology of Formal Organization* (New York: Harper Torchbooks, 1966), p. 220.

[6] Daniel P. Moynihan, *Maximum Feasible Misunderstanding: Community Action in the War on Poverty* (New York: Free Press, Macmillan, 1969).

[7] *Improving the Quality of Urban Life: A Program Guide to Model Neighborhoods in Demonstration Cities* (Washington, D.C.: U.S. Department of Housing and Urban Development, Office of Demonstrations and Intergovernmental Relations, December 1966), p. 11.

[8] Lisa R. Peattie, "Reflections on Advocacy Planning," *Journal of the American Institute of Planners*, 34, no. 2 (March 1968): 81.

[9] Bernard J. Frieden, "The Changing Prospect for Social Planning," *Journal of the American Institute of Planners*, 33, no. 5 (September 1967): 321.

SECTION

D

Broader Concepts, Broader Values

INTRODUCTION

In contrast to the chapters of the preceding section, there is little continuity among the three in this one. One could string them together loosely on a broad conception of values, but let us not belabor the matter.

It is really surprising, at least to the layman, that sociologists, particularly those who concern themselves with communities as locality groups, can point nowhere to a sociologically respectable model of a good-community, and how its various parts and processes would operate to sustain it. In this respect, economists are much further along in describing a state of affairs that can be considered good in the sense that it maximizes utility. They are able not only to describe such a model, but to analyze it into its constituent parts and to trace the dynamics through which the optimization process is sustained. While the theory is highly abstract, it has nevertheless proved of great practical value in application to the individual entrepreneur and the choices he faces, and to the national economy.

Where is the corresponding sociological model? "Toward a Non-Utopian Normative Model of the Community" addresses this general question. It does so in response to the highly challenging effort of an economist who, in the absence of a normative sociological model, constructed one from Parsonian theory and pointed out that its presumed characteristics were diametrically opposite to those of the economists' model. Generally, to promote maximization of utility, the economic model calls for a highly differentiated society with a complex exchange system, a society that is allegedly incompatible with the sociological model, which calls for homogeneity, consensus on values and roles, and a consequent minimum of differentiation and division of labor. The first part of this chapter challenges this economist's point of view on the basis that it is a mistaken conclusion drawn from an admittedly ambiguous part of

243

Parsonian system theory. There is no reason to conclude that a sociological model need be any less differentiated than that which is prescribed for economic optimization.

In constructing a sociological model, it appears inevitable that it will contain certain value assumptions, explicit or implicit. But from sociological theory alone, such value assumptions cannot be validated. Whose values, then, shall be chosen for maximization? One way in which the sociologist can contribute to the answer to this question is to investigate and describe the impact on other values of the attempt to maximize the attainment of a particular value. The analysis of this chapter suggests that three values commonly accepted as desirable by many students of the community cannot all be maximized simultaneously, but that in a certain sense, one value is purchased at the expense of another. As indicated, this is a researchable question, and a small body of empirical research already exists to suggest the feasibility and utility of such analysis. Sociologists should, and can, contribute more than naïve speculation to the great policy issues that beset American communities today.

From a highly abstract and analytical analysis we turn to one that is low in both characteristics, being only a minimal conceptual ordering of an otherwise largely descriptive account. The account is autobiographical, depicting my own two-year experience in a mediatory role in the highly contested situation of a divided Germany. As Quaker international affairs representative in Germany, I was able to gain a considerable degree of legitimation for a virtually unique role—that of friend of all the conflicting parties with the full knowledge of those parties, while playing the role of devil's advocate in political conversations.

Several things stood out in this experience. One was the remarkable degree of similarity between the two opposing thought-action systems and the way they were sustained in interaction; another was the manner in which these two interacting systems constituted a conflict intersystem; still another was the first-hand experience with role innovation, the development of a new social role in relation to the various groups to whom the role was pertinent. A related question, familiar to those who seek to bring about social change, is the problem of entry or access to the system in which they hope to bring about some degree of change. Hence the title: "The Conflict Intersystem and the Change Agent."

Of all the chapters in this book, the last, "Truth, Love, and Social Change," was the most fun to write. It is better thought of as an intellectual romp than as a systematic analysis. Although it ranges over a wide field, it deals with a central theoretical problem that has been of concern to me for many years. When should one stand fast and take on all comers, saying with Martin Luther, "Here I stand, I can do no other. God help me. Amen!" and when should one rather be mindful of the relativity of knowledge, of the ambiguity of values, of the way we often find ourselves looking back on such instances with remorse that we did not instead seek to find a basis for agreement?

The larger question has hovered over many of the chapters in this book. It is implicit in the consideration of censensus and dissensus situations, in the choice of collaborative or contest strategies, in the conception of planning as a unified process related to a social system or as a competitive struggle among representatives of various constituencies, and in many other contexts throughout this book.

In this final chapter, it is given an even broader context for analysis. Truth is given a special meaning here: the sense of assurance we may have that we are right and that the opponent is wrong and that the issue is important and cannot be resolved through compromise. Love likewise is given a special meaning: the alternative path of seeking agreement, of making major concessions, of honoring more the humanity in the contestant than the substantive difference that is at stake.

It will probably seem to the reader a tour de force to relate this issue to a whole series of dichotomies: knowledge by acquaintance versus knowledge about; intuition versus reason; the poetic philosophers versus the systematic philosophers; lyric poets versus logical expositors; I-thou versus I-it; reconciler versus prophet; process orientation versus task orientation. Such a reaction would be entirely plausible, for that is just what it is: a tour de force.

Nevertheless, there does seem to be a conceptual and existential affinity among those alternatives of the respective dichotomies that run along the "truth line" and those that run along the "love line." No presumption is made here of converting these observations into a rigid law of nature. Yet there seems to be more than mere adventition in these juxtapositions. What I am trying to say is that there are many facets to this apparent dualism, along with deep roots and wide applicability.

On a more practical level, the implications for public policy would seem to point toward the advisability of a dynamic pluralism, which affords perhaps the least unsatisfactory resolution to the problem summed up in these two sentences:

We must confront head on the problem of change situations where there is abiding opposition, and where not everyone can be satisfied. We can neither take, nor even allow, the way of pushing one's own value in total disregard of other values, either of one's own or of other people, nor can we take the way of failing to cope sufficiently rapidly and radically with the problems that beset us merely because we cannot reach perfect agreement as to how to proceed.

15

TOWARD A NON-UTOPIAN
NORMATIVE MODEL
OF THE COMMUNITY

Sociologists have eschewed attempts to develop normative models* of such social entities as societies, formal organizations, informal groups, and communities, largely because of a commitment to *Wertfreiheit*. In recent years, though, three developments have changed the basis for this avoidance. First, the value objectivity of sociological investigation has come increasingly to be considered a myth. Second, many sociologists have come to accept the open injection of values into sociological analysis, particularly in order to make their analysis relevant to the great social policy issues of the day. Third, the absence of analytical models has appeared to impede the usefulness of sociological analysis for purposes of social policy formulation. A recent instance is the need for models in determining which social indicators may be important for a social report of the nation, and indeed which direction along the corresponding dimensions is desirable.[1]

Four types of investigation bear in one way or another on the question of normative models in sociology for such entities as communities. The first type covers the series of utopias dating from Plato's Republic to the most contemporary attempt to construct imaginary societies. Such utopias have been useful either in illustrating an abstract philosophical point (in Plato's case, the nature

Reprinted by permission from *American Sociological Review*, 35, no. 4 (April 1970). Adapted from a paper presented at the annual meeting of the American Sociological Association, San Francisco, September 1969. Notes have been renumbered.
* Models that contain implicit or explicit prescriptions as to how a given social entity should be constituted, on the basis of value affirmations.

of justice) or in offering social forms that represent alternatives to the values of the author's own day.[2]

The second type is the study of the historical formation of intentional communities, attempts to enact rather than merely to conceive utopias. Such attempts arise typically as efforts to construct a society that institutes an alternative set of values to those of the contemporary society.[3]

The third type includes the new towns that constitute a focus of current activity. They differ both from the utopias and from the intentional communities in that they usually do not present alternative value bases and social structures to those of the contemporary society, but rather constitute presumably more efficient ways of attaining them. Sociologists are coming increasingly to be consulted on such projects; but on what basis do they consult? What constitutes a good community, in terms more objective than the value position of the individual sociologist?

Fourth are the prescriptive models, attempts to urge the maximization of a particular set of community values: guides to action that swing from value statements to prescriptive admonitions to sociological findings and back again,[4] and attempts at a prescribed set of characteristics that strive for objectivity but nevertheless appear to conceal implicit value preferences. In this category probably belong as well the various representatives of the community movement, that group of social scientists, philosophers, planners, and others who admonish their colleagues that the community is dying and seek to preserve and enhance the values they purport to have found in the preindustrial, agricultural communities of another day.[5]

ECONOMIC AND SOCIOLOGICAL MODELS

Is there an alternative to purely utopian thought or to unsystematic prescription on the part of the sociologist? Harold F. Kaufman writes:

> The social value of community research may be measured by the extent to which it contributes to realizing the types of community that people desire. In this endeavor the sociologist has a continuing challenge to work with action leaders in developing and making explicit various alternative designs for the good community and suggesting conditions under which these goals may be realized.[6]

One might consider the possibility of a model of a local community that would fulfill some of the functions that the economist's model of the market fulfills for him. In a recent article, Mancur Olson dramatizes the need for systematic thinking regarding a community model by taking the bull by the horns and fashioning his own model based on Parsonian system analysis. Although the result is in many respects unconvincing, Olson should at least be congratulated for attempting to provide something that sociologists might better have provided themselves.

Briefly, Olson commences with a conventional economic model, using the example of an international common market, and pointing out that diversification, division of labor, and trade are conducive to the greatest aggregate productivity. Likewise, within a society, diversification, occupational mobility, and differing backgrounds, beliefs, and values are basic to the optimum economic model. He describes this model as do virtually all economists, in terms of aggregate productivity and optimal distribution of utility measured on a unidimensional scale.

> In essence, the economically ideal society would maintain a Pareto-optimal allocation of resources at every moment in time *and* at the same time continually change to the best attainable production functions as knowledge advances. The rate of accumulation of productive knowledge and other forms of capital would be the maximum consistent with the society's rate of discount of future versus present consumption.[7]

Olson emphasizes that such an ideal economic model, based on diversification, is fundamentally incompatible with a sociological model of the ideal society. For his sociological model, he uses his own formulation, adapted from the theories of Talcott Parsons and his followers. He points out that their theory emphasizes institutional integration, and socialization for stable roles about which there is general consensus. The very stability that is necessary to assure institutional integration and to avoid individual alienation makes demands that are the polar opposites of those made by the economic ideal.

> If the demands or values of different groups or associations with overlapping memberships or objectives are incompatible, and different people have conflicting expectations about what people with particular roles should do, then the degree of integration is limited and the possibility of societal disintegration increased.[8]

Olson goes on to point out:

> The continuous reallocations and rearrangements that are needed to satisfy maximally all of our other individual wants (be they material or not) is not usually consistent with the stable or enduring interpersonal relationships that most people apparently value and need.[9]

In this aspect of his analysis he seems to make the different but compatible point that most people desire more of a sense of *Gemeinschaft* than the demands of economic optimization would allow.

Although Olson does not explicitly say so, one can only conclude that he assumes that the ideal sociological model of community is the prototype of the closed-system, commensalistic, custom-bound, sacred, preindustrial community, and that an open-system, symbiotic, contractual, secular, industrialized community is utterly foreign to the sociological ideal. If this seems absurd to most sociologists, three circumstances help account for his position. (1) He takes as his ideal certain principal aspects of Parsons' approach which are strongly contested by many other sociologists—a point he acknowledges. (2) Insofar as sociologists have addressed themselves to normative considerations concerning community, many of them have tended to emphasize *Gemeinschaft* and have indeed looked with nostalgia on the *Gemeinschaft*-like community.[10] And (3) he infers from Parsons' writings a concept of consensus that is not entirely explicit in those writings and whose ambiguity understandably leads to mistaken implications that have constituted the principal basis for the attack on system theory by the so-called conflict theorists. It has to do with the nature of the collectivity, the nature of collectivity orientation, and the commonly accepted value patterns that presumably are necessary for the existence of a social system.

The ambiguity arises from lack of clarity about the system level to which the commonly accepted value patterns are ascribed, a point that is especially important in considering geographic communities. In Parsons' terms:

> The sharing of such common value patterns [which define institutionalized role-expectations], entailing a sense of responsibility for the fulfillment of obligations, then creates a solidarity among those mutually oriented to the common values. The actors concerned will be said to constitute, within the area of relevance of these values, a *collectivity*.[11]

Parsons goes on to translate this attachment to common values into terms of the "common 'sentiments'" of individuals, and adds that the values have a "moral" aspect in that the individual actor has a responsibility for some degree of conformity to these common values.

It is from this emphasis on common values as the indispensable basis for a collectivity that Olson understandably draws his inference regarding the incompatability of the sociological and economic ideal models. To the extent that consensus, in the sense of common values, interests, and life styles, stultifies social and industrial diversification, it is apparently irreconcilable with the economic ideal—and, incidentally, open to the accusation of being both conservative in its side effects and inadequate to account for the strong systemic aspects that are found in a highly diversified and socially differentiated society.

Parsons tends to equate social system and collectivity and tends to emphasize the shared values of the collectivity as a differentia of all social systems, including societies and the substructures within them.

Olson would therefore seem to be justified in his inference that consensus and shared values are to be optimized in the sociological model. But it is a mistake to equate collectivity orientation to the values of a specific collectivity with the shared values that are necessary if that collectivity is to persist as a social system. Many types of sustained, role-structured interaction that can appropriately be considered as social systems show little if any collectivity orientation toward the immediate collectivity in question (i.e., the client-lawyer dyad, the consortium of banks floating a new loan), even though they do embody the shared values that Parsons claims are necessary to sustain patterned interaction. The shared values are not necessarily the values of the specific collectivity, but those of a more inclusive social system. The systemic interaction between lawyer and client is sustained by these values rather than by any significant collectivity orientation to the specific lawyer-client dyad.

The point seems trivial, but it is not. For it invalidates the implication that a sociological model of community can be based only on likeness of roles, interests, and values. In supporting his ideal economic model, Olson gives two examples, which purportedly show the economic nonfeasibility of a sociological model. One is the problem caused by everyone wanting to go on vacation "in August and at the beach." The other is the problem of a society where everyone is socialized into wanting to be a leader.[12] He seems to imply that somehow such common preferences are necessary consequences of the Parsonian concept of shared values as essential to a society or to its constituent collectivities. This is truly a *reductio ad absurdum*.

The diversification and fluidity necessary for economic optimality are compatible not only with the so-called conflict theorists, but also with social system theorists. This is true with two provisos: (1) The shared values necessary to sustain systemic interaction may not be those of the specific collectivity, but those of a more inclusive system. They provide consensus on the acceptable interaction patterns according to which differences of interest, value, objective, and role may be *contested* within the collectivity. This point accommodates the genuine conflict of interest that often exists within collectivities without in any way threatening their continued existence, so long as the norms governing such interest conflicts are shared—norms that derive from a more inclusive social system. This more inclusive system may be the total society, but it may also be less inclusive than the total social system. And (2) the shared values that derive from the more inclusive system accommodate and support the diversification of values, interests, and roles at the less inclusive collectivity level.

On these two bases, it is possible to approach the problem of establishing a normative model of the community based on a social system approach without ending up with the closed-system, commensalistic model that Olson derives from his interpretation of Parsons. By the same token, of course, it is possible to construct a model that would embody these characteristics. My point at present is only that the social system approach does not necessitate this last model.

It is thus possible to conceive of a normative model of the community in modified social system terms that would include Parsons' functional prerequisites of a social system or some counterpart to them, and which presumably would provide for relatively rapid internal modification of the system in order to assure the system's continued adaptability to its environment. Such a model might imply much or little collectivity orientation on the part of individual actors to the community system as such. Kaplan, in what is perhaps the best effort at applying Parsonian system theory to the analysis of a metropolitan complex, points out that there is relatively little collectivity orientation to Metro Toronto among the principal actors in the system. Rather, it is collectivity orientation toward the shared values of the more inclusive Canadian society which sustains the largely ecological interaction that constitutes the configuration of the system:

> Metro Toronto did not approach the level of normative integration described in Parsons' general model. In Metro there was a minimal consensus on goals, values, or norms, outside of a consensus on the liberal, democratic values that pervade Canada and most Western democracies. . . . A normative order was necessary to the Metro system's functioning but was not the responsibility of the Metro system itself.[13]

The Parsonian approach to social systems considers the individual actors or roles from the standpoint of the system itself, while the so-called conflict theorists consider the interaction from the standpoint of the individual actors with their diverse roles, interests, values, and so on. Ralf Dahrendorf asserts the validity of both approaches, as well as the inadequacy of each approach without the other.[14]

In devising his own model for analyzing Metro Toronto, Kaplan asserts that "a partially integrated system, like Metro Toronto, must be described from the bottom up."[15] He refers to this approach as actor analysis, as distinguished from system analysis. He then considers how integration, both normative and nonnormative, is effected in the interaction of individual actors. He asserts that the two disparate functions of integration and adaptation of the Metro system are mutually reinforcing in the long run. They may be caught in a spiral of mutual enhancement or mutual deterioration. In a similar vein, Ramsöy states that where subsystems are parts of more inclusive systems, "various desired levels of subsystem integration and of inclusive system adaptation may be incompatible,"[16] a point that may also have some bearing on an analytical approach to problems of integration and adaptation at the separate levels of the urban community and of the neighborhood.

But in what sense, if at all, can a normative model for the community be constructed which corresponds to the economist's normative model, say, of the free market, which does not make assumptions as to what kinds of values are to be optimized? The economist is able to make his felicitous calculations precisely because he precludes all but a single dimension in his analysis, the maximization of utility. Any counterpart normative sociological model for the community would have to go beyond this and specify what *types* of values are to be maximized—or at least optimized. Otherwise, the sociologist is caught in the dilemma of ascribing value to maintaining the system as such, regardless of what returns it is providing to its environment or to its constituent actors, an implicit commitment that is ideologically repellent to many sociologists such as myself. It is also inadequate to accommodate a situation of low collectivity orientation in Kaplan's sense.

The necessity of somehow building values into a sociological model is the principal reason for the diffidence of sociologists regarding normative models. But must the sociologist build in such values in order to contribute to the consideration of the normative aspects of community alternatives? As indicated earlier, a community model could no doubt be constructed in social system terms, but it is difficult to see how such a model could avoid the problem of value loadings. I shall not attempt here to construct such a model, but I shall consider an approach to the problem of value loadings that may be useful in model construction as well as in other types of investigation.

I shall treat values as dimensions of choice, not prescribing at what point on these dimensions the indicated value should be accepted, but rather showing how, on the basis of empirical investigation, the relationship between specific loadings of these value dimensions can be established. In some instances, a high loading on one value may facilitate the realization of a high loading on another value; in other instances, a high loading on one value may make difficult or impossible, empirically, the realization of a high loading on another value.

In the following analysis, not all value dimensions of possible relevance to a community model will be considered. As in all model-building, certain (but not all) variables must be abstracted for analysis because of their presumed crucial importance.

THE INTERRELATIONSHIP OF THREE VALUES
IN NORMATIVE MODELS

For the present analysis, whose purpose is to illustrate the feasibility of treating values as dimensions and to indicate the possibilities of empirical investigation of the interrelationship of various loadings on these dimensions, three values, or desiderata, will be considered. Each of these values has been given wide currency in the literature on American communities. One need not support them in order to recognize how widely they are held. They are (1) community autonomy, (2) community viability, and (3) broad distribution of community decision-making power.

An examination of the interrelationship of these three values will show the manner in which values may be built into a model as dimensions rather than states, and the implications of specific states of any given value related to those of others.

Community autonomy is at one extreme of a dimension whose opposite extreme is dependence, especially dependence of the community on extracommunity systems such as national corporations or federal agencies. This value prescription for the community often takes the form of a reaction against the mass society and insistence on the need for making local decisions locally.[17]

Community viability is at one extreme of a dimension whose opposite extreme is incapacity to confront problems at the community level. The desideratum here is that a community be able to confront its problems and take action with respect to them.[18]

Wide distribution of decision-making power is at one extreme of a dimension whose opposite extreme is concentration of power in a monolithic structure. The value prescription is for a broad distribution of power among a number of power concentrations, and also a wide dissemination of power within these concentrations. Practically, this involves the issue of a larger number of people participating substantively in decisions (in Selznick's sense)[19] and a decentralization of decision-making—currently to the neighborhood level.

How are these three desiderata interrelated? As community autonomy increases, what happens to community viability and power distribution?

1. Autonomy denotes local control over maximally localized institutions. In operation, it would take the form of the least possible absentee ownership and in general the fewest possible organizational ties, both in the economy and in other sectors, to more inclusive organizations outside the community. To the extent that federal or state or private foundation grant-in-aid programs involve constraints—and they typically involve important constraints—they would be avoided.

Such severe constraints on economic and other activity could be expected to impede the community's viability, its ability to confront its problems and take action with respect to them. These constraints would drastically limit the scope of resources available for such action. Economically, autonomy implies the type of self-sufficiency and lack of diversification *among* communities that Olson correctly points out are incompatible with optimal economic productivity.

But how would the distribution of power be affected by a maximization of community autonomy? Can power be expected to be distributed more widely as autonomy is increased? Two recent studies indicate the contrary. In a summary study of community power research, Claire W. Gilbert reports a "trend in the United States away from centralized forms of power structures in local communities and toward more pluralistic structures."[20] Although the point has not been demonstrated, it seems warranted to assume that part of the reason for this trend toward pluralistic structures is the growth in size of communities and the growth in complexity of their organizational structures, including their increasing ties to extracommunity systems. This assumption is lent strong support by a study by John Walton, which reports a positive relationship "between competitive power structure and the presence of absentee-owned corporations, competitive party politics, adequate economic resources and satellite status."[21] Regarding an explanation for this association, Walton concludes: "Each of the variables associated with competitive power structures reflects the interdependence of the community and extracommunity centers of power or increased emphasis on the vertical axis."[22] Summarizing, he says: "To the extent that the local community becomes increasingly interdependent with respect to extracommunity institutions (or develops along its vertical axis) the structure of local leadership becomes more competitive."[23] Thus, in our terms, he concludes that autonomy and broad distribution of power are inversely related.

2. Turning to community viability, how do community autonomy and the broad distribution of power fare? We have defined viability as the capacity for making community-level decisions that confront problems through action at the community level. We have already described the relationship of viability to autonomy. There are sporadic but increasing data to indicate that the relationship of viability to broad distribution of power is likewise inverse.

Two types of analysis are helpful in exploring the implications of the broad distribution of power. One aspect of this question is geographic: the current agitation in favor of decentralizing citywide decision-making to the neighborhood level, thus building up the decision-making power and prerogatives of neighborhoods vis-à-vis the municipal government and other citywide power loci. Analysis of the relationship between system and subsystem may be relevant to this question. In their analysis of the metropolis as a social system, John E. Bebout and Harry C. Bredemeier have pointed out that the city's adaptive functions may interfere with integrative functions on a still more inclusive level.[24] It may likewise be the case that the adaptive functions of neighborhoods may interfere with the integrative functions of the more inclusive metropolis, and that choices must be made between the objectives of neighborhood adaptation (in the Parsonian sense) and community integration. Lawrence Haworth, a philosopher, has examined this question in his book *The Good City*,[25] and Odd Ramsöy has analyzed it in more general social system terms.[26]

Ramsöy utilizes the concept of complex social systems, where one or more systems are included as subsystems within a more inclusive system. The inclusion of neighborhoods within a larger metropolitan community is an appropriate example of such complex systems. Ramsöy concludes that "if one major strain in complex social systems is between subsystem adaptation and inclusive system integration, another is the reverse process: various desired levels of subsystem integration and of inclusive system adaptation may be incompatible."[27] While one cannot make logically certain inferences from such general statements, this one at least suggests the possibility that neighborhood adaptation, by jeopardizing community-level integration, may decrease community viability.

In a second type of pertinent analysis, several intercommunity studies take a particular type of presumably desirable community action as a dependent variable and various measures of power dispersion as independent variables, and find an inverse relationship between them. They thus suggest that community viability and a broad distribution of decision-making power vary inversely.

Amos Hawley measured the relationship between urban renewal "success," as indicated by reaching the execution stage in an urban renewal program, and the distribution of a city's power structure, as measured by the ratio of managers, proprietors, and officials to the employed labor force. The lower the ratio, the greater the concentration of power. He concluded that his findings "clearly support the hypothesis that the lower the MPO ratio (dispersion of power), the greater the chance of success in an action program such as urban renewal."[28]

Likewise Donald B. Rosenthal and Robert L. Crain found that centralized decision-making authority and a low level of direct citizen participation were among the conditions making for a better chance for consideration and adoption of fluoridation measures.[29]

Herman Turk and his associates found that a concentration of power was associated with a city's taking early and effective action in such programs as urban renewal and the Neighborhood Youth Corps.[30]

The gross relationships indicated above require much more refined research procedures, and it may well be that as further investigation occurs, they may be modified substantially. There is already indication in a number of recent studies[31] that these relationships may not hold in the simple form stated above. But the investigations so far at least indicate that the relationship between broad distribution of decision-making power and community viability cannot simply be assumed to be random or positive, and may well be inverse.

3. Our third desideratum, the broad distribution of power, has already been considered in relation to the other two desiderata, and the relationship was found to be presumptively inverse in each case.

It is perhaps banal to point out that the use of such programs as urban renewal as a measure of success beg the whole question of values by simply making an implicit value assumption in their measure and then pursuing an otherwise "objective" analysis. If viability is to be conceived in terms of a community's capacity for confronting problems at the community level, who is to define

what circumstances constitute problems, decisions, and actions, and what are to
be considered as measures of success in confronting such problems? Competence
in decision-making and action is difficult to divorce from the question of the
goals of the action. Since important goals of various groups within the community often conflict, community viability cannot be considered an objective concept in the sense of being value-free. In a strict sense, a community does not
"have problems." It is one thing to utilize the construct of community to denote
the social organization of any given locality; it is quite another to reify and
even anthropomorphize the construct community as "having problems," "seeking solutions," etc., except in the most deliberately loose and figurative sense.
Various groups within the locality are comprised of people with similar values
or interests, which may or may not be the same as those of other groups. To assume, naïvely, that one "speaks for" any given community by defining problems
from the standpoint of any one of these possible value-interest configurations is
to make a hazardous logical jump. The problem has occupied political scientists
as the problem of definition and existence of the "public interest," and has occupied economists as the problem of aggregating a "public welfare" from a number of disparate individual preference scales. In a different but related vein,
Hillery has argued that "communal organizations," such as communities, are not
primarily oriented toward the attainment of specific goals and should not be
treated as goal-attaining systems. He follows Parsons, however, in considering
primacy of orientation to the attainment of a specific goal as a distinguishing
characteristic of organizations, so that at the level of formal organizations within
the community, rather than at the level of the community as such, it is quite
appropriate to speak of goals, problems, etc.[32]

CONCLUSION

The lack of normative community models in sociology which would provide
comparable analytic leverage to the "ideal" models in economics has been
attributed to the hesitance of sociologists to make normative prescriptions, a
problem which the economist solves by simply taking an abstract, categorical
norm, the maximization of utility. It is maintained that a sociological model
need not posit the high degree of consensus, stability of role structure, and
collectivity orientation that Olson derives from his application of Parsonian
theory. But values must somehow be incorporated within a sociological model.
This can be done without utopian prescription as to what those values should
be. Values can be treated as dimensions, along which certain loadings may be
selected (although the selection is not prescribed by the sociologist). The implications in terms of other values which any particular loading of a given dimension involves can be empirically determined. This procedure has been illus-

trated by an examination (based on as yet scanty data) of the interrelationship of three such value dimensions: autonomy, viability, and broad distribution of community decision-making.

Thus values can be incorporated into a community model, providing a framework for specific normative choices as to specific value loadings. The implications of specific value-loading choices in terms of "costs," available resources, or other values can be empirically determined. The model thus becomes a series of equations rather than a specific utopian prescription, just as the economist can contribute to the analysis of utility maximization without prescribing what preference scales are to be used.

This brief examination of the relationship among three commonly accepted desiderata for the good community also has important substantive implications for practitioners such as community planners and others who strive for purposive community change related to one or more of the three. It indicates the essential naïveté of simply accepting all three simultaneously as desiderata and failing to consider the price in terms of the other two which a given advance in one of these goals may entail. Although it is not yet possible to state these inverse relationships in precise quantitative terms, there seems to be no important methodological or theoretical consideration barring progress in this direction.

The practical implications of such analysis for policy decision are apparent. It does not dictate the content, but provides the decision-makers with the cost in one value which an increase in the realization of another value will entail. In this it is analogous to the economist's analysis of the relationship between level of employment and inflation. Since it appears that these two variables are positively correlated, it is presumably not possible to check inflation while maintaining full employment. This relationship poses a difficult value choice to the policy-maker, but two aspects of the choice are significant for the present analysis: (1) the economist does not prescribe which value shall be maximized; (2) the economist makes the value choice more explicit and precise for those who do make it.

NOTES

[1] Mancur Olson, Jr., "Economics, Sociology, and the Best of All Possible Worlds," *Public Interest*, no. 12 (Summer 1968).

[2] A frankly utopian approach, involving the explicit construction of perfect societies, has its contemporary advocates. See Myron Orleans, "Towards Utopia" (a paper delivered at the annual meeting of the Eastern Sociological Society, New York, 1969).

[3] See Rosabeth Moss Kanter, "Commitment and Social Organization: A Study of Commitment Mechanisms in Utopian Communities," *American Sociological Review*, 33, no. 4 (August 1968).

[4] For example, Irwin T. Sanders, *Making Good Communities Better: A Handbook for Civic-Minded Men and Women* (Lexington: University of Kentucky Press, 1950), and Roland L. Warren, *Studying Your Community* (New York: Russell Sage Foundation, 1955; paperback ed., Free Press, Macmillan, 1965).

[5] Outstanding examples are Arthur E. Morgan, *The Small Community: Foundation of Democratic Life* (New York: Harper, 1942) and Baker Brownell, *The Human Community: Its Philosophy and Practice for a Time of Crisis* (New York: Harper, 1950).

[6] Harold F. Kaufman, "Toward an Interactional Conception of Community," *Social Forces*, 38, no. 1 (October 1959): 17.

[7] Olson, "Economics, Sociology, and the Best of All Possible Worlds," p. 111.

[8] *Ibid.*, p. 112.

[9] *Ibid.*, p. 116.

[10] This is especially true of rural sociologists, who have concerned themselves primarily with the rural community. An early example is E. Dwight Sanderson and Robert A. Polson, *Rural Community Organization* (New York: Wiley, 1939).

[11] Talcott Parsons, *The Social System* (New York: Free Press, Macmillan, 1951, 1964), p. 41.

[12] Olson, "Economics, Sociology, and the Best of All Possible Worlds," p. 107.

[13] Harold Kaplan, *Urban Political Systems: A Functional Analysis of Metro Toronto* (New York: Columbia University Press, 1967), p. 17.

[14] Ralf Dahrendorf, *Class and Class Conflict in Industrial Society* (Stanford: Stanford University Press, 1959), p. 163. See also his "Out of Utopia: Toward a Reorientation of Sociological Analysis," *American Journal of Sociology*, 64, no. 2 (September 1958).

[15] Kaplan, *Urban Political Systems*, p. 22.

[16] Odd Ramsöy, *Social Groups as System and Subsystem* (New York: Free Press, Macmillan, 1963), p. 199.

[17] This theme runs through Robert A. Nisbet's *The Quest for Community* (New York: Oxford University Press, 1953), and is treated in a more explicit way in Roland L. Warren, "Toward a Typology of Extra-Community Controls Limiting Local Community Autonomy," *Social Forces*, 34, no. 4 (May 1956). The theme is ubiquitous in the literature of the community movement.

[18] The theme is treated in Arthur J. Vidich and Joseph Bensman, *Small Town in Mass Society: Class, Power, and Religion in a Rural Community* (Princeton: Princeton University Press, 1958), and is central to community organization books such as Murray G. Ross, *Community Organization: Theory and Principles*, 2nd ed. (New York: Harper & Row, 1967).

[19] Philip Selznick, *TVA and the Grass Roots: A Study in the Sociology of Formal Organization* (New York: Harper Torchbook, 1966), p. 220.

[20] Claire W. Gilbert, "Community Power and Decision-Making: A Quantitative Examination of Previous Research," in *Community Structure and Decision-Making: Comparative Analyses*, ed. Terry N. Clark (San Francisco: Chandler, 1968), p. 155.

[21] John Walton, "The Vertical Axis of Community Organization and the Structure of Power," *Southwestern Social Science Quarterly*, 48, no. 3 (December 1967): 362.

[22] *Ibid.*

[23] *Ibid.*, p. 363.

[24] John E. Bebout and Harry C. Bredemeier, "American Cities as Social Systems," *Journal of the American Institute of Planners*, 29, no. 3 (May 1963).

[25] Lawrence Haworth, *The Good City* (Bloomington: Indiana University Press, 1963).

[26] Ramsöy, *Social Groups as System and Subsystem*.

[27] *Ibid.*, p. 199.

[28] Amos H. Hawley, "Community Power and Urban Renewal Success," *Community Structure and Decision-Making*, ed. Clark, p. 405.

[29] Donald B. Rosenthal and Robert L. Crain, "Structure and Values in Local Political Systems: The Case of Fluoridation Decisions," in *ibid.*, pp. 241–42 *et passim*. See also Robert L. Crain, Elihu Katz, and Donald B. Rosenthal, *The Politics of Community Conflict: The Fluoridation Decision* (Indianapolis: Bobbs-Merrill, 1969).

[30] Herman Turk, *A Method of Predicting Certain Federal Program Potentials of Large American Cities* (Los Angeles: Laboratory for Organizational Research, University of Southern California, 1967). A finding contrary to those given here was reported by Wayne Paulson, Edgar W. Butler, and Hallowell Pope in "Community Power and Public Welfare," *American Journal of Economics and Sociology*, 28, no. 1 (January 1969). They suggest that the difference may be attributable to the fact that they studied *smaller* communities. In any case, such analysis is still at a relatively rudimentary stage. It nevertheless suffices to illustrate the problem under consideration here.

[31] Terry N. Clark, "Community Structure, Decision-Making, Budget Expenditures, and Urban Renewal in 51 American Communities," *American Sociological Review*, 33 (August 1968): 576–93; Michael Aiken and Robert R. Alford, "Community Structure and Innovation: The Case of Urban Renewal," mimeographed (paper presented at the annual meeting of the American Sociological Assn., September 1969); and Wayne Paulson, Edgar W. Butler, and· Hallowell Pope, "Community Power and Public Welfare," *American Journal of Economics and Sociology*, 28 (January 1969): 17–28.

[32] George A. Hillery, Jr., "The Community Theories of Talcott Parsons: A Critique" (a paper presented at the annual meeting of the Society for the Study of Social Problems, San Francisco, 1967), and *Communal Organizations: A Study of Local Societies* (Chicago: University of Chicago Press, 1968), pp. 142ff.

16

THE CONFLICT INTERSYSTEM
AND THE CHANGE AGENT

This paper attempts to analyze conceptually a recent two-year experience in a mediating role in East and West Berlin. It concerns two problems:

1. How do two diametrically opposed belief-action systems sustain themselves respectively in adaptive response to continuing new developments and in hostile interaction with each other?

2. What are some of the implications of this analysis for the role of a mediatory change agent?

As international affairs representative in Germany for the American Friends Service Committee, I lived in West Berlin and developed and maintained contacts with high officials of the German Democratic Republic as well as of West Berlin and the Federal Republic. It was part of my function to talk with officials who, because of the difficulties of the German situation and the Federal Republic's policy of nonrecognition of the German Democratic Republic, were not talking to each other. A considerable amount of time was also spent with State Department officials in Berlin and in the U.S. Embassy in Bonn (Bad Godesberg) and officials in the Foreign Ministry of the Federal Republic. Contact was likewise maintained in much weaker fashion with Soviet Embassy officials both in East Berlin and in Bonn (Rolandseck).

It is possible to give some quantitative indication of the activity, at least in its external aspects. During the first twenty-two months I held a total of 245 conversations, of which 151 were with people I had not met before and 94 were repeats. Of these conversations, 153 were with officials and 92 were with non-

Reprinted by permission from *Journal of Conflict Resolution*, 8, no. 3 (September 1964): 231–41.

officials. Ninety-five were held in West Berlin, seventy-one in the Federal Republic, and seventy-nine in East Berlin and the German Democratic Republic. There were 139 conversations with individual persons and 106 with two or more persons. Thirty-nine of the people with whom I had appointments added third persons to the interviews without consulting me. Of these, four were in West Berlin, nine in the Federal Republic, and twenty-six in East Berlin and the German Democratic Republic. Political questions were touched upon or discussed at length in 236 of the conversations, only 9 being completely nonpolitical in nature. In addition to these interviews, there were nine interviews refused or otherwise not granted. I also made fifteen group appearances in which I discussed political questions, nine of which were confined mainly to German Quakers.

In these conversations, whether with officials or nonofficials, I tried as far as possible never to say or agree to anything on one side of the Berlin Wall which was inconsistent with anything said or agreed to on the other. Since considerable pressure toward fuller agreement was exerted on each side, this policy, based essentially on religious values, had several practical consequences:

1. It presented an excellent occasion for significant dialogue (part of the intervention strategy, as explained below), for in this intense conflict situation each side would seek reassurance that I, as a mediator rather than a partisan, nevertheless agreed with the essential justice of its position.

2. It subjected me to considerable psychic strain, since I continually disappointed people on both sides of the conflict by not agreeing with them sufficiently to satisfy them.

3. It was a constant antidote to one-sided thinking, to the false logic that slips past easily when one's conclusions have already been drawn from arguments other than those advanced. Thus it was not only a question of wishing assurance that one's own conclusions were sound, but the much more immediate and practical matter of needing to be able to defend one's position before conceding agreement with one's conversation partner.

This, parenthetically, is a discipline to which people are relatively seldom subjected. Rigid adherence to it in all cases would perhaps be undesirable, since it might reduce that minimal free area for role inconsistency which facilitates personal adjustment by individuals in what is usually for them a series of mutually interdependent but also partially inconsistent or incompatible social roles. (Nevertheless, one wishes that one's conversation partners in this particular situation, with their mutually exclusive all-or-none interpretations of the East-West conflict, could be subjected to such a discipline more than they are. And, of course, it was part of the intervention strategy to complicate their conceptions in just this way, however minimal the impact.)

There were other kinds of functions, activities, and strategies, but this report concerns only the reciprocal interaction between the two hostile belief-action systems and the practical implications for the mediational change agent's role. The report is necessarily largely subjective, since I was not only participant and observer, but also reporter. The conceptualizations employed to describe this somewhat unusual series of conflict-related situations are open to theoretical discussion, which I hope this analysis will stimulate.

How, then, are these two mutually exclusive thought systems sustained despite their obvious inconsistency with each other, despite their obvious one-sidedness, and despite their constantly being subjected to attack from the other side?

TWO BELIEF-ACTION SYSTEMS

The two belief-action systems are the official positions of the East and West regarding the dispute over the divided city of Berlin and the divided German nation. Data for the description of these positions come from newspapers and broadcast accounts, from official documents, and from interviews with high officials in both East Berlin and the German Democratic Republic and West Berlin and the Federal Republic.

The Eastern system is monolithic, thus presumably easier to establish and investigate. The Western system, despite the apparently greater room for divergence of opinion, is also remarkably unified and monolithic in content if not in method of opinion formation.

Each system contains a "complete" explanation for the deterioration since 1945 of the hopes for a unified Berlin, which would become the capital of a unified Germany. Thus, though the content varies, the systems purport to describe the same events.

The following propositions are made by both systems:

1. The other side is completely to blame for the failure of German reunification, and continues deliberately to thwart this purpose. This is true even though our side may possibly not be perfect and occasionally may have made a tactical error.

2. We have a true picture of how the situation has deteriorated. Their picture is devised to confuse the real issues and to take attention away from their own primary and deliberate responsibility for the deterioration.

3. We are willing to negotiate and have made countless offers to do so, but they have either ignored these offers or set such impossible terms as deliberately to doom any such efforts to unacceptability.

4. They have continuously followed policies and engaged in specific actions that were provocative and risked war, and war might well have occurred were it not for our patience and the utter necessity of avoiding atomic war.

5. The social system they have devised since World War II is in many vital respects a revival of Nazi doctrines and behavior patterns.

6. The people on the other side really want peace, just as we do. But they

have been victimized by their leaders, do not have access to the truth about what is going on, and are unable to develop under present conditions any vital alternative to the destructive policies of their leaders.

7. They are not willing to accept the status quo, but constantly precipitate crises and are an abiding danger through their dedication to changing the existing situation, which they try to justify by claiming that the present situation is "unnatural."

8. On the more fundamental level of the structure of the social order, they are equally aggressive. They openly assert that they want to destroy our social order and set up their own instead.

9. You can't be neutral in a fundamental dispute like this. If you are for peace and a just social order, you must agree completely with us and join us in eradicating this menace.[1]

How do these two juxtaposed belief-action systems sustain themselves? For analytical purposes, let us consider first the systems as systems, then consider them in their interaction.

Underlying each system is both an ideology (Marxism-Leninism or Western democracy) and a history of world struggle against the other system's ideology. Underlying each system is a social structure that arose because of the exigencies of the occupation period—on the one hand, the social structure imposed on its part of Germany by the Soviet Union, on the other the social structure imposed by the Western allies.

Each system involves various processes for the interpretation of new events in a way that is ideologically correct and for preventing "contaminated" thinking from the other side from reaching the ideologically unreliable or making an impact on them. Here, as well, the Eastern system is more monolithic and the procedures are more clearly identifiable and more closely related to the activity of the state; but the Western system also provides for these system-sustaining functions, and virtual unanimity of interpretation of events approaches one-party monolithism.

SOCIAL CONTROL

Each system involves both external and internal types of social control through which new accommodations are made and equilibrium is maintained under changing impacts, and through which participants are kept in line with the system's interpretation. Three aspects of this control appear to be particularly important:

First, there is the substantive pull of the line, the predisposition of the individual to interpret new events within the usual pattern, a pattern that commands his emotional loyalty.

Second, by the same token it is difficult on the intrapersonal level to admit chinks in the ideological wall. Emotional safety resides in accepting the line and adapting the perception of reality to fit the line rather than the line to fit reality. The latter would be particularly problematical since, unless this is done virtually monolithically by those whose legitimated function it is to do so when needed, confusion would result and the ranks would be divided in a situation where there is widespread recognition of the importance of presenting a solid front against the antagonist.

Third, on the interpersonal level, admitting inadequacies in the line would present similar difficulties. Strong social control processes operate to keep the individual in line. Challenging any of the important assumptions of the ideology or any important conclusions of the legitimated decision-makers could bring effective sanctions, both formal and informal. This reality takes form on the intrapersonal level as a resistance against points of view dissonant to the ideology.[2]

Even when direct exposure to the other side's propaganda is necessary (it is hindered in many though not exactly equal ways on both sides for the great masses of people), the exposure comes through the usual newspaper diatribe or the highly inflammatory speech of a leading functionary of the opposing side, an account of events which is so obviously one-sided that it is easy to write it off as propaganda.

Thus each system has its own ideological content basis for its respective view of recent history, its own basis and procedure for interpreting new events in accordance with this view, and its own system of social control for gaining assent to the prevailing view.

THE INTERSYSTEM

The two systems, though logically mutually exclusive, are from the standpoint of social process reciprocally supporting. Each is sustained in part by the existence of the other system and by the pattern of hostile interaction with the other system. Thus the two systems in their reciprocal interaction can be viewed as a significant sociological unit, an intersystem, if you will.

In Adenauer's time there was a cynical saying among disenchanted Germans on both sides of the divide that "Adenauer needs Ulbricht and Ulbricht needs Adenauer." The statement expressed the recognition of the existence of an intersystem, a system in which the response of the one strengthens the preconceptions of the other and lends credibility to the leaders, who then give this response as proof of the necessity of a hard course. The situation is almost puncture-proof—the opponent is damned if he does and damned if he doesn't. If he does something that our side believes he should do, then that proves that our side's hard policies are having a beneficial effect. If he does something that our side believes he shouldn't do, then this proves his moral culpability and serves as a reason for redoubling our efforts against such inhumanity.

The hostile systems interact and communicate with each other in this inter-action, despite the nonrecognition policy of the Federal Republic. However, aside from technical agreements—on water, sewage, postal systems, and numerous other matters below the political level—the method of communication between systems is limited, almost as though by mutual consent, to indirect communication of two types. One is the official pronouncements of the leaders in the form of extreme statements of the respective positions. The other, somewhat similar, is the interpretation given to these and other developments by minor politicians, opinion leaders, and the mass media. These latter, in both cases, follow the cues of the top leaders. Thus the typical official hears an account of what the other side has said or done which already has been strained through the ideological adapters and comes to him in the form of radio or television newscasts from his own side, or newspaper accounts or editorials, magazine articles, and so on. Only a relative minority of officials on either side, as a result of a combination of both internal and external controls, has direct and constant access to the newspapers and broadcasts of the other side. Even when they do, these media, as mentioned earlier, have already oversimplified the issues in such a provocatively hostile way that the internal controls of the top leaders are more than adequate to resist any siren melodies. It is easy enough to write it all off as war and hate propaganda, as subversion.

Thus the communication within the intersystem is such as to strengthen differences rather than to weaken them. Further, there is no provision for face-to-face contact and an open airing of differences within a responsible interaction framework. There is no mutual negotiating of a common reality perception of what has happened or what is happening. The intersystem functions not to further agreement but to strengthen each belief-action system in its disagreement with the other.

The situation is accompanied by many phenomena familiar to students of conflict processes:

1. A tendency to view events increasingly in moral disjunctions involving the good guys against the bad guys.
2. The tendency to warp reality perceptions to fit the preconception rather than vice versa.
3. A pressure on middle-of-the-roaders to come out strongly for an all-or-none position.
4. A tendency to delineate rather clearly the roles of partisans—be they journalists, clergy, generals, or politicians—and to leave relatively undefined and incomprehensible the role of noncommitted or only partly committed neutrals.

5. A tendency to bring larger and larger chunks of social reality and cultural activity into the political dimension, a progressive politicization of various aspects of the culture.

6. A tendency toward the self-fulfilling prophecy: We have to take measure A because we are practically sure that they will take measure B (but in taking measure A we add to the likelihood that they will take measure B).

This analysis evolved out of experience in the situation. Like most AFSC appointees abroad, I was given extensive leeway in performing my functions, which were generally understood to be those of becoming knowledgeable about the country involved; taking up contacts with appropriate high officials and other persons of relevance to the international field; soliciting their opinions on various developments; and occasionally offering an opinion myself. It is fairly clearly understood that international affairs representatives should not be "valueless" in the sense of being morally neutral, but that they nevertheless should attempt to see both sides and not be captured by a "we against them" spirit. The underlying goal is to facilitate communication rather than to sell a set of preconceived answers. In the case of Germany, it was hoped that a viable set of relationships could be established between East and West.

THE PROBLEM OF ENTRY

Looking back, I find it useful to conceptualize the experience as the problems of entry and interaction of a change agent and a social system. As indicated above, there were two belief-action systems involved, but because they are so interdependent in a rather stable mode of interaction it is perhaps preferable to consider the intersystem that includes them both.

In this instance, although the change agent had not been invited, he was not necessarily unwelcome. Quakers, to the extent that they are known at all, have a remarkably good name in Germany chiefly because of the Quaker feeding during the allied blockade following World War I. Many of their activities in the international field, such as their East-West diplomats' conferences, are well known and highly regarded. Their traditional pacifism, based on religious conviction, gains increasing relevance in the days of possible total annihilation. Such apprehension as is shown at confronting, on a personal basis, people on the other side of various controversies has usually with the course of time given way to outright approval.

A brief anecdote will serve to illustrate the nevertheless difficult entry problem. After I had finished explaining my duties to a high Communist official in East Germany, including a recital of contacts with some of his counterparts in West Berlin and Bonn, I acknowledged that my activity was somewhat unusual and that I realized it would take some time before I could expect or hope for the necessary good faith from both sides.

The official replied: "I think I understand what you are doing; but you are right that it is unusual and that there will be some initial mistrust. After all, if you were a journalist or a diplomat, people would know exactly how to deal with you. Nevertheless, people on this side will give you no difficulty, because they want peace as you do. But on the Western side, they will give you trouble, because they don't really want peace."

I thanked him, adding that a Western official had said virtually the same thing to me just a day or two before, only with the fields reversed.

The entry problem, as this official realized, consisted of devising a role of interaction in relation to the intersystem, and of differentiating this role from a number of other possible roles, some of which might have permitted entry and all of which were at least fairly clearly established in relation to this intersystem: journalist, diplomat, spy, agitator, pro-Communist American, missionary. In addition, there was the problem of esteem within the role, particularly concerning qualities on which I felt myself being assessed both in East and in West. The first was basic good faith that I was dealing honestly and openly and was not using my intervention in any way that intended harm for either side. The second was the ability, regardless of motivation, to avoid causing embarrassment or difficulty to one of the parties through stupidity and inadvertence. The third was the ability to establish myself as someone worth talking to—for these were all busy officials with responsible positions in an extremely sensitive and explosive international situation.

There was an additional factor, somewhat unexpected, though related to the others. This was the factor of boundary maintenance on the part of the intersystem. It might be expressed by the attitude indicated in the following words (which, however, were never spoken overtly): "Look here. We are engaged in a fateful struggle. If you want to get into this struggle, regardless of which side you're on, there is a role for you, and both sides will know the appropriate behavior for you and issue appropriate positive and negative sanctions if you violate the norms. But don't come around wanting to interact with us if you don't want to be a participant in this struggle. If you want in, just choose your side and come on in."

Working against this boundary maintenance and this lack of a well-established interaction role were the advantages of my identification as a Quaker, with the attendant set of expectations that I would be quiet and tactful and would mean no harm. But there were two other much more specific factors.

First, it was important for me to tell about the kinds of contacts I was making with high officials of the other side. This was more than name-dropping. It was necessary to show my good faith by being frank about these contacts with people who were perceived as the enemy. Further, as a matter of self-protection, it was best that they first hear of these contacts from me. Of course, such firsthand contacts immediately created a great deal of interest. Here was somebody who had just talked with the enemy, with whom direct contact was impossible. What did he think? What did he say to this, to that? The advantages in relation to the entry problem are obvious.

Second, given this set of contacts with friendly as well as with enemy officials, I was naturally a subject of scrutiny. What kinds of communications might possibly be going across this human bridge? Both sides felt it important to know.

There was another favorable factor. The lines were drawn, the thinking tended to be highly oversimplified—all or none, right against wrong. Some of the supports in the intersystem for this kind of thinking have already been indicated. Nevertheless, there exists room for doubt. Each side knew how its reasoning was derided by the other side; but it dismissed the other side with relative ease. There still remained the question of how its position would look to a presumably dispassionate observer. Each side wanted reassurance.

It is remarkable how often the conversation really began with such a question as "Well, then—and what *do* you think? Don't you agree with our position?" The context and the attitudes tended to vary, though. In the East, the attitude tended to be very highly aggressive against the West, with extensive verbalization and a recital of the well-known arguments of militarism, revanchism, and fascism, as though the official really supposed I had never heard them before. In the West, the attitude tended to be one of self-assurance, of simply assuming that since I seemed to be a decent sort of person, I must be well aware that they, over there, are 100 percent wrong, and one doesn't protest this any more than one protests that he loves his mother.

While the Communist expected rather complete disagreement and was gratified at the least indication of understanding of his point of view, the West German or American expected agreement and was disappointed at the slightest indication of acceptance of any Communist point. As for me, I expected agreement from fellow democrats, and was disappointed to find the Western officials so often "unreasonable," while I was aware of basic disagreements in point of view with the Communists and was gratified at small indications of "reasonableness."

It thus became possible to solve the entry problem in a minimal way, at least, and to establish a rather unusual type of role relationship for interaction with officials in both parts of the intersystem.

INTERVENTION STRATEGY

The intervention strategy was relatively simple: I was to be one of the few people in touch with and talking with important officials on both sides of the Wall—in a situation where face-to-face communication had almost completely broken down. This seemed reasonable and desirable, and little deliberate attention was given to the tangible outcomes, if any. As experience was gained, however, the strategy became more clearly defined.

The attempt to be truthful and consistent while talking with officials of diametrically opposed views soon directed attention to the completeness of the gap that separated the two ways of looking at things. Countless times I heard one man argue vigorously for a particular interpretation of an event or situation, only a couple of hours later to hear his counterpart in the other side of Berlin argue equally intently and logically (within his ideological perspective) the absurdity of the very same interpretation. There followed the realization of the existence of completely different thought-action systems, so far out of line with each other that objective reality as seen by one side had virtually no similarity to what was seen by the other. Both sides were distorting the truth, principally by selective perception but also by the process of impugning motives. Something that one does and approves is condemned as vicious when done by the other side because of the different ideological context in which it is seen. There was, as mentioned earlier, no provision for direct face-to-face interaction in which reality perception could be negotiated.

Such negotiation of reality perception became the chief objective of my strategy. I assumed that, in the process, the oversimplified viewpoints might be cut down somewhat, and that an area of overlap in reality perception might be achieved. I assumed that this would increase the possibility of resolving some of the differences—though it would not assure it, for even if the problems were defined in relatively the same manner, there would still remain basic differences of interest and of value.

Implementation of this strategy took a fairly simple form. In essence, it consisted of presenting the arguments used by the other side: "Well, I was talking about that with Soandso over there the other day, and here is the way he sees it." In doing this, I neither identified myself with the viewpoint I was recounting nor rejected it. I did employ one rule of thumb, however. I recounted only the arguments that I felt had some logic *on the other side's terms;* that is, arguments that seemed feasible enough to me so that I thought I could present them adequately and was prepared to assert that, whether or not I agreed with them, they were sincerely held and had at least a modicum of validity as seen by the other side.

There were some associated rules of thumb:

I tried to avoid what some people call the "win-lose trap." If I figuratively started pounding the table, then I became associated with the other side and lost all my pull, being easily written off as a simple dupe to the other side's fallacious arguments. I simply tried to give the reasoning and indicate my belief that it was sincerely held.

As a related point, I always tried to avoid straining a relationship. That is, I avoided using arguments or getting into subject matters where I felt that my relationship to my conversation partner was not sufficiently strong to bear the weight of such explosive issues. (Those who have been in either part of Berlin in recent years will recognize just how thin-skinned Berliners can be.)

Another procedure was to acknowledge the truth—and there was always at least a kernel of truth—in the point that the conversation partner mentioned. When it could honestly be done (which in both parts of Berlin was most of the time), I expressed my own misgiving about the very same thing that bothered the person with whom I was speaking. The matter under consideration usually seemed to me to be a matter of legitimate concern expressed in highly exaggerated terms.

EVALUATION

Was the strategy effective? Did the change agent induce change? Evaluation is extremely sketchy and thoroughly unscientific. Here are some of the assumptions on which the intervention strategy was based:

1. The idea that "you can't influence a Communist because they're all the same and they never change" is false both in its premise and in its conclusion. I assumed rather that while Communists, like any other members of an establishment (including the American State Department), must in general support official policy—at least in their official capacity—these Communists, again like American State Department officers, covered a wide range from rigidity to flexibility in their responses. As someone has pointed out, they have their John Birchers, too, but they are not all John Birchers. Generally, my experience supported this assumption.

2. I also assumed that the range of flexibility might be narrower among the Communists than among the Western officials. My experience here was mixed: the Communists seemed to me less flexible than the American officials, but not than the West German officials.

3. Another assumption had to do with dissonance. Many people in the West pointed out that, to the extent that I succeeded in the slightest degree in creating an increased understanding for the West's position, I would be placing my respondent in a difficult position. Even if the latter agreed, he could do nothing about it. The same point was also made in the East, but less frequently. I assumed this argument to be false, on the grounds that dissonance is not always resolved 100 percent in favor of the system. Everyone has some room for dissonance, both in living with it subjectively and at times in expressing it to others. An aggregate of dissonance regarding current problems may constitute the basis for a potential change—part of what is meant by "the time is ripe."

Not only among the liberals but also among the John Birchers, dissonance may be a factor making for change, even though the positions from which the two groups change are at opposite poles. This applies in Communist states as well as in the West. Recent years have seen the accumulation of such dissonance in most of these states, and policy adjustments have occurred to resolve some of it.

4. On a different level, I made an assumption of reciprocal causation. In East-West interaction this means that what the East does by way of reaction to some Western move has the tendency to strengthen the position of people in the West who advocate a certain course and to weaken those who advocate its opposite. The same applies to actions taken by the West. Thus the actions of each side are to a certain extent controlled by the other, giving validity to a policy of evaluating various response alternatives—hard or soft—in terms of what segments of the political spectrum on the other side they tend to strengthen or weaken. More specifically, and in highly oversimplified fashion: Do they strengthen the liberals over there, or the John Birchers? This assumption, which did not rise out of this experience and was neither proved nor disproved by it, nevertheless constituted a mode of reasoning that formed the basis for fruitful discussions in both East and West.

5. On a still different level, there was a paired assumption: that total ideological victory is not a feasible short-run goal (whether or not it is desirable); and that this is not necessarily a bad thing. The assumption is relevant to the strategy, although it does not account for it completely. Its relevance lies in the fact that it was not the intent of the strategy to work toward a victory for the ideology either of the East or of the West. Rather, both parties will be around for quite some time, and perhaps better communication will facilitate accommodation. The relative accommodation in which Catholics and Protestants have lived together in Germany for the past three hundred years, while each side holds fast to its view that the other is wrong and to its hope of converting the other side, is not a totally irrelevant precedent.

Needless to say, I hardly aspired to make a dramatic impact on the complex, many-layered situation in a divided Germany during the two short years I was there. Only one thing can be said with assurance: I found it possible in this highly tense situation, with lines clearly drawn, to establish a meaningful set of relationships with some of the many people who occupy positions of importance in the various parties to the German problem; to do so quite openly; to converse quite freely on all sides, even to say things that are seldom said on either side; and to do so while I was constantly prodding and prying at comfortably held oversimplifications—a process that was not always pleasant for either me or my respondent.

There would have been great benefit in having reports from others who had engaged in similar activity, particularly if these reports had been analytical rather than completely descriptive. To be most helpful, such accounts must make use of an adequate scientific conceptualization and relate themselves to relevant parts of social theory. It would seem that social system analysis and role analysis offer at least a modicum of promise for such conceptualization.

NOTES

[1] The phenomenon is reminiscent of Urie Bronfenbrenner's experience in the Soviet Union: "Slowly and painfully, it forced itself upon me that *the Russian's distorted picture of us was curiously similar to our view of them—a mirror image.* But of course our image was real. Or could it be that our views too were distorted and irrational—a mirror image in a twisted glass?" ("The Mirror Image in Soviet American Relations: A Social Psychologist's Report," *Journal of Social Issues,* 17, no. 3 [1961]: 46).

[2] See Leon Festinger, *A Theory of Cognitive Dissonance* (Evanston, Ill.: Row, Peterson, 1957).

17

TRUTH, LOVE, AND
SOCIAL CHANGE

There are two kinds of values to which people orient themselves in thinking about social change. They can be depicted in their extreme form, as will be indicated presently. In this extreme form they become mutually exclusive, although we are seldom aware of this. Most of us carry both orientations around with us, applying them in different admixtures in this case or that—so far as I can see without any systematic examination of their interrelation, and thus without recognition that, pressed beyond a certain threshold, they are in fact incompatible. Our orientation toward these two kinds of values has important implications for the whole question of channeling social change, and the posture we take—as individuals, as groups, as organizations, as nation-states —toward social changes that are on the fringe of feasibility. Such changes involve issues which at a particular point in history become increasingly relevant; so much so that people find themselves taking sides as to whether they want the change or whether they do not, and they find themselves believing that their side-taking has something to do with the outcome, so that it becomes more than relevant, it becomes fateful.

THE CONFLICT OF TRUTH AND LOVE

The two basic orientations toward change can be termed "truth" and "love." By truth is meant here not the truth of the dispassionate scientist, aloof

Paper prepared for the Seminar on Channeling Social Change, Institute on Man and Science, Rensselaerville, New York, October 1967.

from the world of events as he pursues knowledge, but rather the impassioned conviction of the zealot, the person who is convinced he has come upon some fundamental moral value and wishes to see it embedded in the warp and woof of events. His truth is that of the prophets of old, who prefaced their statements: Thus saith the Lord. They saw this normative truth as something greater than themselves, yes, greater than those who opposed them—something whose authenticity called to them with absolute conviction, something that must override less important things, something for which they were willing to sacrifice their own happiness, their lives, if need be, as well as others'. This is the sense in which I am using the word "truth"—the conviction that we somehow represent the fundamental order of things in calling for the changes that we propose to bring to the social order.

I am using "love" in a special sense, too. I am using it roughly in the sense of the Latin *caritas* and the Greek *agape,* and Corinthian I. I am using it not in the affective sense, but in the appreciative sense, as a relationship of infinite appreciation and respect, perhaps best expressed in the concept of Stoic and Jew and Christian alike that all men are brothers, being children of the same loving Father. However it is described—and I use this language only figuratively—it constitutes roughly a commitment to the infinite value of each human being, and the corollary, expressed by the philosopher Kant in more formal terms, that human beings are to be considered as ends, rather than merely as means.

As I say, most people live comfortably with these two commitments, often honoring them more in the breach than in the observance, until they are confronted with a situation where the two values meet each other head on over an important issue, and they are faced with the problem of deciding whether they are to force their truth—of compelling value—on the person who disagrees, or whether, out of love for him in the sense of respect for his infinite worth as an autonomous individual, they are going to seek a *modus vivendi* with him which will prevent them from acting in an unloving way but will leave them, in Browning's words, with a sense of the unlit lamp and the ungirt loin.

Truth and love come into conflict distressingly often, not least in the field of social change. When we speak of channeling social change, do we really mean getting people to jump through our hoops?

There are at least two issues involved here. One is the question whether we really know enough about social change to know whether it can be channeled, and if so, whether we have the knowledge necessary to do the actual channeling. The other plummets us into the value questions. If we can channel change, and do so, we must presumably guide change in accordance with some preconceived end. But whose end? On the other hand, if we do not have a preconceived end or goal, can we really be serious when we use a term like channeling, which means guiding?

Finally, if it is our end toward which we wish to bend the course of events, are we not in effect trying to get people to jump through our hoops? Are we not, in effect, saying that we want to help people decide things for themselves so long as they decide them in our way, but that if there is any danger that they may decide them in some way unacceptable to us, we must set limits? Do we show sweet reasonableness and willingness to negotiate *within* the channel while at the same time exposing the iron fist of compulsion if people decide they would prefer to go *outside* the channel?

A consideration of the strain and turmoil in this generation indicates the complex interrelation of these two sets of questions. We have not yet found a way to revise national boundaries and in other ways accommodate changes in power, aspiration, and international configuration without resort to war. Such changes occur peacefully, within or outside of international institutions set up for this specific purpose, only when great power coalitions are present to enforce the peaceful changes on lesser powers.

On a different level, we appear unable to make a serious impact on the bundle of tormenting problems at the center of our great cities. We have poured billions of dollars into low-income housing and have attempted through federal policy to desegregate our Negro ghettos, both with highly equivocal results.

On both the international level and the community level we see the confusion raised by the uncertainty of our ability to control change and of how the direction of change shall be established. With great-power agreement, many things are possible in the United Nations. Similarly, where major parties to the community dialogue have achieved consensus, the way is open for prompt action, and we seem to know how to proceed. Unfortunately, on both levels, circumstances that permit important problems to be solved in an atmosphere of consensus as to goals among the principal parties are few indeed.

Most of the great issues of our day have become issues because they involve a variety of interests and points of view, passionately held. The passionately held point of view which differs from our own we tend to think of as resistance to change, and we look for some pathology behind the inability or refusal of our opponent to see the wisdom of our own view. Reflecting the large changes in viewpoint in which our century is engulfed—and over which we have little if any control—we tend increasingly to look at the viewpoint of our opponent from a causal rather than a moralistic approach. His condition is thereby transformed in our minds from one of deliberate malice to one of pathology. Instead of being evil, he is simply sick. We seem unwilling to admit to ourselves—and to proceed with the necessary implications—that there are genuine conflicts of interest and genuine conflicts in value—two different but related things. Not all interests can be reconciled by increasing trust and intercommunication, although no doubt some of them can. Nevertheless, our global remedy for conflict of interest appears to be based on the false premise that such interest conflicts are at least theoretically reconcilable but that such reconciliation is prevented by faulty comunication, faulty reasoning, and pathological traits of the individual or nation, which prevent them from adopting the necessary posture of goodwill and rationality which would produce agreement and permit necessary and desirable changes to occur without conflict. Although the differences are extremely great, they are not necessarily irreconcilable, we asume.

Part of our difficulty is that we don't recognize the hard fact of conflicts over interests and values. Our apparent inability to face this fact squarely, and thus realistically to go about getting on with things, lies in our implicit adherence to a great Socratic truth—or perhaps, if all its implications are considered, one should call it a great nontruth—namely, that the truth is one, and that it is dicoverable and demonstrable through some such reasoning process as the Socratic dialectic. Ultimately, then, it is only ignorance that keeps you and me from acknowledging the same basic set of values, and once you have overcome your ignorance, you will see that your interests and mine coincide. For our true interests lie compatibly in the realization of the same set of values, which cannot be considered to imply anything but the same real situation for all men.

Now, this is patent nonsense. Yet it holds us immobilized. It keeps us looking for the fool's gold of agreement in situations where we will never find it, and it keeps us explaining away the disagreement in terms of ignorance, malice, or pathology. We have taken this same nonsense over into our Jewish-Christian theology, and assumed that in some ultimate sense, all people have the same set of values and that all valid values can be realized simultaneously. We appreciate Greek tragedy, but do not understand its fateful lesson—that values of loyalty and honor and love and religion often conflict with each other in most fatal ways, and that such conflicts cannot be reasoned away.

CHANGE AS A "NATURAL" PROCESS, AND PURPOSIVE CHANGE

But let us return to our prior question, for it is indeed a formidable one. *Can* change be channeled? Or, perhaps more precisely, what is the relationship between the process of social change and the attempt to influence this process by deliberate intervention?

It is interesting to note that the so-called grand theories of social change are primarily concerned with understanding how change takes place, rather than with bringing about change. They try to understand social change as a natural process. I think one can fairly say this about the various cyclical-change theorists, such as Plato and Sorokin and Toynbee, although it is interesting that in each case, admonitional lessons were drawn which the authors wrote down by way of feeding them back into the social process.

Much the same can be said of the evolutionary theories of change. One thinks of Hegel's concept of history as the unfolding of absolute reason in a sort of logical dialectic that is acted out in the rise and fall of civilizations, in a way that makes purposive intervention seem minuscule and irrelevant. Or in quite other terms, one thinks of Spencer's all-pervading concept of evolution, including social evolution, which assures a steady progress as history unfolds, provided that natural laws are not tampered with by deliberate interveners.

Obviously, a theory that explains change without resorting to the efficacy of purposive intervention must be enervating in its implications: Leave things alone, you can't possibly do any good. Karl Marx struggled with this problem throughout his life, and he apparently never was able to reconcile satisfactorily his insistence on scientific socialism as the theory of a natural change process, on the one hand, and his desire to influence that change process, on the other. Presumably men are capable of courage, dedication, and sacrifice, but not in the interests of a movement that does not depend on them for its implementation.

One of the leading threads woven into the multicolored garment of grand theories of change is the question whether values and aspirations are efficacious in history, or whether they are not merely epiphenomena, the kinds of things people think as they behave inexorably in accordance with a natural law that functions independently of their values and aspirations. As I have indicated, Marx never finally resolved this question in his own mind, even though he quite explicitly favored the epiphenomenal view, putting his chief emphasis on dialectic materialism. This materialistic dialectic, it will be remembered, constituted on his part a conscious "Copernican revolution" as over against the Hegelian dialectic idealism, which saw in ideas the dynamic of history. And it will be recalled that Max Weber was deliberately aiming his discourse at Marx when he pointed out the crucial efficacy of the Protestant ethic, a set of ideas, in bringing about capitalism.

Generally speaking, systematic thinking about social change has been of the grand type, concerning itself with the rise and fall of civilizations and of great nations and coalitions. It has sought to make order out of history by "explaining" events in accordance with a few basic laws of change, and in the process has treated the events as though they occurred independently of the willing of specific individuals and groups. There are two major exceptions to this general statement. These are the interrelated concerns with social movements and with revolutions. Both of these topics involve purposive effort to change society or a part of it, and both of them have received considerable attention from students of social change.

Let us turn for a moment from the question of theories of change to the matter of social change itself. While it is obvious that the efforts of individuals may have some effect on the course of events, this course is itself channeled by forces that are largely beyond the effective control of any single human being or any group of human beings to alter in any major way.

Although it is possible to describe all human social behavior as purposeful, this is far from saying that the aggregate decisions of individual human beings and of groups of human beings to behave one way or another can be or are purposefully controlled. Let us take a simple example: urbanization. I shall employ this term to mean the actual growth of cities and also the spread of city ways to the countryside. This phenomenon is worldwide. It is part of a complex network of other closely related developments. It is widely acknowledged that the process is inexorable, irreversible, and extremely difficult even to slow down or in any way divert. In this respect, it is very much like automation, or the growth of scientific knowledge, or the resurgence of nationalism in the Communist countries.

To point out the apparent autonomy of various social change processes, however, is not to deny the efficacy of all purposive intervention in these processes. The economists have long since demonstrated the efficacy of deliberate national economic strategies in preventing depressions. Likewise, there is little doubt that the deliberate policy of the Puerto Rican government to promote industrial growth through Operation Bootstrap was notably effective. The federal policy with respect to racial desegregation in North and South is more indicative of the difficulty of planned intervention, and ironically, more effect from this intervention is so far ascertainable in the South than in the North.

What seems to emerge from such considerations is a conception of the relationship between social change processes, as such, and those smaller components of change processes which are thought of as purposive change efforts. The relationship might be summarized in this way: Purposive attempts to influence the course of social change are themselves part of the dynamic forces producing social change. While they are only a part, and sometimes a minor part, they nevertheless are important. Often they are secondary, in the sense that the purposive attempts at change are themselves responses to changes that are occurring quite independently of them. Thus, for example, various purposive changes may be made in order to cope with the effects of increasing urbanization, even though that primary phenomenon is itself difficult to alter.

Likewise, greater or lesser deliberate control may be attempted by a government over the course of industrialization, through encouraging certain industries and discouraging others, influencing plant location, and so on. But there is little indication that the process of industrialization can be halted or reversed. The same can be said for responses that are made to the increasing division of labor, which itself seems quite incapable of being deliberately halted or reversed.

The concept of channeling does convey the notion that change is going to flow on, but that perhaps it can be kept within certain bounds, through appropriate measures that will not attempt a reversal of the main direction of flow, but rather will apply a retaining wall here and do a little dredging there, as well as putting up a few markers to indicate the channel.

INDUCEMENT OF CHANGE, RESISTANCE TO CHANGE

There are two modes of viewing change, the passive and the active. The passive mode, in this case, is analogous to the passive mode in grammar. It implies that ego is on the receiving end. The individual is the object of change. The active mode, on the other hand, puts ego, the subject of the sentence, on the initiating end. The individual is the initiator of change. Change is seen as resulting from ego's behavior. Obviously, both modes have their validity, but let us pursue further the active mode of change, that which considers change as the object, at least in part, of human volition.

It is interesting that in doing so, most of us tend to empathize with the individual who is trying to bring about the change. One might just as readily empathize with other individuals in the environment who oppose the change, but we do not customarily react in this fashion. We seem to be conditioned to assuming that change is good and that the person who resists it therefore constitutes a problem. Why do we do this? I suppose there are at least two reasons. The first is syntax. We tend to identify ourselves with the subject of the sentence, rather than with the object. The other is more complex. We (the "we" being people who deliberate at all about such things) tend to take a problem-oriented view toward society, an essentially utopian view which looks at the situation, recognizes aspects of it that are less than satisfactory, and begins to think about altering the more unsatisfactory aspects.

Actually, the opposite basic orientation is equally appropriate. We could look at society and see the great merits in the existing situation and be concerned with preserving it so as not to lose its merits in the uncertain search for improvement.

The tendency to empathize with the change agent and to see the change resister as a problem begs the question in a highly naïve way. Often, when we say someone is resisting peaceful change, the case actually is that he is not resisting peaceful change at all, he is simply resisting our change, whether peacefully or nonpeacefully. He doesn't like it. It goes against his own selfish interests, or his larger values, or both. But since our change is by definition right, then we must account for his disagreement.

How will we overcome his resistance? Perhaps we should get to know his culture better, so that our change can be made more palatable to him on his own terms. Perhaps he should be educated, since his disagreement with something which is obviously beneficial is an indication of his ignorance of the true situation. Or perhaps he is sick. He isn't free to think creatively with us. Theoretically, if we could rid him of his illness, he would be able to reason correctly and see the light even as we have seen it.

All of this may of course be so, but it is highly debatable. There are two alternative ways of accounting for his disagreement. The first is to accept our implicit premises that the true and the good are one and that therefore only one of us can be right, but that he happens to be the one who is right, and we are in error. *We* (if you will forgive me the absurdity) are in need of being educated; or perhaps *we* are sick and thus unable to follow his flawless reasoning.

The other explanation is more acceptable from my own point of view. Granted that neither he nor we are ignorant or sick (although either or both may be, of course), he simply disagrees with our evaluation, basing his own on a different scale of values, or on a different set of selfish interests from ours, or both.

Perhaps all I am trying to say is that we should not fall into the naïve blunder of thinking that the problem lies with the person who resists change. It may conceivably be the other way around.

SOME IMPLICATIONS OF TRUTH AND LOVE

Let us return now to the original consideration of truth and love as two fundamental modes of orientation toward social change. Actually, the relationship here is not simply one of orientation toward social change, but rather a deep-rooted polarity that permeates many aspects of our lives and extends to the most diverse fields. The truth-love relationship is at one end of a broad, inclusive spectrum. At the other end are orientations toward experience itself, a fundamental epistemological dichotomy perhaps best captured by the difference between what William James calls "knowledge by acquaintance" and "knowledge about." Somewhere in between these extremes there is an area that can be described by the term "savoring of existence" and which extends on one side toward a fundamental orientation toward ways of knowing and on the other toward a fundamental orientation toward change. Let me begin in the middle and work out toward both ends, first in the direction of orientation toward knowing.

Starting in the middle, in the area of "savoring of existence," I shall begin with the lyric poets. This is highly appropriate, since in my judgment that is what lyric poetry is all about. It is the plea of the poet, embodied in words, that we savor existence, not merely exist. The lyric poet therefore points out to us the immediate sense of color and smell and taste in the countryside or on

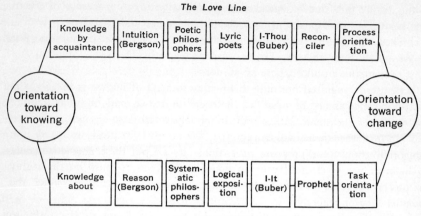

the city streets, in a mansion or in a hovel. Or he takes the everyday occurrence, the everyday emotions, and holds them up to us in a way that attracts us to their immediate qualities, not thinking of them as task-oriented events, but rather as visceral experiences. And so we see in a direct and intense way a field of daffodils, or the boom and bustle of the young, energetic city of Chicago, or we are invited to share the experience, the inner tone, of a man's love for a woman.

What a contrast from a different use of words—a use that describes facts about situations, or points out their logical interrelationships, or seeks, within the situation, to pursue some goal outside of the situation, to concentrate on those aspects of the situation that have to be dealt with in order to achieve something else!

As we move from this set of alternatives within a situation—savoring it for its immediacy, for its flavor, or pursuing it for understanding, for rational ordering—over toward two alternative ways of knowing (not a far move at all), it is interesting to note the variation among philosophers in their ways of approaching their subject matter. At the one extreme are the philosopher-poets, at the other the philosopher-scientists. On the one hand there is the long line of attempts through word pictures to inquire into the essence of reality. One thinks of Plato's cave analogy, or of the charioteer in the tenth book of the *Republic*. How different from Aristotle, who is in turn much more analytical, much more prosaic, much more systematic, emphasizing logical interrelationships almost to the exclusion of the attempt to portray a sense of the immediate reality. One does not expect poetry from Aristotle. But think of the other poetic philosophers, of Nietzsche, of Santayana, and others who deliberated in a mode that was essentially poetic. They wanted to give full value to one side of the duality indicated by Pascal, himself an interesting admixture of the two: The heart has its reasons which reason itself does not understand.

They contrast markedly with another line of philosophers, represented by Aristotle's great adapter, Thomas Aquinas, and by Descartes, Spinoza, and most contemporary philosophers of science.

Bergson recognized not only this duality in ways of knowing, but also the partial incompatability of what he contrasted as reason and intuition. Opting for the latter, he insisted that only intuitively could nature's essence, which was process rather than state, be captured. Reason can only break up reality into categorical chunks for purposes of analysis. It can put these chunks together again in only a mechanical way. In doing so, it loses its grasp on the reality of process, the *élan vital*. Only through intuition can man encounter the essential flow of reality.

It is interesting that English does not have two forms of the verb "to know" which account for this basic difference in approaching reality. Many other languages, particularly the Western European ones, do have a pair of terms corresponding to the distinction being made here: the Latin *scire* and *noscere,* the German *wissen* and *kennen,* the French *savoir* and *connaître,* and so on. It is these pairs that William James indicated through his use of the somewhat clumsy terms "knowledge about" and "knowledge by acquaintance."

Having explored the end of the continuum that has to do with the dichotomy in ways of knowing, let us move toward the other end, which has to do with our relation to other people, particularly in regard to social change and to the alternative emphasis on truth or love in respect to it.

Buber gives a striking depiction of the alternatives in his description of the I-thou relationship and the I-it relationship. The one is to the whole person, the other only to a part of the person. And similarly, the one relates the whole self, the other only part of the self. The one relationship looks to the other person as a being of infinite worth in itself.

> But this is the exalted melancholy of our fate, that every *Thou* in our world must become an *It.* . . . As soon as the relation has been worked out, or has been permeated with a means, the *Thou* becomes an object among objects—perhaps the chief, but still one of them, fixed in its size and its limits.[1]

Here we see an implied reference to Kant's dictum of treating humanity in oneself or in another always as an end, never as merely a means. Buber describes the first alternative, man as an end, the I-Thou relationship, in terms of love.

> Love ranges in its effect through the whole world. In the eyes of him who takes his stand in love, and gazes out of it, men are cut free from

their entanglement in bustling activity. Good people and evil, wise and foolish, beautiful and ugly, become successively real to him; that is, set free they step forth in their singleness, and confront him as *Thou.*"[2]

THE PROPHET AND THE RECONCILER

Now it seems to me that the way of truth, in the sense of moral truth as I described it earlier, is addressed not to the whole other person, but only to a part of him. It seeks to bend the other person to one's own purposes—an utterly indefensible effort except for the assurance conveyed by psychological certainty of one fact: that one's own purpose is of transcendent value—or, in religious language, is God's purpose. "Thus spake the Lord!"

This sense of inner certainty that the ideals for which one is striving are sanctified, that they are God's truth, is best exemplified in the Biblical prophets. For them, it had a number of implications. First, they were sure they were right, for the Lord had spoken to them. Second, they considered the truths that God had spoken as being of the highest value, more valuable than their own comfort, safety, or life. They therefore showed extreme courage in proclaiming God's truth, often under extreme antagonism aroused by their proclamations. Third, they seemed to be so charged with the importance of their message that they hardly raised the question of a loving relationship to their fellow men. Theirs was not the way of understanding and reconciliation. How could they understand and reconcile themselves to evil? Their mission was to condemn evil, and to condemn the evildoer as well. "Wherefore, O harlot, hear the word of the Lord," says Ezekiel to Jerusalem, and proceeds to document his accusation in hardly conciliatory terms.

Many of the prophets of old and their latter-day counterparts have suffered beatings, imprisonment, and worse because of the antagonism they created. One can hardly withhold the observation that much of the antagonism might have been mitigated by a more conciliatory approach, or, as some modern change agents might put it, by more attention to process and less to task. But psychological certitude about knowing the truth has a way of going to extremes, of sacrificing other values to this truth, and of combatting viciously those who cannot be swayed to it.

Hence the way of truth has led to the condemnation of Socrates, the crucifixion of Jesus, the burning of Giordano Bruno, the excommunication of Spinoza, Calvin's tyranny in Geneva, and a host of other instances of the pursuing of one's own truth, experienced as *the* truth, to the sacrifice of other values, and—especially important for our discourse—to the sacrifice of love. It is needless to tell others or ourselves that a sense of psychological certitude is no guarantee of truth. He who finds himself afire with the zeal of allegiance to a commanding ideal needs no further certitude.

If we think of the prophet as a sort of ideal type who maximizes truth, we can set up a corresponding ideal type, particularly in controversial issues such as the prophet engages in, which maximizes love. That ideal type can be designated as the reconciler. The reconciler, as he faces a dispute, is more concerned with reestablishing an amicable relationship between the contestants than he is with the question of which truth triumphs. In order to be effective as a reconciler, he must persuade both parties to the dispute that he wishes them not ill but good. They must be able to consider him as unprejudiced—not in the sense that he may not have any convictions in the issue at stake, but rather that he can be utterly relied upon not to allow his own personal predilections to influence his relationship to either of the parties as he attempts to resolve their conflict.

He cannot function as a reconciler while he affirms the good of one side and the evil of the other. To the extent that he does so, he has stepped over into the role of the prophet and vitiated his role as reconciler.

But by the same token, to the extent that he holds his own conception of the truth in abeyance, seeking not to impose what he thinks is the right solution but rather engaging in a process of helping the contenders agree on a resolution, he is submitting to a constraint on his own ability to prophesy, to proclaim God's truth.

There does not appear to be any way out of this dilemma. The individual either seeks to impose his way or subordinates his commitment to what he considers the right way to a conflicting commitment to amity.

Truth and love cannot be maximized simultaneously. The prophet maximizes truth, but at the expense of love. The reconciler maximizes love, but at the expense of his own truth. It is possible to take various positions in between, all of which involve maximizing neither.

All of us experience this incompatibility on various issues with which we are confronted. How far shall we enforce our truth on the antagonist? But the problem is not a vexing one on all issues in which we find ourselves in disagreement with someone else. For on many of these issues, although we have an opinion, we do not feel so strongly about it that we must have our way. We are willing to go along with whatever resolution is found.

Moving farther along in the direction of our concern with social change, we find here also two disparate emphases that seem to permeate the gamut of change postures and issues. One has to do with accomplishing a particular outcome, achieving a particular task. The goal is clear, and the problem is only to acquire the necessary support from other parties for its accomplishment. This task orientation corresponds to the prophetic one, to the emphasis on truth.

The other, equally relevant in considering purposive social change, may be called process orientation. It emphasizes not the accomplishment of this or that specific task, but rather the building of a set of relationships among the principal parties, encouraging communication and discussion among them, so that they will then set for themselves whatever goals they may wish to set. The emphasis is on the man-to-man relationship, not on the task to be accomplished. It is not organized toward tasks, toward people as means, as "its," toward rationality, toward truth, but rather toward process, toward people as ends, as "thous," toward sentiment, toward love.

I do not want to overstress this series of dichotomies. What I have sought to do so far is to string these various beads along on two strings. On the one string, the truth string, has been knowledge about, reason, the systematic philosophers, logical exposition, the I-It relationship, the prophet, and task orientation in social change. On the other string, the love string, has been knowledge by acquaintance, intuition, the poetic philosophers, lyric poetry, the I-Thou relationship, the reconciler, and process orientation in social change.

In doing so, of course, I am implying that the dilemma we face in purposive change is not an isolated phenomenon, but part of a dualism that runs through the whole question of our relation to our fellow men and our ways of comprehending reality. And I have been explicit on one other related point—that there truly is a conflict between truth and love, and that in matters where positions are strongly held, it is illusory to assume that the problem is merely one of helping both sides to see or find the one truth, in a Socratic sense, and much more realistic to acknowledge deep-rooted and abiding differences of interest and value that rational deliberation can seldom be expected to reconcile.

This is not to say that true agreement is impossible when two or more parties hold different points of view. We have seen the contrary much too often to believe that. Mary P. Follett's book on *Creative Experience*[3] is not only a strong logical argument for the possibility of "emergent" resolutions which each side of a controversy can affirm even more readily than they affirmed their initial conflicting positions; it is also replete with illustrations of cases in which this has occurred. I am asserting, though, that we cannot expect either that it always will occur or that it is always possible for it to occur.

TASK GOALS AND PROCESS GOALS IN CHANGE

Let us examine another aspect of the truth-love problem, the question of task orientation and process orientation in purposive change, from the standpoint of the change agent in the community. By change agent I simply mean any person or group, professional or nonprofessional, inside or outside a social system, which is attempting to bring about change in that system. To take the classic example, let the change agent be a public health worker who is attempting to introduce inoculation against a contagious disease. He has his goal already established. It was established, let us assume, not by people of the community who felt a strong need and desire for inoculation, but rather by an outside health organization's determination to seek to prevent deaths from the contagious disease in that community by means of a mass inoculation program.

Let us contrast this public health worker with a different type of change agent, a general-purpose community development worker. This worker does not have a task-oriented goal. He is not concerned primarily with whether a bridge gets built or illiteracy is reduced by 20 percent through an intense literacy campaign or a mass inoculation program takes place. The community development worker is concerned with engaging in a process with community people through which they will come into closer relation to one another and will begin to form viable patterns for decision-making and to utilize these patterns for making their own decisions as to what goals they care to pursue, and in what order, and then to go about implementing the decisions they have made.

Two decades or so of community development work have indicated that there is indeed an abiding problem whether to emphasize specific preconceived tasks or rather to emphasize community growth in decision-making ability. The difficulty, of course, lies in the fact that it is always much more satisfying to be able to show tangible indications of task accomplishment; the accomplishment achieved through stimulating local people to make their own decisions and implement them may be painfully slow in coming, and may evaporate as soon as the community worker leaves the scene.

Since community development has been conceived primarily as a means toward national social and economic development, which involves goal-setting at a level more inclusive than the community, thus establishing specific goals and quotas for various communities, it is readily apparent why the task-oriented approach has won out over the process-oriented approach in most community development ventures. Putting this another way, most ventures are fairly explicit about the dual goals of the accomplishment of specific tasks *and* the social process of enhancing community decision-making capacity. But when the chips are down, it is the task goals that hold sway, and rather than attempting to help community people decide what they themselves want, the change agent attempts to persuade community people to do what he wants.

It is interesting that community change agents tell each other in their literature that they should be emphasizing process rather than task, but they also keep admitting that task continues to eclipse process. Somehow they assume that this is not good community development, or at least that it is not democratic community development. Some of the theorists seem to be quite clear that they favor the emphasis on process, even when the chips are down and there is precious little task performance to show for it.

Others, however, can't bring themselves to make this decision. They seem to think it is possible both to help people do what they themselves want to do and at the same time to ensure that specific goals get accomplished. They assume not only that the people, because they are now confronting their problems rationally or democratically, or because various barriers to free communication within the community have been broken down in the community development process, will be able to make viable decisions, but that these viable decisions will somehow magically correspond to what some outside agency (the national plan) thinks the community should be doing. They are often disappointed.

Of course, there are some change agents who are simply committed to task accomplishment, and acknowledge no special commitment to building any sort of more viable or more democratic or more anything relationships among the people of the community. The task-oriented community worker corresponds to the truth line, while the process-oriented community worker corresponds to the love line. As we have seen, the man who tries to combine them does not have it easy.

CONFLICT, CONSENSUS, AND CHANGE

Since we are on the community level let us consider a different but related kind of problem in the community setting. The problem is usually described in terms of the alternatives of conflict strategies and consensus strategies in bringing about community changes. As is well known, recent years have seen an eruption of controversy within American communities involving such issues as birth control, fluoridation, urban renewal, and civil rights. Any of these issues is an excellent example of the "dilemma of partisans," as Wayne A. R. Leys has called it: the dilemma of having to choose between seeking to force one's way on others and renouncing one's own good in favor of amity with opponents.

The trend in the last decade has been noticeably in the direction of affirming conflict as a desirable state of affairs, or at least as an indispensible prerequisite to the accomplishment of worthwhile goals that are not in accordance with the interests of some power structure or other. The way of trying to work through consensus, through moral appeal, through persuasion has seemed too slow for many advocates of social change.

The body of practice theory that has had most directly to do with the social aspects of planning for change in the community is the branch of social work called community organization. Until comparatively recently, its model for change called for cooperation with community people in establishing decision-making channels, defining goals, and choosing and implementing appropriate courses of action. Let us recall again Murray G. Ross's definition:

> Community organization is a process by which a community identifies
> its needs or objectives, orders (or ranks) them, develops the confi-
> dence and will to work at them, finds the resources (internal and/or

external) to deal with them, takes action in respect to them, and in
so doing extends and develops cooperative and collaborative attitudes
and practices in the community.[4]

This definition assumes that a community has only one set of needs or objectives,
and that these are the same for all its varied inhabitants and interest groups. I
have commented earlier on the questionable nature of this assumption. The
definition goes on to describe a process of goal setting and implementation
based on a consensus of all the principal parties. It does not take conflict situations into account.

Yet some of the most important issues confronting American communities
are rife with conflicting viewpoints.

The implicit assumption of consensus as a basis for purposive change is
apparent in the structure of such community planning agencies as the old-style
councils of social agencies or the newer community welfare councils. They have
been based on a commitment to consensus, and as a result have tended to be
relatively conservative organizations. They have in general avoided controversy
by means of limiting their membership essentially to like-minded persons, coming overwhelmingly from the middle class (to the relative exclusion of Negroes,
the poor, labor unions), and they have also tended to shun direct confrontation
with "controversial" questions such as birth control, the organization of protest
groups among the poor, and open housing. Likewise, they have avoided conflict
tactics, such as demonstrations, picketing, and so on, as "inappropriate." Such
tactics are indeed inappropriate to an organization with a strong commitment to
consensus.

Recently there has been a change in intellectual climate within the profession of community organizers, partly because of the increasing realization that
the most important issues that cry for resolution do involve controversy, partly
because there has been a growing number of leaders in the field who have come
out for a positive, task-oriented role on the part of the community organizer,
rather than simply that of an enabler. The community organizer no longer merely
seeks consensus among community people. He attempts to achieve a consensus
for the goals that he, for whatever reason, thinks are worthwhile.

It is perhaps justified to say that he has moved over toward truth and away
from love.

APATHY AND OPPOSITION AS OBSTACLES TO CHANGE

In some of my own research on processes of purposive change at the community level, it has been interesting to note an important difference between two

kinds of community action. By community action I mean temporary, sporadic efforts to further some community purpose, such as to establish a new art museum or to institute a new set of social services or to attract a new industry to the community. Such projects as I have in mind usually start with relatively few people, who expand their circle as they move on with the project, in order to avail themselves of the resources of other people and groups, and, once the goal of the project is developed—the new art museum is established, the new social services are instituted, the new industry has come to town—they either dissolve their coalition or transform it in some way into a formal organization.

In one review of thirty-five action projects of this general type which a colleague and I made,[5] it was apparent that there were two kinds of change efforts. In the first kind, the principal problem confronting the change agents was that of setting up a viable coalition to work toward its specific objective, and to hold this coalition together long enough to acquire the necessary resources and apply them effectively to the goal. In these cases, the principal obstacle seemed to be apathy. Most people either didn't care or were in only mild agreement with the goals of the change agents. Interest had to be generated and sustained in order to acquire the needed resources and apply them to the objective.

In the other kind of action project, the principal obstacle was not apathy, but opposition. People were interested, people cared, but they were divided into two groups: those who supported the change agent's objective and those who opposed it.

We found that these two kinds of change efforts took different forms with regard to a number of variables, including the type of change strategy employed, the types of goals they set for themselves, the stance of key leaders regarding the proposed change, and even the success or failure of the change venture.

There are certain implications here for the channeling of social change. In the first cases, those in which there was general consensus in approving the change goal but where the problem was apathy, not only was it possible to work with collaborative techniques in bringing about change, but the use of these techniques apparently contributed favorably to the outcome by serving to stimulate people's interest and support through participation in decision-making.

In much of our thinking about channeling social change, we tend to assume that all channeling problems are of this first type—the need to exchange views, to stimulate interest, to iron out differences, to pull together.

But this happy model does not fit all cases. For in the others, those in which there is dissensus regarding values or interests or both, there are real differences that cannot be dissolved by bringing people together for face-to-face talks, or by bringing them into the decision-making process, or by other processual means. Of course, one might coopt them by permitting them a voice in goal-setting as an investment in their subsequent support of the change effort, but the price may be too high. That is, they may not lend their support unless the project's goals are changed so radically as to defeat the purposes of the change agent.

Putting this another way, the change agent is faced with the problem posed earlier—he must either force his values on others or give them up in the interests of amity. He can achieve his goal only by defeating the opposition. He is in a zero-sum situation. You win, I lose, or vice versa.

Now let me point out one of the weaknesses of this study, for it has implications for the channeling of social change. The analysis I have just made leaves out an important variable—the strategy of the change agent. It more or less assumes that if there is opposition, you must either fight or give up your goal. It leaves no room for the third alternative, which is mutual give-and-take in the search for a solution acceptable to both sides. Let me say that we approached this particular study with this third possibility in mind, and we found relatively little evidence of the process in the cases investigated. We had little difficulty in classifying all the cases into either the consensus or the dissensus category.

Nevertheless, let me make an observation about this possible third category, which seems so hopeful yet so elusive. I have indicated that there are many change situations in which consensus is not only possible but actually realized, but that there are others in which it is not realized and perhaps not even possible. Earlier I asserted the fallacy of assuming that this second category never exists, of assuming that there is only one consistent, valid set of values, and that thus all men can find agreement on this one set of values and its implications, if only they are well informed and if they are psychologically freed from the personal deficiencies that interfere with finding the truth and affirming it. I indicated that this was a sort of Socratic conception that was untenable.

The third possibility—that agreement can be found through a creative process of interaction, so that an emergent truth, rather than a preexisting truth, can be discovered and can form the basis for consensus in what was earlier opposition—is simply a modification of the first position, and it still retains the weaknesses of that position. Rather than saying, with Socrates, that agreement is possible because there is only one truth and we shall find it, it says, with Hegel, that agreement is possible because there is only one truth, which we shall create in the synthesis of our conflicting partial viewpoints. Now this may be possible occasionally, but if we are to be realistic, we must acknowledge that many situations do not fit this model, and that a lot of people get hurt before the conflict gets itself resolved in a long-range historical synthesis. We can hardly be satisfied with a complacent view that history is the unfolding of absolute reason and that newer and ever higher syntheses will work themselves out as the centuries go by. This position, wherein everything that is is right, as Hegel put it, is hardly more tenable to the person deeply concerned with the misery that social change problems bring in their wake than is Pangloss' vapid assurance that everything is for the best in this best of all possible worlds, or the assurance of the social Darwinists that progress is a built-in process and will take place automatically if only we don't tamper with the social organism.

DYNAMIC PLURALISM

There must be an alternative to the way of the loveless prophet and the truthless reconciler, but the idea of the creative synthesis of opposing viewpoints, while helpful and perhaps applicable in some cases, does not completely fill the gap. We must confront head on the problem of change situations where there is abiding opposition, and where not everyone can be satisfied. We can neither take nor even allow the way of pushing one's own value in total disregard of other values, either one's own or others', nor can we take the way of failing to cope rapidly and radically with the problems that beset us merely because we cannot reach perfect agreement as to how to proceed.

This implies the need for neither consensus nor knock-down, drag-out conflict, but for a creative confrontation, a dynamic pluralism, if you will. To me, this seems to place a high priority not on glossing over differences, but quite the contrary, on emphasizing differences. It would imply a sense of discomfort not when people have not reached consensus, but when they have. By the same token, it must imply, if we are not to be at each other's throats or destroy the firm ground on which we claim to stand, the strengthening of the ground rules of the process of opposition—channeling, if you will, this opposition, keeping it within the bounds of an acceptable and tolerable confrontation, rather than letting it engulf all other values and all other parties. We need the mechanisms that will encourage the prophet in proclaiming his truth, but will not permit him to destroy himself and the rest of us if we do not care to accept it. We need mechanisms that will permit and channel the seeking of agreement, but which will not suppress important parts of the whole picture in the name of an illusory consensus. We need mechanisms that will fall short of satisfying every party to every controversy, but which will assure the right of the dissatisfied to be heard and to continue their efforts to persuade the rest of us.

Although my own principal frame of reference is the local geographic community, I think the above needs, which seem to me to fit the community context, likewise fit other contexts. These include the international context, where abiding differences in ideology and national interest preclude perfect agreement on all important issues, and where so often nations pursue their own interests and ideological positions with the loveless zeal of the prophet. They include the field of issue resolution on the national scene, and other political decision-making contexts; formal organizations of various types; and informal groups, including the family.

SOME PRECONDITIONS FOR DYNAMIC PLURALISM

If we need to encourage different points of view, if we need to encourage the confrontation of these points of view, if we can feel easier about not achieving agreement before moving ahead in compelling decisions, and if we need strong ground rules for making decisions that not all parties will completely welcome—if we are to have a dynamic pluralism, is it possible to consider some of the preconditions for such a state of affairs?

The problem is how to encourage that confrontation of strongly held viewpoints, of at least partially opposed interests, which is necessary for change, without literally or figuratively killing one another off.

Let us consider some of the preconditions for such a state of affairs.

1. The first precondition is to find ways of overcoming the simplistic dichotomization built into verbal language forms. Either-or, for or against, right or wrong, true or false, good guys or bad guys—they form patterns of thinking that encourage the worst in the prophet, namely, his temptation to see the moral differences in such extreme form that hostility and coercion appeal to him as means for assuring that his truth, which is of course God's truth, will prevail. This tendency to see things along a single dimension often makes differences of degree seem differences of kind, excludes consideration of other aspects that should be taken into account in evaluating possible courses of action, and thus operates to vitiate whatever possible basis may exist for creative synthesis or compromise or at least a *modus vivendi.*

In our individual struggles to think more inclusively, to assess complex situations and alternatives, we are terribly handicapped by this trick that our language plays on us. Mathematics and symbolic logic afford alternatives to verbal language in only the most limited cases. In others, we shall have to continue to talk to each other in highly imprecise language that burdens us with thinking in highly imprecise fashion.

But there are many things that can be done. Children, as they learn language in their formal schooling, can be taught to express relationships in a discriminating fashion; they can be taught to avoid reification, making things out of words; they can be taught to express dichotomous statements in terms of continua, and in other ways learn to employ language in ways that help elucidate the problem under analysis, rather than obscuring the nuances.

2. A second precondition is to assure fluidity among the parties to various issues, so that they find themselves in different combinations of collaboration and opposition as they confront different issues. One might describe this sug-

gestion as emphasizing the value of coalitions, in preference to alliances. In this distinction, a coalition is thought of as a temporary collaborative relationship among a number of autonomous actors in order to further their common interests respecting a specific ad hoc goal. An alliance, on the other hand, is a more permanent collaborative relationship among a number of autonomous actors in order to further their common interests on a wide range of goals. The coalitional arrangement not only permits the individual party greater flexibility in choosing his collaborative partners according to a number of separate issues, but also makes it more difficult for a bloc to maintain discipline within its membership as it seeks to include more and more issues under the headings of "ours" and "theirs." The type of pluralism I described above is furthered by the coalitional type of arrangement. Let me give only two examples, one theoretical, the other practical.

The theoretical example is taken from Karl Marx. His prediction of ultimate revolution of the proletariat in the most advanced capitalist countries was based on his assumption that class consciousness would grow as the proletariat became increasingly oppressed. Capitalist society would become even more polarized than he found it in nineteenth-century England into an exploitative class of capitalists and an exploited class of workers. This polarization would affect so many aspects of life that an ultimate confrontation would be inevitable.

Part of the reason the predicted revolution has not occurred in the advanced capitalist countries is that the predicted polarization has not occurred. Rather, people of various incomes and in various relationships to the instruments of production have found themselves in a plurality of coalitions on issues that did not divide along worker-owner lines, but along lines of religion, geography, political preference, and so on. Society never became polarized into two hostile alliances.

My other illustration is the recent breakup of the two major power blocs, the Warsaw Pact countries and the NATO countries. There are no doubt differences of opinion on the matter, and it is of course difficult to separate out other developments that have altered the international field. But many people, including me, believe that the situation in which the two blocs were monolithically arrayed under the clear hegemony of the Soviet Union and the United States respectively was a highly dangerous one, more dangerous than the existing situation, and that it was dangerous precisely because each powerful bloc leader could feel confident of his ability to command the collaborative loyalty of his whole bloc on all major issues that separated the two blocs. And, parenthetically, there were too many major issues that did.

As the situation becomes more confused, as bloc leaders lose their inordinate control over bloc members, as bloc members begin to form loose coalitions across bloc lines, as issues get sorted out along lines that do not coincide with bloc lines, states leave their complete dependence on alliances and engage in more discrete, less inclusive ad hoc coalitions based on ad hoc interests. Let me emphasize the point: a coalition is preferable to an alliance as a context for collaboration in a world that makes pluralistic tolerance a necessity.

3. The next suggestion may simply beg the question, but there may at least be some advantage to being explicit about it: new techniques must be found for effecting peaceful change in situations where full agreement cannot be reached. Let me give three examples:

The first is the adjustment of international boundaries. We know, for example, that in many of the newly formed African states, the national boundaries were set merely as a continuation of lines drawn on a map in highly adventitious fashion at some point or other in history. We know that boundary changes would be highly desirable here and perhaps in other parts of the world, but how to effect them? Must it be through war? Or, in order to prevent war, must we maintain boundaries that work hardship and make little sense?

The second example is the settlement of labor disputes. Airline, railroad, and postal strikes, as well as strikes in major industries, can have drastic effects on the entire economy. When their secondary costs are added up, the means seem fantastically disproportionate to the ends. So far, we have come up with mediation, conciliation, the cool-off, arbitration, calling in the national guard, and applying presidential and other governmental pressures as means of settling wage disputes. Like the Wise Men in *Amahl and the Night Visitors,* "we still have a long way to go."

The third example is the civil rights revolution and its attendant violence. Whether or not it is true—as I believe it is—that ghetto riots and calls to violence by the fringe of the Black Power movement are responses to the failure of the white man to respond to moral pressure, it is nevertheless also true that rioting is a poor way of bringing about social change, even if it seems the only effective way open. It seems to me that the extent to which the black revolution will remain substantially nonviolent—as it has been, surprisingly, in the past— will be determined by the ability of blacks and whites to devise ways of bringing about equality of opportunity rapidly enough to meet the rising expectations of blacks for social justice.

In each of these examples there are important conflicts of interest. But in other areas of controversy, important conflicts of interest are amenable to legislative, judicial, or other types of issue resolution that are not so costly as wars, strikes, and race riots. There is a technological aspect, in addition to the moral one. Of course, another alternative in each of these cases is no change, the status quo. But in each case, the status quo becomes increasingly untenable, and one thing becomes certain: The status quo will not survive. The issue cannot be status quo or change. The issue is only: Will change come peacefully, and at a not inordinate cost generated by the process of reallocation itself?

4. If we are to have a creative pluralism, still a fourth prerequisite must be

met. We must devise ways of adjusting our formal systems to accommodate new power relationships among the actors; ways, again, which will not be excessively costly. One obvious area in which this adaptation of formal mechanisms is particularly important is the international field. The United Nations must somehow find ways to deal realistically with shifts that have taken place among the great powers since the permanent membership of the Security Council was determined, and thereby to compensate for the inadequacy of equal representation of unequal states in the General Assembly. But the most obvious example of nonadaptation of the formal mechanism to accommodate changes in power is the absence of the People's Republic of China from the United Nations and from its Security Council.

At the local level, a particularly challenging change in power relationships is occurring through the emergence on the city scene of a new source of power—organized blacks. Just what form this exercise of power will take in its informal aspects, and how this power will be incorporated into the deliberative bodies that set or help set community policy, remain to be seen. But here, as elsewhere, the issue is not status quo versus change. The issue is how we will achieve the change that will accommodate the community's institutional structure to the growing power of black citizens as they become organized, develop an explicit position on community issues, act through representatives, and take their place at the hard bargaining table where powerful interest groups hammer out community policy. Will ways be devised to incorporate them rapidly into the important decision mechanisms, or will they have to fight their way in at considerable cost to themselves and to whites?

5. A fifth prerequisite for tolerant pluralism will have to be a willingness to float with situations rather than forever insisting on controlling them. The days of the Pax Romana or the Pax Britannica or the Pax Americana are largely past. Great powers can be expected to wield inordinate influence; but their attempts to control all situations with prophetic zeal can only lead to the extravagant side costs that are so apparent in Vietnam, costs not only to the Vietnamese, but to the rest of the world as well, insofar as they constitute barriers to the solution of still other problems that are also important, problems of atomic nonproliferation in international relations, problems of the urgent tasks of the Great Society, whose programs are being rolled back at home. If peaceful ways of resolving problems of true conflict of interest are to be taken seriously, then it must logically follow that not all nations, or even all great powers, will be satisfied with all issue resolutions. The quest for total control, the aspiration of any country to police the world can only create excessive costs.

6. We need to improve our knowledge in at least three ways:

First, improved knowledge through better communication is needed to explore those situations, referred to earlier, which seem like stubborn conflicts of basic interest but in which ways may possibly be found to avoid the zero-sum situation, ways that both sides can affirm. This may not be possible in every case; but without trying, we will never know. And without the kind of communication that illuminates possible pathways to agreement which lie in the shadow, we can't even try. This is no cure-all, but a full exploration of possibilities for mutual agreement would seem an obvious course of action.

Ironically, as conflict grows, communication between the parties tends to narrow rather than widen. A process of sealing off the parties from interaction except in a conflict situation begins to take place, with the result that less and less opportunity presents itself to explore possible ways to agreement. As tension mounts, the willingness to explore paths to agreement is interpreted increasingly as a sign of disloyalty, while partisans on both sides call for victory in the name of the prophetic truth they claim to represent. Yet there is indication, even at the national level, that the readiness to take steps toward such exploration is a variable that can be widened. In such instances, of course, the good offices of third parties can be invaluable.

Second, we need better data about the issues at stake, about the effect that alternative courses of action might have, about how seriously the other party takes the controversy, about where he is willing to compromise and where he is not.

Third, we need better understanding, in a scientific sense, of conflict and conflict-resolving processes. Much of the research on war and peace is related to this in that it gives a more precise way of calculating the moves an opponent may make, particularly in a zero-sum situation. There is some indication that such knowledge is already being used to devise strategies of deterrence that, though hardly a cure for war, have nevertheless enabled the great powers to move more knowledgeably and therefore more cautiously through improved calculation of the anticipated ripostes of the opponent. On a quite different level, we have much knowledge, but need a great deal more, on the genesis of long-time hatreds between particular peoples, on the psychological concomitants of extreme nationalism, on the relation of frustration and relative deprivation to aggression of various types, on the possibilities of escalation of disarmament, rather than armament, and so on through a long list.

Here again a note of caution is in order. Knowledge can be used for various ends, and there is no guarantee that scientific knowledge of any type will be used for worthy ends. The presence of improved knowledge is itself no guarantor of peaceful change, though I count myself among those who believe it is an aid.

Finally, we need to take into consideration the various aspects of both conflict and cooperation.

It would seem to me that every situation in which conflict or cooperation becomes an issue has at least four components, none of which should be neglected:

First, there is a structural component. The situation may be so structured that a principal party can protect its vital interests only through conflict and violence; or, on the other hand, it may be so structured that other courses of action are open.

Second, there is the matter of interests. We have already considered situations where interests conflict and situations where they do not, and have asserted that some situations involve interest conflicts that are real and enduring and cannot be resolved to the complete satisfaction of all parties.

Third, there are the personal aspects. There is little doubt that if the leaders of the United States and the Soviet Union in 1962 had had personal characteristics different from those they in fact had, the outcome of the Cuban missile crisis might have been fatefully different. It is quite apparent that some people are more predisposed toward hostile aggressiveness than others, and that some of these predispositions may be culturally induced.

Fourth, there are the processual elements in the situation. Given the structural, interest, and personal elements, it is still possible that because of faulty communication, or types of interactional strategy that are less than optimal, solutions that would have been really satisfactory to both sides may never emerge as genuine possibilities; or, on the other hand, through adroit strategies and good communication, what seemed like a zero-sum conflict may turn out to be resolvable to the satisfaction of all parties, and at relatively modest side costs.

The acknowledgement of the importance of each of these components in interactional situations prevents us from affirming or denying partial solutions that are offered as panaceas for war, or for violence, or for other excessive costs of conflict resolution. Education for peace, development of well-adjusted personalities, setting up adequate international machinery, developing a cosmopolitan culture, assuring adequate communication, employing the "appropriate" strategies for conflict resolution—all are relevant, but by the same token, all are misleading as go-it-alone candidates for resolving change peacefully. Every situation where change must be undertaken under conditions of conflict of interests has the four aspects mentioned above, and none of them should be neglected.

TRUTH, LOVE, AND SOCIAL CHANGE

Let me summarize this discourse briefly by saying that it explores the concepts of truth and love in relation to purposive social change, relating truth to the specific goal that the change agent desires, but on which other people may have deep disagreements, and relating love to the contrary value that most of us acknowledge, a value that admonishes us not to impose our truth on others in these deep interest conflicts, out of respect for their value as autonomous human beings. We cannot do both principles complete justice at the same time, even though there are occasional instances when a conciliatory approach may show paths to agreement where none seemed previously to exist. In effect, I have suggested not a solution to this dilemma, but rather a *modus vivendi,* an uneasy resolution in which different truths may compete for acceptance, and resolutions short of full agreement may become implemented.

In conclusion, I should like to return to Buber's dichotomy between the I-Thou relationship and the I-It relationship, the one loving, the other exploitative; the one seeing one's fellow human as an end, the other seeing him as merely a means. If there is any validity in the preceding discourse, it indicates that in most important situations involving alternative courses of social change, neither relationship can be completely relevant. What is more troublesome, they are, in Buber's presentation, essentially incompatible.

Someone has suggested that we need to think of a third kind of relationship —an I-You relationship. It is not the relationship of the I-Thou in the sense of an immediate relationship of love for one's fellow human, particularly for one's opponent. Nor need it be that of the I-It, in the sense of seeing one's fellow human only as an object for manipulation to one's own purposes.

Between the two, can there not be a whole broad spectrum of morally responsible relationships that are neither pure love nor pure manipulation, which seek indeed to persuade, but never to coerce the conscience; which do not love, but nevertheless respect; which are concerned with task, but are not oblivious of process; which behave in anticipation of the future, but with a sense of living in the present; which seek to understand, but also to experience directly; which have a trace of the prophetic, but also a trace of the reconciler?

I may not be capable of considering everyone at all times as a Thou (Buber himself implies that this is God's role), but that need not free me to consider anyone as simply a pawn to be manipulated. There is an intermediate stage between the category of "friends" and that of "the masses." It is that of Yous, to whom one responds if not with love, then with integrity; if not by walking a second mile, at least by walking a first.

It seems to me that there is such a possibility, and that this is perhaps best categorized in Buber's terms as the I-You relationship, and that far from being nonexistent, it is the modal type of relationship into which human beings come. It is a relationship in which I cannot always follow my own truth and reach agreement with my neighbor, but it is at least a way in which we can live together in a richer and more colorful world than we could if truth and love always went hand in hand. Above all, it is a world of dynamic pluralism, a world in which you will always put a question mark beside my Q.E.D., a world in which, because you and I cannot both have our way, we are forced into compromise. We need to find ways of channeling change which will assure that you and I will reach the optimum agreement possible, but that our remaining disagreement will neither immobilize us nor result in our destroying each other and those around us.

NOTES

[1] Martin Buber, *I and Thou* (New York: Scribner, 1952).

[2] *Ibid.*

[3] Mary P. Follett, *Creative Experience* (New York: Longmans, Green, 1924).

[4] Murray G. Ross, *Community Organization: Theory and Principles* (New York: Harper, 1955), p. 39. The definition has been slightly shortened in this quotation.

[5] Roland L. Warren and Herbert H. Hyman, "Purposive Community Change in Consensus and Dissensus Situations," *Community Mental Health Journal,* 2, no. 4 (Winter 1966).

NAME INDEX

SUBJECT INDEX

PRINTED IN U.S.A.